Ski, Climb, Fight

CAMPAIGNS & COMMANDERS

GREGORY J. W. URWIN, SERIES EDITOR

CAMPAIGNS AND COMMANDERS

Ski, Climb, Fight

The 10th Mountain Division and the Rise of Mountain Warfare

Lance R. Blyth

University of Oklahoma Press : Norman

THIS BOOK IS PUBLISHED WITH THE GENEROUS ASSISTANCE OF
THE McCASLAND FOUNDATION, DUNCAN, OKLAHOMA.

Library of Congress Cataloging-in-Publication Data

Names: Blyth, Lance R., 1966– author.
Title: Ski, climb, fight : the 10th Mountain Division and the rise of mountain warfare /
    Lance R. Blyth.
Other titles: 10th Mountain Division and the rise of mountain warfare
Description: Norman : University of Oklahoma Press, [2024] | Series: Campaigns and
    commanders; vol 77 | Includes bibliographical references and index. | Summary: "A military
    history about the storied 10th Mountain Division, perhaps best-known as the ski troops of
    World War II, both in their founding and how they shaped mountain warfare through the
    present day"—Provided by publisher.
Identifiers: LCCN 2024009749 | ISBN 978-0-8061-9465-3 (hardcover)
Subjects: LCSH: United States. Army. Mountain Division, 10th—History. | World War,
    1939–1945—Mountain warfare. | World War, 1939–1945—Regimental histories—United
    States. | Mountain warfare—History.
Classification: LCC D769.3 10th .B59 2024 | DDC 940.54/1273—dc23/eng/20240301
LC record available at https://lccn.loc.gov/2024009749

Ski, Climb, Fight: The 10th Mountain Division and the Rise of Mountain Warfare is Volume 77 in
the Campaigns and Commanders series.

The paper in this book meets the guidelines for permanence and durability of the Committee on
Production Guidelines for Book Longevity of the Council on Library Resources, Inc. ∞

CONTENTS

Illustrations

Tables and Maps

Tables

Maps

Acknowledgments

The initial idea for this project came during a ski tour with Christopher Coates above Camp Hale; my thanks for his companionship on several adventures. I am grateful to Brian Laslie, Adam Kane, Maurice Isserman, Alexander Statiev, Tait Keller, and Roger Taylor for reading earlier versions of this work. I appreciate the research assistance of Keli Schmid and her team at the 10th Mountain Division Resource Center, Denver Public Library. Information from Chris Juergens of History Colorado, Doug Schmidt of the 10th Mountain Division and Fort Drum Museum, and David Little of the 10th Mountain Foundation proved crucial. Christian Beckwith kindly provided me the opportunity to sharpen my thoughts on his podcast. Marine Corps strategist Brian Donlon unselfishly shared his research. Farnham St John gave me crucial insights into ski instruction. Pete Lardy of Pikes Peak Alpine School patiently answered my technical questions and provided his mountaineering archive. Greg Urwin, Kent Calder, and Andrew Berzanskis did their editorial due diligence, grasping what I was trying to do and holding me to it, as did the University of Oklahoma Press's two peer reviewers. Thanks to Benjamin Folger for his help, Helen Robertson and Robert Fullilove for their editing assistance, and Amy Hernandez for marketing. I am grateful to the United States Air Force Academy Department of History for giving me an academic home. My greatest thanks is to my wife, Gretchen Merten. Her love of the high mountains and my love for her regularly put us near or above tree line in all seasons and conditions. Look for us there.

The views expressed in this book are mine and do not necessarily reflect the official policy or position of the US Department of Defense or the US government.

Acronyms and Abbreviations

AAC	American Alpine Club
ADC	assistant division commander
AGF	Army Ground Forces
AIARE	American Institute for Avalanche Research and Education
AIS	Arctic Indoctrination School
AMGA	American Mountain Guides Association
AMWS	US Army Mountain Warfare School
AT	alpine touring
CPX	command post exercises
CT	combat team
ECWCS	extended cold weather clothing system
FM	Field Manual
MCRP	Marine Corps Reference Publication
MSS	Military Ski System
Mt	mount or monte
MTC	Mountain Training Center
MTG	Mountain Training Group
MWI	Mountain Warfare Instructor
MWTC	Mountain Warfare Training Center
MWWSTC	Mountain and Winter Warfare School and Training Center
NSA	National Ski Association
NSP	National Ski Patrol
NWTC	Northern Warfare Training Center

OCS	Officers Candidate School
OQMG	Office of the Quartermaster General
PCU	protective combat uniform
RCS	Rock Climbing Section
RCT	regimental combat team
TC	Training Circular
TM	Technical Manual
T/O	table of organization
TRADOC	US Army Training and Doctrine Command
TRST	tactical rope suspension technician
WPD	War Plans Division

PROLOGUE

The standard origin story of the US Army's 10th Mountain Division goes something like this: In February 1940 the chairman of the National Ski Patrol, Minot "Minnie" Dole, was having après ski drinks with some friends at the Orvis Inn in Manchester, Vermont. Talk soon turned to the success of the Finnish army, which utilized skis in holding off the Russians in the Winter War. Concerned the US Army was unaware of the requirements for winter warfare, Dole engaged the War Department to offer the assistance of the National Ski Patrol (NSP). Rebuffed at several turns, Dole persisted into the fall of 1940 when his efforts culminated in a meeting with the army chief of staff. While Dole offered his ski patrols as auxiliaries in defense of the United States, his efforts began a process of experimentation, advising, recruiting, and training. This resulted in the activation of the 10th Light Division (Alpine) on July 15, 1943—redesignated the 10th Mountain Division on November 6, 1944, the first and only American formation ever specially organized, trained, and equipped for mountain warfare.[1]

Like most origin stories, that of the 10th Mountain, as it is called here in Colorado, is mostly true—meaning it is also partly false. The army did know of the requirement for winter and mountain warfare prior to Dole's entreaties, though it did not know much, particularly of the technical aspects. Further, Dole's successes in convincing the army to begin initial ski experiments, then to organize a test force, came not solely as a result of his persistence; changes to the strategic situation in Europe also caused the army to reassess its plans and requirements to move beyond winter and ski warfare to mountain warfare. The emphasis in the origin story on skiers and the NSP obscures the role mountaineers and the American Alpine Club (AAC) played, especially in training and equipping the division. Concluding the story with the end of World War II also misses important continuities to the present day. Most importantly, the standard narrative misses the larger context of mountain warfare.

Mountains introduce a "retarding element," as Prussian military theorist Carl von Clausewitz termed it, into operations. Mountain warfare thus comprises the ways and means military forces employ to overcome this retarding element of the terrain.[2] The hindering effects of mountains arise from a combination of several factors. Steepness is paramount, with mountains having elevation differentials of 1,000 feet or more from their lowest to highest points. Mountains are rugged terrain, divided by ridges into compartments connected by a few passes, with slopes 45° and steeper; climbing requires careful movements, often only one limb at a time. Most mountains are cold in winter with persistent snow depths of one or two feet and freezing ambient air temperatures. They can have arctic conditions with persistent windchill temperatures below −25°F, resulting in a high risk of frostbite on exposed facial skin in ten to thirty minutes. At mountain altitudes of 5,000 to 8,000 feet, individuals can suffer from acute mountain sickness. Above 8,000 feet there is a risk of altitude sickness, and above 18,000 feet no human habitation is possible.[3] Military forces operating in mountains overcome these inhibiting factors by surviving through being mobile, in order to maneuver in the mountainous terrain. However, the best techniques and technologies for survival and mobility are found in the civilian mountaineering and skiing communities, not the military. The pursuit and adaptation of civilian practices for military usage is an underlying current in mountain warfare.

This work presents how the US military has pursued mountain warfare capabilities from 1940 to the present day. It is a military history concerned with strategy, doctrine, procurement, organization, and training. By necessity, it also engages with the history of mountaineering and skiing, particularly in discussions of gear and skills. The many details may challenge the reader's patience, but I ask you to keep reading, as you are likely to find much of interest.

The bulk of the book, six of nine chapters, covers the 10th Mountain Division year by year from 1940 to 1945. As noted above, the army's knowledge of mountain and winter warfare in 1939 was insufficient. Following the fall of France in the summer of 1940, the army was thus receptive to offers of assistance from the National Ski Association (NSA) and the American Alpine Club. Their assistance and advocacy would ultimately encourage the army to create a mountain test force in the fall of 1941. Throughout 1942 the army's early mountain troops tested techniques and equipment, adapting civilian gear and practices. The National Ski Patrol of the NSA contracted with the army to locate volunteers for the mountain troops, and members of the AAC also tested equipment and proposed training methods. By the end of the year, the army settled on Camp Hale, Colorado, to host its Mountain Training Center (MTC). By the start of 1943, the army was able to issue skiing equipment, based on civilian models, and conduct ski training using modified civilian skills and recently enlisted civilian experts; in addition, it taught several thousand men the basics of glacier travel, winter camping, and avalanche knowledge.

From July 1943 the army was training an entire division, the 10th Light Division, at Camp Hale in rock climbing, mountain movement, and alpine survival, again adapting civilian mountaineering techniques and technologies. The division also conducted mountain unit training and supported mountain training detachments in the eastern United States and the Mediterranean theater.

In the next year many men became accomplished enough with the skills and gear to be military ski mountaineers, while the rest of the division were increasingly competent military skiers. This was necessary as they underwent combined arms training in several feet of snow, culminating in the infamous "D" (for division) Series field exercise. Despite the extreme conditions, the men performed quite well. By the summer the army accepted the value of mountain training and reorganized the 10th into a true mountain division, before dispatching it to Italy at the end of the year. In Italy the division benefited from the production of mountain warfare doctrine, written and reviewed by its members. In just over one hundred days of combat, the division patrolled, conducted a limited attack, and then spearheaded the spring offensive, which broke the German lines in the Northern Apennines. With the end of the war, the division enjoyed an alpine interlude—climbing, skiing, and glacier training—before returning to the United States and being discharged in November 1945. Thus ended the story of US mountain warfare in World War II.

The last three chapters of this book bring the story of US mountain warfare up to the present day. The army maintained a training center for mountain warfare in the postwar period, initially for a regimental combat team (RCT), at Camp Carson, Colorado, with summer training in the Front Range and winter training at Camp Hale and Cooper Hill. The Korean War saw a new mountain warfare school at Carson that trained overseas replacements, mountain warfare instructors, and cadres for units undergoing mountain and cold weather exercises. After 1960 these efforts faded as mountain warfare took a back seat to cold weather considerations. By the end of the decade, however, the army realized that it once again needed civilian mountaineering expertise.

The military soon discovered that mountaineering had radically changed in the postwar period. After the final high mountain conquests in the Himalayas, multipitch big wall rock climbing came to dominate. Skiing had changed even more, becoming focused on downhill, alpine skiing at resorts. Thus, during the 1970s the military slowly adapted civilian techniques and technologies into new doctrine and equipment. In the 1980s new requirements, such as the deployment of marines to Norway and the return of mountain units to the army's rolls, accelerated the process. After 2000 mountain warfare underwent a renaissance. Intellectual engagement in mountain operations continued into the new century, as did the operation of mountain schools. Civilian backcountry skiing and alpine climbing proved to be extremely adaptable to military use. In particular, the US invasion of Afghanistan resulted in updated techniques, technologies, and doctrine. This renaissance has held to the present day; how to keep it going I consider at the end of the book.

CHAPTER 1

MOUNTAIN WARFARE,
1940–1941

In 1908 Capt De Witt C. Falls, adjutant of the New York National Guard's fashionable Seventh Regiment, observed the Italian, French, and Austrian mountain troops during their summer maneuvers in the high Alps. A talented sketch artist and witty commentator, Falls noted that France, Italy, and Austria had "specially organized corps" to patrol and protect their mountain frontiers. But he believed that "it is extremely doubtful if any emergency will arise to make it necessary for the Government of this country [the United States] to organize any troops on these lines [for mountain warfare]." Such an "emergency" indeed came to pass thirty-one years later, with the outbreak of World War II. The summer of 1939 found American mountaineers Robert H. Bates, who was part of the 1938 American K2 expedition, and Adams "Ad" Carter, a member of the 1934 US Ski Team, climbing in the Swiss Oberland region. They heard the rumors of a coming war between Germany and Poland and observed mobilized Swiss mountain troops. Bates and Carter wondered if the US Army knew about mountain warfare and if it "could make good use of mountain troops, too."[1]

The army did know about mountain warfare. Army officers educated at the Command and General Staff School in Fort Leavenworth, Kansas, in the interwar period read German general William Balck's treatise, in translation, on the development of tactics during the Great War, which included a section on "Mountain Warfare." There they learned that the German army had been taken by surprise by the need to conduct mountain warfare, which required special training, and that "only well trained mountain troops who in their sports do not forget the objects of war, are suited for this special work." "The main thing," Balck wrote, quoting Austrian regulations, "for troops in the mountains is mobility and endurance." Balck also alerted American officers

ALPINE TROOPS (Italy).

AUSTRIAN OFFICER—ALPINE TROOPS.

CHASSEURS ALPINE (France).

The mountain troops of Europe (1908), from Falls, "Mountain Troops of Europe," 30, 36.

to the potential usefulness of skis, translated as "snowshoes," for the infantry, artillery observers, and staff officers.[2]

Students could also read translations of foreign articles, such as the 1933 German "Attack in Mountain Warfare," which argued from the experience of the world war that seizure of mountain heights had to accompany attacks up mountain valleys. The 1935–36 class at the Command and General Staff School carried out a series of map exercises in mountain warfare in February 1936. At the end of 1937 *The Military Engineer*, the professional journal of the Society of American Military Engineers, printed an article concisely encapsulating "the principles and lessons of modern mountain warfare." The article noted mountains had severe winters, but lacked shelter and lines of communication. This required adaptation of doctrine, organization, equipment for a war of position, and movement without a continuous front. Ridges provided the primary routes for movement and offensive maneuvers, while the defense needed fewer troops in forward positions, but more in reserve closer to the front. The battalion was the primary tactical unit, reinforced with an engineer platoon, a mountain artillery battery, and pack animal units. Machine guns, mortars, and lighter mountain guns were the main support weapons available to mountain units. Provision of medical and logistic services were of greater importance in the mountains, the latter utilizing not just pack animals, but cableways, motor transport, and narrow-gauge railways. Finally, soldiers had to be physically fit and possess a capacity for endurance to live and fight in the mountains, for which they also needed adequate clothing.[3]

The "principles and lessons" of mountain warfare permeated the General Staff to the extent that the *Tentative Field Service Regulations, Operations,* signed by Gen George C. Marshall, chief of staff of the army on October 1, 1939, included for the first time in US Army doctrine a section of eighteen paragraphs on "Combat in Mountainous Terrain." Marshall recognized that "mountainous terrain offers no insuperable obstacles to the conduct of military operations even in cold weather if the troops are properly equipped and clothed, and are inured by previous training." Yet Marshall and the army did not know what the equipment and clothing should be or what training would be required. Ironically, it would be the Russo-Finnish War, or Winter War, of 1939–40, fought in a flat, frozen landscape, not the mountains, that would set off the energetic efforts of skiers, not mountaineers, to provide technical assistance.[4]

Skiers

"FINNS SMASH A RED DIVISION" the headline of the *New York Times* read on January 1, 1940, with similar top lines in papers across the world and the United States, apparently including that taken by Assistant Secretary of War Louis Johnson. His interest piqued, Johnson wrote to Marshall on January 6, asking what consideration had been given by the US Army to the requirements for fighting in winter conditions. Marshall, viewing the question mainly as one of equipment and clothing, passed it on to the G-4 (Supply) Division of the General Staff. Three weeks later Marshall replied that winter operations were under study, particularly in relation to the defense of Alaska, and he intended to continue tests, accelerating them where possible, to determine the best winter equipment, techniques, and practices.[5]

The Winter War that so interested Secretary Johnson began on November 30, 1939, with a broad Soviet advance into Finland. Finnish fortifications on the Karelian Isthmus, the Mannerheim Line, and skillful counterattacks on the shores of Lake Ladoga combined with severe winter conditions to bring the Soviets to a halt. Around Suomussalmi Finnish troops maneuvered on skis along the flanks of the road-bound Soviets, reducing their advancing columns into pockets (*motti*) and destroying one division by the end of December. It was this event Johnson read about in his newspaper. The fighting continued with a second Soviet division chopped up in January and a third in early February. This may well have been the topic of conversation among Minnie Dole and his ski partners, including Roger Langley of the National Ski Association, that Saturday night in Vermont. But on February 11 the Soviets launched a new offensive, ground through the Mannerheim Line, and forced an armistice on March 13. Ultimately the Finns lost not due to a lack of skiing, but to a lack of the implements of modern warfare: aircraft, artillery, and tanks.[6]

Yet many Americans, including Dole, focused on the role of Finnish skiing "because we were skiers." American skiing exploded in the decades after World

War I. A new European-style, social, Alpine ski culture took hold in New England practiced by urban, educated professionals, who made up nearly two hundred ski clubs. New American skiers benefited from laminated skis with metal edges and metal bindings and from structured, disciplined instruction in the Arlberg technique of Austrian ski instructor Hannes Schneider. They also enjoyed increased mechanization with rope tows, then one-person J-bars, then two-person T-bars, then chairlifts. Snow trains took weekend skiers in a sociable setting from Boston and New York to New Hampshire and Vermont. Here ski clubs, locals, and eventually governments cleared trees to make increasingly wider ski runs. In the 1930s many people who wanted to ski could now go to the mountains on their days off where they could learn to ski without uncomfortable exertion. At least a million Americans, perhaps as many as three million, were skiers by 1940.[7]

Not surprisingly, thousands of them were injured skiing. Minnie Dole, insurance executive and a member of New York's Amateur Ski Club, was one of these; he broke his ankle at Stowe, Vermont, on New Year's Day 1937. He laid in shock in the snow for several hours until some friends moved him down to a road on a short piece of tin roofing. A few months later one of those friends died from a punctured lung after a ski race crash. The Amateur Ski Club formed a committee with Dole in charge, and he convinced the other ski clubs in the Northeast to form patrols to respond to dangerous accidents and ensure evacuation off the slopes. Incorporated into the National Ski Association in 1938 with Dole as chairman, in three seasons the National Ski Patrol (NSP) grew to over 4,000 patrolmen, of which 455 were registered patrolmen, the rest being junior or in training. Registered patrolmen completed over thirty hours of first aid and snow safety training, after which they wore a blue diamond with an orange cross on their sleeve. (The distinctive rust-red jacket would come into use only in 1946.) Each of the nearly 180 ski patrols in the NSP consisted of five to fifteen patrolmen under a patrol leader. Five to fifteen patrols made up a section under a section chief, who reported to a division chairman in one of seven divisions: Northeast, Central, Northern Rocky Mountains, Southern Rocky Mountains, Inter-Mountain, California, and Pacific Northwest. The majority, over a hundred, of the ski patrols were in the Northeast Division.[8]

So when talk turned that Saturday night in the Orvis Inn in February 1940 to how the US Army would not be able to replicate Finnish skiing feats if called on to defend the United States in a winter campaign, Dole's thoughts landed on the NSP's ski patrollers. They were competent skiers, familiar with basic lifesaving, organized into patrols, sections, and divisions, and knowledgeable of their locales. Could they be useful in a winter defense of the United States? President Franklin Delano Roosevelt directed that the entire hemisphere be defended at a meeting on November 14, 1938. It was generally understood that, if the Germans and Italians defeated France and the United Kingdom in the imminent European war and incorporated part of their navies, the resulting fleet would be much larger than the US Navy, which would place the United States and the Western Hemisphere at risk of attack. Others were also having thoughts similar to Dole's at the time. One Californian imagined unnamed hostile mountain troops invading the High Sierras in 1940. *Life* magazine mapped out "Six Ways to Invade U.S." One illustration showed Japanese mountain troops on the slopes of Mount Rainier, while "Plan Six" posited a seaborne invasion of Canada via Iceland and Greenland, with the attack continuing down the Saint Lawrence River into the heart of the northeastern United States.[9]

Dole and his comrades knew their geography and their history. Any invasion force ensconced in the Saint Lawrence River would turn, as so many had done in the past, down the Champlain Valley and into the Adirondack Mountains where they skied. While the National Ski Association's offer of services to the War Department that spring received "a most frosty brush off," Dole, increasingly certain of the need for ski troops particularly after the German invasion of France in May 1940, polled his patrol leaders in June for permission to offer the NSP's services to the army. Nine of ten members agreed. Dole met with the chief of staff of the Second Corps Area in New York, responsible for defense of the Northeast, in early July, who encouraged him to reach out to Washington, DC. So Dole wrote to the White House, proffering the NSP's assistance to train ski troops, for which some of the two million skiers Dole calculated were in the country could be recruited, as he believed it would be easier to "make soldiers out of skiers" than skiers out of soldiers. The White House thanked Dole and passed his letter on to the War Department, where it sat. Dole persisted, and by exploiting his Yale and business connections, he secured a meeting with Arthur E. Palmer, special assistant to the new secretary of war, Henry L. Stimson. Dole offered the services of NSP patrollers as ski scouts and guides for the army in case of a winter invasion. Palmer was impressed and the secretary's office arranged a meeting next door with General Marshall.[10]

At 1000 on September 10, 1940, the chairman of the National Ski Patrol met with the chief of staff of the US Army for fifteen minutes. Marshall proved receptive to Dole's offer of the NSP as auxiliaries. Two days later Marshall passed on a memo on winter training Dole left to his operations chief, noting that Dole was "quite a person" and the NSP was "not a fly-by-night affair." While Marshall did not see the army creating whole units of ski troops at that time, he did perceive the usefulness of ski training for morale and for potential operations by those divisions stationed in the northern latitudes of the United States. In November Marshall formally accepted the National Ski Patrol's offer of assistance, directing ski patrols to become familiar with their local terrain, to locate shelter for use by military ski patrols, to be prepared to serve as guides, and to cooperate with antiaircraft and antiparachute warning services. Dole incorporated this mission into the first ever ski patrol manual in 1941 as chapter 6, "Your Patrol and the Defense of the U.S.A."[11]

Marshall and the War Department were far more receptive to Dole and the NSP's offer of assistance in the summer of 1940 than they had been to the NSA's overture in the spring as the army was now preparing to execute "Joint Army and Navy Basic War Plan—Rainbow No. 4," approved by President Roosevelt on August 14, 1940. Rainbow 4 outlined the defense of the Western Hemisphere in light of France's being out of the war and the United Kingdom's tenuous position, as the Battle of Britain was still raging. Major portions of both the French and British fleets could fall under German control, triggering a US mobilization before the Germans could strike. Among the army's tasks for defense of the hemisphere were securing Alaska westward to the Aleutian island of Unalaska and defending, in alliance with Canada, Newfoundland and Greenland. Rainbow 4 called for up to thirty thousand men to embark at New York for the latter task and over six thousand to embark at Seattle to secure Alaska. As all of these areas had snowy winters, it made sense to prepare those units nearest to the embarkation ports for winter warfare and to train at least some personnel to ski.[12]

Thus, by early August 1940, a month before Dole's meeting with Marshall, the General Staff directed the preparation of training guidance for winter warfare training and experiments to determine what equipment would be necessary for winter operations. The army realized that "it is conceivable that our ability to fight in winter terrain might be of major, even decisive importance," yet it simply did not have the units ready for such specialized training, most having not even completed their basic training. By the end of October, the G-3 (Operations and Training) Division noted that "the desirable training objective is the immediate creation of divisions fully equipped and highly trained" for winter warfare, but it was necessary to "begin this training on a small, more honestly, inadequate scale."[13]

On December 5, 1940, the War Department directed the six divisions mobilizing in the Northeast, Upper Midwest, and Pacific Northwest to form ski patrols of varying sizes with the technical assistance of the National Ski Association. The patrols were to learn to use skis and snowshoes and the fundamentals of travel and camping in snow and mountains. The experiment, with an intentional variety of practices and experiences, lasted from December to April 1941. The army learned that it took two months to teach a soldier to ski, if the man selected was physically fit and capable. But for a ski soldier to be of use in the field, he would need to spend a winter season snow bivouacking and ski touring. The final report of April 28, 1941, noted that winter warfare was "not simply a phase of training" but constituted a separate "form of warfare which requires the most careful planning, equipment and training."[14] But by the spring of 1941, due to the efforts of civilian mountaineers, the army understood that skiing and winter warfare were a part of mountain warfare.

Mountaineers

In the fall of 1940, Bob Bates took James Bryant Conant, the president of Harvard, and his son climbing in New Hampshire. While climbing the Pinnacle on Mount Washington, Bates recounted his experiences in Switzerland the previous summer and "talked much the time about how mountain troops could be useful to the American army." Conant was to meet with General Marshall in a few days and promised to bring up the importance of beginning to train mountain troops. Bates did not stop there. He joined with members of the 1938 K2 expedition and arranged a meeting of the American Alpine Club (AAC) to discuss what role the club might play in national defense. The AAC set up a defense committee that then reached out to the War Department via one of its former members: Secretary of War Stimson.[15] So even as the National Ski Patrol approached Stimson and Marshall about winter warfare, the AAC was raising the issue of mountain warfare.

The American Alpine Club, formed in 1901, initially functioned as an elite social club with fewer than one hundred members. Its focus was largely on its annual meeting and dinner, though it did begin publishing the *American Alpine Journal* in 1929. This exclusivity left American mountaineering loosely organized in seventy regional clubs, such as California's Sierra Club, which were federated as the Association of Mountaineering Clubs by 1925. Increasing numbers of college mountaineering clubs also came into being in the interwar period. Lacking access to the Alps, American mountaineering clubs were a generation or two behind their European counterparts, and they concentrated primarily on mountain climbing, hiking to summits via the safest routes. But by 1930 there was a growing knowledge of, and interest in, more sophisticated techniques and tools for rock climbing.[16]

In 1932 a group of California Bay Area climbers who frequented the Yosemite Valley formally affiliated with the Sierra Club as the Rock Climbing Section (RCS). The RCS embraced rope work techniques—tying into, belaying, rappelling—taught by Robert L. M. Underhill. It also became interested in European climbing tools, particularly as described in a 1933 translated article by German climber Leo Maduschka. Maduschka added pitons, hammers, carabiners, and slings to the list of essential gear and introduced the use of the Prusik knot, which can be pushed up a climbing rope, but holds when pulled down. But none of these tools were available in the United States, so the RCS had to order them from Europe, particularly German suppliers, thus introducing into American mountaineering a necessary obsession with gear.[17]

American mountaineers too developed their own style of expeditions. From 1930 Bradford Washburn of the Harvard Mountaineering Club (HMC) led regular expeditions to the Alaskan and Yukon ranges with a number of up-and-coming American mountaineers and climbers, including Charles Houston and Bob Bates. Compared to the Himalayas the high north was more glaciated, colder, and lacked a population to serve as porters, so Washburn did without the systematic buildup of base camps via laborious hauling. Instead, he used aerial transport into the mountains, landing on lakes and glaciers, to airdrop supplies ahead of a party, and radios to coordinate the aerial support. Several of the HMC "Alaskans" went on to join expeditions into the Himalayas. When the American Alpine Club secured permission to send a small party to attempt to climb the K2 peak for the summer of 1938, it settled on Charles Houston as its leader. Houston secured the participation of Bates, but the rest of the HMC alumni were unable to join, so the AAC invited Wyoming "packer and guide" Paul Petzoldt, though there was some concern that he would not fit in socially. With Petzoldt's inclusion American climbing joined American mountaineering, as Petzoldt insisted, and Bates accepted, that the expedition would need far more pitons and carabiners than the more traditional Houston had procured. The team purchased the extra kit on its way through Paris. While the American 1938 K2 expedition failed to reach the summit as Houston and Petzoldt turned back three thousand feet below the peak, it symbolized the coming of age of American mountaineering.[18]

When the army responded to the AAC's overture to the secretary of war, in early December 1940, it was Bates who set up a display of up-to-date mountaineering equipment for Maj Gen James A. Woodruff. Bates displayed pitons, hammers, carabiners, ropes, ice axes, and crampons and the layers of wool underwear, flannel shirts, Shetland sweaters, scarves, and wool mittens worn under windproof and water-resistant jackets, pants, and gauntlets of densely woven cotton gabardine. He showed Woodruff wool balaclava helmets and venting snow goggles, nailed leather boots with differing sizes of socks to layer, marked by colored tape, and puttees to keep the snow out. Two-man tents, weighing twelve pounds, double down sleeping bags lined with flannel weighing seven and one-half pounds, and half-length air mattresses of four pounds completed the layout. Bates must have impressed upon Woodruff that all this equipment came from outside the United States, primarily England, and that it took time and required mountain terrain to learn how to use properly. Bates's presentation clearly had an impact, for after Woodruff reported back to the War Department, Col Henry L. Twaddle, acting assistant chief of staff for G-3, concluded that the winter warfare efforts of the divisional ski patrols would not be enough. On December 13, 1940, Colonel Twaddle sent a memo to General Marshall recommending training troops for mountain operations. A week later he sent a memo to the AAC requesting information on mountaineering equipment.[19]

Civilian skiers and mountaineers, many of whom were inducted into the army after the outbreak of war, would determine what equipment the army would need for winter and mountain warfare and the specifications for its production. In late November 1940 Lt Cols Charles E. Hurdis and Nelson M. Walker from the G-3 attended the National Ski Association convention in Lacrosse, Wisconsin, to determine what kind of equipment would be needed for winter warfare. They were amused to discover that the ski experts could not even agree on what type of binding would be best. The NSA thus established an equipment committee under Californian Bestor Robinson, a member of both the NSA and the RCS. Robinson's committee's remit was to collect, analyze, and make recommendations to the War Department "on necessary equipment and technique of ski troops . . . who could live out of their packs on expeditions of several days duration." Robinson understood the army needed not just to train skiers, but also to train and equip men to live and fight in the snow.[20]

The equipment committee quickly realized that of the several million skiers Dole estimated were in the country, the vast majority only skied prepared slopes. There were few skiers who knew how to spend days snow camping and ski touring. Ski and equipment manufacturers focused on the civilian downhill market and skis, boots, poles, and clothing had not been developed with potential military use in mind; many items, such as lightweight stoves, were not made in the United States. In looking at foreign practices, the committee found that European ski troops made use of their more established settlement patterns and transportation networks. It also realized that polar exploration relied on dog sleds and motorized equipment across relatively flat terrain. Himalayan mountaineering expeditions relayed heavy loads of supplies by porters from camp to successive camp. None of these experiences were applicable for American ski troops in the wilds of Alaska or on the glaciers of Greenland.[21]

Robinson decided that the equipment committee would have to rely on an "indigenously evolved" set of techniques and equipment such as had been developed by himself and his fellow climbers in the RCS, who reorganized themselves every October into the Ski Mountaineers Section of the Sierra Club. Taking advantage of a more stable maritime snowpack and comparatively temperate winter conditions in California's Sierra Nevada, these early backcountry skiers toured into the mountains, using skins, or "climbers," erected a camp, summited a mountain, and skied long runs back down. Technically minded—many were scientists or engineers—they eliminated all unneeded equipment and carried multiuse items, thus reducing the weight of their packs to just eighteen pounds plus two and a quarter pounds of food and fuel per day, even in −30°F temperatures. This weight would give an ample margin, as Robinson put it, for military loads.[22]

In April 1941 Robinson led twenty Ski Mountaineers, including a young David Brower, into the Little Lakes Valley of the eastern Sierra Nevada backcountry, west of Bishop, California. Capt Paul Lafferty, a former University of Oregon ski coach, who had recently led the 3rd Division ski patrol on a two-week circumnavigation of Mt Rainier, accompanied the party. Utilizing the equipment list developed from their experiences, the Ski Mountaineers took multiple examples of every piece of kit from civilian suppliers to test. Their testing included skis from Northland, boots by L.L.Bean, sleeping bags and tents from Abercrombie & Fitch, and clothing from Montgomery Ward. In heavy snow, low temperatures, and high winds, they tried different stoves, waxes, rucksacks, ropes, sunscreens, goggles, pants, and parkas. Robinson, now a civilian adviser to the quartermaster general, reported the test results to Washington, DC. Meanwhile the Ski Mountaineers, having provided recommendations for equipment, were busy writing up their techniques.[23]

Skiers were not the only ones providing the army with recommendations on equipment and technique; mountaineers also provided input and expertise. On December 20, 1940, after Lieutenant Colonel Woodruff's meeting with Bob Bates, the G-3 wrote to the AAC asking for information on essential items of mountaineering equipment that could be used by the army. The detailed reply listed twenty-one items of equipment and where each might be needed, broken down by temperatures and regions. At the same time, at the beginning of 1941, the AAC tasked member Kenneth Henderson to "prepare a mountaineering manual that could be used for the instruction of troops." In the spring Twaddle accepted the AAC's offer of Ad Carter to perform intelligence work on mountain warfare, translating books and articles from German, French, Italian, and Swiss sources, for the G-3. Carter's work was crucial since the War Department's translators had no mountaineering experience and translated mountaineering terms literally, rendering *piton* as a "nail" and *skier* as an "off-walking snowshoer."[24]

In March 1941 Twaddle asked Walter Wood and Bates, who were preparing a summer expedition to the Saint Elias Range in Alaska, to conduct tests with supplies airdropped onto glaciers. Twaddle assigned two B-18 bombers for the task and an official observer, Capt Albert Jackman. Starting on July 4, the Wood Yukon expedition airdropped a number of supply boxes along their routes to the summits of Mounts Wood and Walsh. Bates and Jackman tested a number of other items of equipment along the way, including survival rations and tents, and discovered that 94 percent of their five thousand pounds of air-dropped supplies had survived.[25]

That fall Bates began serving as a civilian adviser for winter and mountain warfare to the Office of the Quartermaster General (OQMG), which determined the specifications of any piece of equipment to be procured. Bates, who was eventually commissioned as a captain, brought on William House from the K2 expedition, Ad Carter came over from the G-3, and now-Maj Bestor Robinson soon took command of the Cold Climate Unit, concentrating much of the mountaineering expertise in the country in the OQMG. The Cold Climate Unit faced the challenge of determining a mountaineering kit to be used in almost any mountain range in the world including in the Arctic, to consist of as few pieces as possible, that would stand up to the use and abuse by soldiers, and that could be manufactured in the United States rapidly enough to be fielded within a year despite material shortages. They thus focused on five critical items: ice axes, mountain boots, mountain rope, crampons, and tents. By the end of 1941, as Bates saw it, the army had "many prototypes of mountain, cold-weather, and emergency equipment that had been adapted from civilian models to army use," but "there was a great need for testing before procurement began."[26]

Ultimately the NSA's and AAC's efforts toward identifying equipment and techniques for the army led Colonel Twaddle to recognize the need for mountain, vice just winter, warfare. Twaddle and his staff realized quite early on that all the specialized equipment and specialized techniques needed for operations in the mountains necessitated specialized mountain troops. Twaddle thus argued for a mountain warfare requirement in the US Army through the winter of 1940–41 and into the spring. Twaddle held that the American military needed to be ready to undertake any type of operation in any type of terrain, including mountains, even if the specific theater had yet to be identified. If it became "necessary to undertake operations in mountain terrain" then "at least a Division trained in mountain warfare should be available for this purpose."[27]

Mountain Divisions

Mountain divisions had occupied Capt Ridgely Gaither on the General Staff since at least the summer of 1940. Gaither had been tasked to determine how troops should be trained, organized, and equipped to fight in special environments including jungles, or on shores during an amphibious landing, or upon dropping from the sky in parachutes or gliders, or in mountains. Gaither gained traction for jungle, amphibious, and airborne divisions, but mountain warfare and mountain troops took longer, given the "mighty thin file" he had to work with. He finally received authorization to plan for twelve divisions for jungle, airborne, and amphibious warfare and three divisions—to be designated 10th, 12th, and 14th—for mountain warfare. Gaither planned for mountain divisions since this was how the US Army mobilized, equipped, trained, deployed, and employed forces for most of the twentieth century.[28]

Now–Brigadier General Twaddle continued to push for organizing a mountain division in April and May 1941, informed by the work his staff was doing on updating the 1939 FM 100-5 *Operations* and writing a brand-new field manual, FM 31-15 *Operations in Snow and Extreme Cold*. Both field manuals emphasized the need to train, equip, and organize troops to operate in the mountains and in winter. While the 1939 version of FM 100-5 had a section of eighteen paragraphs on "Combat in Mountainous Terrain." the 1941 revision, signed by Marshall on May 22, doubled this to over forty paragraphs on "Mountain Operations." Mountain warfare was defined "primarily by difficulties which terrain offers to movement," but such mountainous terrain required the troops be "properly *equipped, clothed, supplied, and trained*." The 1941 operations manual also included for the first time a section on "Combat in Snow and Extreme Cold," identifying the uses of ski troops. FM 31-15 *Operations in Snow and Extreme Cold*, in its first paragraph, stated, "Special equipment and a high state of training are of paramount performance." FM 31-15 would not be approved until September 18, 1941, likely because the War Department had first to determine what that special equipment and training would be.[29]

Twaddle's spring push to organize a mountain division to train in the coming winter came to naught, however. Faced with the same problems in 1941 as in the year prior—lack of troops to train, lack of funds to train them, no immediate requirement for mountain operations—Marshall chose to defer any decision in May. For his part, Twaddle did not stop, instead shifting to bureaucratic guerrilla tactics. On May 7 he sent a memo to his fellow assistant chief of staff of the War Plans Division (WPD) emphasizing the need for early development of clothing, equipment, and organization for winter and mountain warfare. He sought the WPD's support for the creation of a small force by autumn to initiate tests and provide a nucleus of experienced personnel for later expansion into a division, particularly as mountain and winter warfare instructors. Twaddle apparently spent May and June seeking the support of the rest of the General Staff while the G-3 continued work on the organization of a mountain division.[30]

On July 15, 1941, Twaddle, ready to reattack, proposed to Marshall the mountain division "as a distinct type" that could not be improvised by attaching specialized units, "but must be specially organized and trained." While such a division "specifically organized and trained for combat in the high mountain terrain can operate in the lowlands or in any terrain, the reverse is not true." Further, a mountain division could "be more readily adaptable to air transport" than a standard division. The table of organization (T/O) described a mountain division slightly smaller than an infantry division of the time (14,965 officers and men compared to 16,175) with fewer heavy weapons. Mountain division artillery had only forty-eight 75 mm pack howitzers vice the thirty-six 105 mm and twelve 155 mm howitzers of an infantry division. The mountain infantry regiment was to be nearly a thousand men smaller and lack the antitank guns and heavy machine guns of its flatland counterpart. The weapons companies of the mountain infantry battalions only had four light machine guns, not the eight heavy machine guns of standard infantry units. Where the mountain division was truly different was in the use of 7,893 horses and mules for transport and supply, compared to none in the infantry division.[31]

Twaddle's efforts to garner support for an American mountain division supplied by American mules clearly paid off in the responses to his proposal. The WPD agreed, stating there was a "definite need" for a mountain division and that "one such division be organized at an early date and trained in high mountain terrain." The chiefs of infantry, artillery, and cavalry all supported the proposal, even as they proposed changes to the tables, as did the chief signal officer and the surgeon general. Only the G-1 (Personnel) and G-4 Divisions of the General Staff disagreed as they saw no immediate requirement for a mountain division. Yet the endorsement of the general headquarters (GHQ), responsible for mobilizing, organizing, equipping, and training the US Army, under Lt Gen Leslie J. McNair, was the most important. Twaddle had apparently worked with GHQ staff officers as several supported his proposal. Lt Col John M. Lentz, in a memo to McNair, stated that "all concerned agree in need for organization of the Mountain Division," though he suggested adding a squadron of autogyros to it for reconnaissance work. McNair's own director of operations, Lt Col Mark W. Clark, recommended his boss concur with the mountain division organization, arguing that "at least we may get one more division."[32]

However, on August 5, 1941, Lieutenant General McNair rejected the G-3's mountain division. No specific theater of mountain operations had yet been identified for US mountain troops, he stated. He deemed the animal transport in the proposed division "inefficient" compared to motorized transport. McNair did not see the need for an entire specialized mountain division; instead, adapting an infantry division or specific elements of a division for operations in difficult terrain was sufficient. He accepted for the moment Twaddle's May proposal for a test force, an infantry battalion and artillery battalion "capable of operating in mountainous terrain," but held out that it should contain "a minimum of pack transportation and a maximum of motor transportation." The same day McNair responded, the WPD learned that a decision on a mountain test force was being withheld pending results of cost estimates.[33]

The American requirement for mountain warfare and mountain troops stalled by August 1941, but changes in the international situation, to war plans, and in requirements to execute those plans would soon revive and cement it. From January 29 to March 29, 1941, American and British planners conducted secret staff talks, agreeing that, when the Americans entered the war, their focus would be combined offensive action against Germany. Thus, the basic American war plan changed. The Joint Planning Committee revised War Plan Rainbow 4 into Rainbow 5 in April, and it was approved by the joint board of the chief of naval operations and chief of staff of the army in May. Rainbow 5 called for defending the Western Hemisphere, protecting US possessions in the Pacific, deterring Japan, and dispatching forces for overseas operations, particularly in Europe and the Mediterranean. The president read the plan but neither approved nor disapproved it. Yet, it clearly remained on his mind for in early July he asked the secretary of the Navy and secretary of war to provide estimates of the personnel and equipment necessary to execute the plan.[34]

For the Army Ground Forces (AGF), the task of preparing an estimate fell to Maj Albert Wedemeyer of the WPD. Wedemeyer planned for most of the army's units to be used for the offensive mission of Rainbow 5. He envisioned raising three large expeditionary armies, two of which would include mountain divisions. Wedemeyer assigned two mountain divisions to the two armies as he expected they would have to conduct operations to seize bases in the mountainous Scandinavian or Iberian Peninsulas or fight in the Andes Mountains of South America or the Alaskan ranges. Further, as the army could not be certain of the exact military situation it would face, Wedemeyer also called for a large strategic reserve, including six mountain divisions. Of the 215 divisions he estimated the army would require, 10 were to be mountain divisions.[35]

Wedemeyer specifically justified the need for mountain units in his estimate by citing the example of the Norway campaign in 1940 where the Germans deployed two mountain divisions while the British sent no mountain troops. Such specialized units required planning for and creating the necessary equipment quickly. Wedemeyer provided a requirement for American mountain warfare in potential specific locales—the Alps and other mountains of Central Europe, the Pyrenees, Norway, Alaska, the Andes—and called for specially trained and equipped mountain troops organized into divisions. Wedemeyer finished his report, the "Ultimate Requirements Study Estimate of Army Ground Forces," in early September 1941.[36]

Wedemeyer's specific mention of the German use of mountain troops during the Norwegian campaign echoed what many staff officers, including Twaddle, had argued during the spring and summer of 1941—namely, that Norway and the Italians' experience against the Greeks illustrated the need for American mountain troops. In Norway, mountain troops were used primarily at the iron ore–exporting town of Narvik, north of the Arctic Circle. There one regiment of German mountain troops (*Gebirgsjäger*) seized the port on April 9, 1940. The British and French response did not come until the end of the month, but ultimately it included three battalions of French mountain troops, or *Chasseurs Alpins*. (There was also a Polish *Podhalian*, or Highlander Brigade, a mountain unit in name only as it was recruited mainly from Polish émigrés in France.) Given the up to eight feet of snow on the ground, the Gebirgsjäger and Chasseurs Alpins did equip subunits of skiers. Fighting alongside the Norwegians, the Allied forces managed to retake Narvik and push the Germans back against the nearby Swedish border by the end of May. However, the impending fall of France led the Allies to evacuate their troops from Norway. American intelligence would later find that German "methods of winter combat in mountainous terrain were tested and proved sound" during the Norwegian campaign and that the equipping, and most importantly the training, of forces for this combat was critical.[37]

On October 28, 1940, Italian forces, based in Albania, invaded Greece, including the 3rd *Alpini* Division Julia. The Julia mountain division attacked in the center of the offensive in the Pindos Range, driving deep into the mountains aiming for the Metsovo Pass in the Greek defenders' rear. The Alpini got only about halfway there when a Greek counterattack in early November nearly cut them off and then drove them back, along with the rest of the Italian forces. In response the Italian high command deployed more forces, eventually including three more Alpini divisions, but initially did so piecemeal. Most of these forces were not equipped or trained for mountain and winter warfare, and the US military attaché to Italy reported "ten thousand were frozen." The attaché, whose report would circulate widely among the General Staff during the summer of 1941, concluded from the Italian experience that "an army which may have to fight anywhere in the world must have an important part of its major units especially organized, trained, and equipped for fighting in the mountains and in winter. . . . Such units cannot be improvised hurriedly from line divisions. They require long periods of hardening and experience, for which there is no substitute for time."[38]

Minnie Dole certainly agreed with this assessment. In July 1941 he met with Twaddle to discuss the proposed mountain division. Dole sent a letter to General Marshall at the end of the month arguing that if such a unit was created then many experienced mountaineers and skiers already in the army would transfer to it. If not, he feared they would leave the service when their one-year enlistments ended that fall and winter. In early October the treasurer of the National Ski Patrol, on a visit to Washington, learned that mountain and winter warfare proposals were still blocked, and Lt Col John Walker also called Dole to relay much the same information, asking him to consider intervening. Dole organized a resolution from the National Volunteer Winter Defense Committee of the National Ski Association and sent it to Marshall on October 8, with copies to the president and Secretary Stimson. The resolution recapped that the army might have to fight in any place and at any time, including in the mountains and in winter. Such training took time, he reiterated, noting the Germans had spent four years raising and training mountain troops prior to the war. The committee thus urged "that at least a test force be organized and trained this coming Winter in order to secure the necessary experience with regard to training and equipment for a future mountain division or divisions."[39]

By the middle of October 1941, Marshall had a war plan backed by a requirements study that made it clear that the US Army might have to fight in mountains somewhere in the world, most likely in Europe. He had long recognized that mountain warfare required proper mountain troops, something the experience of Germans and Italians in Norway and Greece, respectively, only reinforced. And Marshall had the urging of the civil National Ski Association, National Ski Patrol, and American Alpine Club to raise, equip, and train mountain troops. But the United States was still at peace, and the army still had neither the men nor the money to raise a full mountain division. Marshall opted for the test force Twaddle proposed in May. He issued orders on November 15, 1941, to constitute the 87th Infantry Mountain Regiment at Fort Lewis, Washington, and to activate its 1st Battalion (Reinforced). (*Infantry Mountain Regiment* would soon be changed to *Mountain Infantry Regiment*.) The 1st of the 87th was to "develop the technique of winter and mountain warfare and to test the organization and equipment and transportation of units operating in mountainous terrain in all seasons and in cold climates in all types of terrain" in accordance with FM 100-5 *Operations* and FM 31-15 *Operations in Snow and Extreme Cold.*[40]

From January 1940 to December 1941 the US Army General Staff, with the support and insistence of civilian skiing and mountaineering organizations, determined a broad requirement for mountain warfare. Initially the requirement was to defend outlying mountainous territories to protect the mobilizing nation. It then shifted to potential offensive actions in the mountains of Europe or possibly South America. This type of mountain warfare would require mountain divisions with specially equipped and trained mountain troops. The army now had to determine how to man those potential mountain divisions, where to base them, what equipment they would use, and who would train them.

CHAPTER 2

Mountain Troops, 1942

At the start of 1942, the US Army understood that it could require a specialized division of mountain troops at some point in the near future. Yet, a lot of questions remained. Who would man the mountain troops, and how would they be recruited? What skills and techniques would the mountain troops need to learn, and how were they to be taught? What equipment and transportation would the mountain troops need and with what specifications and in what numbers? And finally, when would the army activate the mountain division, which division would it be, and where would it train? To answer these questions, 1942 would prove to be a year of experimentation by the nascent mountain troops.

Mountain Recruits

A first question to be answered was who would fill the ranks of the 1st Battalion of the 87th Mountain Infantry Regiment. Minnie Dole was well on the way to providing a solution by late November 1941. Working with officers from the G-3, Dole and the NSP "developed a questionnaire for interested skiers" to determine if they wished to enlist in, request assignment to, or transfer to the mountain troops. The questionnaire asked for education, occupation, previous military experience, skiing and mountaineering and other outdoor ("camping") experience, and three letters of recommendation attesting to the same. The American Alpine Club also mailed questionnaires to a select list of club members and encouraged any who had already volunteered or been inducted into the army to advise the club whether they wished transfer to the new mountain unit.[1]

The National Ski Patrol, through its parent organization the National Ski Association, contracted with the War Department as a consultant in March 1941. The War Department consulted with the NSP to locate qualified members for the mountain troops. The first NSP recruit, Dartmouth ski team captain

☆ ☆

Fight in the Mountains

★ ★ ★

The National Ski Patrol System

CALLING ALL SKIERS

THROUGH the efforts of THE NATIONAL SKI PATROL SYSTEM all men desiring service with MOUNTAIN TROOPS may have it. The WAR DEPARTMENT is seeking qualified men, enlistees, voluntary inductees and inductees for service with MOUNTAIN TROOPS and has asked THE NATIONAL SKI PATROL SYSTEM to help get them. It is only necessary for you to contact our office at 415 Lexington Avenue, New York City, and ask for our Bulletin 10-C. Men recommended by us proceed within ten days to the Mountain Training Center in the Colorado Rockies, for basic training before assignment to mountain units. There is no red tape. Only regular Army physical exam on induction is required. Skiing and rock climbing ability is not demanded. Past outdoor experience and familiarity with camping, mountains, and general all-round toughness comes first. You don't have to be an expert. Men are given an opportunity to apply for officers' training upon completion of thirteen weeks basic training.

Germany, Italy and Japan have many mountain outfits. They are tough. Ours must be tougher.

The motto of THE NATIONAL SKI PATROL SYSTEM is "Service to all Skiers." We are only trying to continue our work and help YOU, but YOU can help us carry out our important task for the WAR DEPARTMENT.

Inquire today for full information regarding service with our MOUNTAIN TROOPS who

"Climb to Conquer"

THE NATIONAL SKI PATROL SYSTEM

NATIONAL HEADQUARTERS: 415 LEXINGTON AVENUE

NEW YORK, N. Y.

☆ ☆

National Ski Patrol System recruitment advertisement, from *American Ski Annual*, 1943.

Charles McLane, reported to Fort Lewis on a "sleepy Sunday" at the end of November 1941 with just a suitcase and "a pair of skis." McLane joined a cadre of forty-five men drawn from the previous winter's divisional ski patrols, particularly those of the 3rd and 41st Divisions in the Pacific Northwest; the California National Guard; and volunteers with skiing experience from other units. In the days and weeks after Pearl Harbor, the cadre steadily added more NSP-vetted volunteers, other outdoorsmen, and muleskinners ("leader, pack animal" in army nomenclature). The officers had either winter experience or experience with pack animals. Capt Paul R. Lafferty was among the former, an experienced skier and mountaineer who had led a ski patrol on Rainier and accompanied Bestor Robinson's Ski Mountaineers into the Sierras earlier in the year. The commanding officer, Lt Col Onslow S. Rolfe, was of the latter, intimately knowledgeable about mules for supply and support of mountain troops. Lieutenant Colonel Rolfe admitted he knew little about mountain and winter warfare and so was willing to listen to his more experienced corporals and privates, thereby setting a precedent in the mountain troops.[2]

Rolfe's first few months in command were taken up with the organization of the battalion, basic military training of the new recruits, and preparation for specialized training. The battalion formed under a tentative table of organization developed that summer, T/O 7-135 Mountain Infantry Battalion. It authorized twenty-six officers and 718 enlisted men with twenty-two riding horses and ninety-nine pack mules organized into a headquarters and headquarters detachment, three mountain infantry rifle companies, and a mountain infantry heavy weapons company. The mountain infantry battalion was more than a hundred personnel smaller than a standard infantry battalion, with no motor transport and no antitank guns or heavy machine guns. Its smaller size enabled it to maneuver in rough terrain where few roads existed, supplied by pack mules. Rolfe's headquarters included himself as commander, Maj Robert L. Cook, previously assigned to Alaska, as executive officer, a captain as plans and training officer (S-3), and a first lieutenant as adjutant and intelligence officer—all mounted on horses. The headquarters detachment had forty-eight enlisted men in a headquarters section including three mounted orderlies, a message center with three mounted messengers, an intelligence section, and an ammunition section with fourteen muleskinners and mules.[3]

The T/O authorized the battalion's three rifle companies—lettered A, B, and C—six officers and 186 enlisted men each. A horse-mounted captain commanded, with a first lieutenant as executive officer, another as weapons platoon commander, and three second lieutenants as platoon commanders. Three 60 mm mortars with nine mules paired with two light machine guns with six mules made up the weapons platoon. The three rifle platoons consisted of three eight-man rifle squads and an eight-man automatic rifle squad with two automatic rifles and a pack mule for ammunition. Company D, the battalion's heavy weapons company, had a captain company commander, first lieutenant executive officer, and two lieutenants as platoon commanders—all on horseback. The light machine gun platoon had four guns and six mules, and six 81 mm mortars and twenty-four mules composed the mortar platoon. In addition to thirty muleskinners, Company D's roster included the battalion's stable and packmaster, farrier, and saddler.[4]

At the new battalion's first formation, Lieutenant Colonel Rolfe disabused the men that they would only be ski troops, stating that "we are mountain troops" and that "skiing will play only a small part." This meant the new recruits had to be "good soldiers" first, necessitating several weeks of basic military training in the articles of war, military courtesy and customs, army regulations, hygiene, and sanitation, all per the proper army manual. They drilled in close and extended order, not only for discipline and cohesion but also to allow orderly movement by large units. They practiced rifle marksmanship and use of the bayonet. McLane remembered the time as one of standing guard, drilling, shooting on the range, and running the bayonet course. By the end of January 1942, the battalion completed its organization and initial training and was issuing specialized equipment such as rucksacks and skis, preparing for winter and ski training. But the army had no manual for such training. The 1st Battalion, 87th Mountain Infantry, thus turned to lesson plans from the Rock Climbing Section and Ski Mountaineers Section of the Sierra Club. These lessons, drawn from the soon-to-be-published *Manual of Ski Mountaineering*, covered equipment, ski safety and avalanches, winter first aid, snow transportation of the injured, signals for help, and nutrition.[5]

Rolfe was uncertain of what he was organizing, training, and preparing his battalion for. Was he to create small units of instructors? Or was he to develop a "large tactical unit" for combat operations? Higher headquarters proved to be unhelpful and even a hindrance in defining Rolfe's mission, focused as they were on mobilizing units and preparing to defend the West Coast. The American Alpine Club was certainly in favor of training the new unit as mountain warfare instructors (MWIs). In October 1941 the club's treasurer, hearing that a mountain battalion was to be established, quickly produced a two-page "Outline of Proposed Course of Instruction for Mountain Troops at Fort Lewis." This memo recommended a yearlong course for the new battalion focused on the men developing mountaineering skills by utilizing the AAC mountaineering handbook and the officers studying the "strategy of mountain warfare"; it then proceeded to describe training a division by the summer of 1943. The AAC's position, however, found no purchase in the War Department.

Rolfe thus fell back on the tasks assigned in his activation directive: "develop the technique of winter and mountain warfare and test the organization and equipment and transportation in accordance with training doctrine and technique prescribed" in Field Manual (FM) 100-5 *Operations* and FM 31-15 *Operations in Snow and Extreme Cold.*[6]

Rolfe and his S-3 were specifically referred to Sections V "Mountain Operations" and VI "Combat in Snow and Extreme Cold" of FM 100-5. Section V stated mountain operations required properly equipped, clothed, supplied, and trained troops. Mountains made mobility difficult, could "render tactical considerations subordinate" to survival requirements, and placed the highest importance on small-unit maneuvers. Necessary training for the mountains listed skiing and snowshoeing first. Section VI repeated the requirement of specialized equipment, training, and organization for winter warfare, particularly infantry trained in the use of skis and snowshoes. Such units could operate as patrols, raiding parties, or a major force, especially as the critical reserve element in the offense or defense. FM 31-15 emphasized the challenges of operations in snow and cold to moving troops and supplies, keeping troops and animals warm, and preventing low temperatures from causing equipment or weapons to malfunction. Mobility issues could be partly overcome by equipping a part of each combat unit with skis or snowshoes. Again, infantry on skis were seen as crucial, operating in squad or platoon patrols upward of fifty miles in front of the lines, as "speed and stealth are the two fundamental advantages of ski troops."[7]

Mountain Techniques

Given the emphasis on skiing in the field manuals and the fact that it was now winter, despite having initially insisted to his men that they were not just ski troopers, Rolfe directed the development of military skiing techniques. Captain Lafferty and Lt John Woodward, a ski racer who had trained the 3rd Division ski patrol, assembled an instructor cadre of thirty men, many of whom had been ski instructors prior to joining the battalion as NSP volunteers. Over a day of discussions and demonstrations, the instructors settled on Austrian Hannes Schneider's Arlberg method, popularized in the United States by Otto Lang's 1936 book *Downhill Skiing*, as their basic training reference. Woodward remembered, "We formally agreed to utilize the Lang book as the final arbiter of stylistic disputes. It worked. Nobody killed anyone else over issues of technique."[8]

As presented by Lang, the Arlberg method taught students first to stand, then walk, climb, and fall on their skis. They then progressed to the snowplow, then the snowplow turn. Addition of a cross-slope traverse between their snowplow turns led to the stem turn. Learning to swing one's upper shoulder back and through the turn, while bringing one's skis together, resulted in a stem christie turn. All these techniques were part of a "chain" with each technique being "the logical development" of the previous technique. Importantly, the Arlberg was already adapted for military ski training. In May 1941 Lang, the director of the Sun Valley, Idaho, ski school, filmed Woodward and four of his ski patrolmen and three of Lang's instructors in uniform. The resulting training film, *The Basic Principles of Skiing*, demonstrated skis, boots, and bindings and progressed though the Arlberg technique. Numbered 11-168, it became part of the US Army's extensive list of training films.[9]

On February 15, 1942, the battalion's three rifle companies, nearly six hundred men total, moved from Fort Lewis into the Paradise and Tatoosh Lodges located five thousand feet up on the slopes of Mt Rainier in the national park. Ski instruction began the next day. The battalion spent six hours a day, for six days a week, for the next two months on skis. For McLane, an accomplished skier, the training was "eight weeks of concentrated snowplowing, a painless monotony." The instruction ended on April 17 with a military ski test drawn from the *Manual of Ski Mountaineering*. The troopers ran through a two-mile course—up, down, level—with a thirty-pound rucksack and ten-pound rifle. At stations along the course instructors graded soldiers' ability to link four stem turns, conduct two stem christies, sideslip, kick turn, step turn, and perform one- and two-step glides. Three-fourths of the men qualified as third-class military skiers, the rest as second- or first-class. They also conducted a battalion ski march carrying packs and rifles for seven miles, climbing four thousand feet to The Sugarloaf, then skiing down Paradise Glacier, and over Mazama Ridge back to the lodges.[10]

In developing the techniques of military skiing, the 1st Battalion, 87th Mountain Infantry, learned that military skiing was quite different from civilian skiing. Rolfe would later note that "civilian skiing is nearly all downhill skiing, with no excess weight being carried. Military skiing teaches the individual to operate not only downhill but across country with a heavy pack and accessories, and to develop proper stamina and form." Military skiing instruction was based on the Arlberg method, even though its emphasis on a shoulder swing into turns, when done with a pack and rifle, risked throwing the skier off-balance and to the snow. But it was good enough, suitable for larger groups, and already known to most American skiers and instructors. As Schneider had perfected his method instructing Austrian troops to ski during World War I, the Arlberg was effectively returning to its roots.[11]

US military ski technique as developed on Rainier aimed to enable a mountain soldier to maneuver on skis at the highest possible speed consistent with absolute stability. The Mountain and Winter Warfare Board envisioned a five-week course of instruction in "U.S. Army Ski Technique." It kept the Arlberg method's focus on progression, adding in classification tests at days seven, eighteen, twenty-four, and thirty-one, rather than just one at the end. Cross-country techniques received a four-day block, as did downhill techniques that utilized rope tows to move the students back uphill. After eighteen days, the instruction began again from the start, but now with increasingly heavy packs over four days. The students concluded training with advanced techniques conducted with full packs on difficult snow. An instructor cadre of four officers and twenty-four noncommissioned officers (NCOs), two per platoon, was needed to train an infantry battalion.[12]

While Companies A and B left Mt Rainier after the final ski test in mid-April, Company C stayed on, joined by Company D, the battalion's weapons company, and the ammunition section of the battalion HQ detachment. For two weeks these units determined the techniques necessary to transport the machine guns and mortars the rifle companies would rely on for support and the immediate ammunition resupply all required. The T/O expected that the heavy weapons and ammunition would be carried by mules, but these animals were not an option in deep snow. Therefore, the battalion conducted tests with skis, snowshoes, and sleds. Despite their general unpopularity with skiers, snowshoes proved to be crucial. The battalion learned that heavy weapons and seventy-to-eighty-pound ammunition packs were best carried on packboards by snowshoers, as such weights were far too "treacherous" for skiers. Placing the weapons or ammunition onto sleds or toboggans and hauling them with skiers or snowshoers proved to be too difficult, a "man-killing job," in mountainous terrain.[13]

Companies A and B returned to Mt Rainier in May, each for two weeks of unit training to develop the techniques of maneuvering in the mountains on skis, handicapped by the prohibition on firing weapons in a national park. Despite this, the officers and men learned that infantry tactics had to take the terrain and weather into account. They ascertained the effectiveness of snow camouflage, of wide flanking maneuvers, and of hit-and-run attacks on skis. They learned how to use higher elevations to their advantage. They learned everyone in a squad had to ski at the same ability level in order to maneuver together. They also came to realize they still had much to learn about operating in the mountains with snow. On at least two occasions, only luck prevented avalanches from wiping out entire platoons. Given this level of ignorance, the company officers and noncommissioned officers followed their battalion commander's lead and listened to their better-skiing and more mountain-experienced enlisted men in the after-action critiques.[14]

With the coming of late spring and summer, the battalion next looked to develop mountaineering techniques, moving up rock and ice and across snow fields and glaciers. At this time, the army decided to expand the single mountain infantry battalion into a full regiment, and the development of mountaineering techniques "foundered in the whirling waves of regimental expansion." Most of the newly arriving men needed to receive basic training overseen by members of the original battalion. Plans to create separate groups of instructors were discouraged, so as not to denude new formations of experienced personnel. The new regiment was thus unable to move to a suitable site on Mt Rainier to develop mountaineering techniques. "In desperation" the regiment built three thirty-foot walls of logs in a sand and gravel pit at Fort Lewis, chopping out notches for hand- and footholds and placing pitons at the top. Here a small group of instructors taught the use of ropes for belaying and rappelling via pitons, which was about all they could teach under the circumstances.[15]

Finally, in August 1942, after shooting scenes for a rock and ice climbing training film, the regiment began sending classes of anywhere from twenty to nearly one hundred men to a five-day mountaineering school on Mt Rainier. This short course gave the men a brief exposure to mountaineering techniques derived from the American Alpine Club's just-published *Handbook of American Mountaineering*. Much theory and little practice was crammed into the course. The morning of the first day covered climbing pace and aids and elementary rope technique, with ice and snow techniques in the afternoon. The second day began with a discussion of avalanche factors and rescue techniques, including from crevasses. Elementary rock techniques took up that afternoon and into the next morning. The afternoon of the third day involved rappelling and advanced climbing, with advanced rock and rock piton techniques on the fourth day of class. The last day covered advanced rope and rock techniques and "mountain freighting"—hauling weapons and equipment up cliffs and carrying casualties back down. But the school only ran for a few months, as the 87th Mountain Infantry received orders to conduct maneuvers in the "low, snowless mountains" of the Coastal Range of central California in the fall of 1942.[16] Much work still remained to be done to develop the techniques of military mountaineering.

From the winter to the fall of 1942, the 87th Mountain Infantry attempted to "develop the technique of winter and mountain warfare" and "test the organization." The 1st Battalion was somewhat successful creating techniques of military skiing, but less so in the techniques and organization of winter and mountain warfare, being largely hamstrung by its inability to conduct battalion-level live-fire maneuvers. But the nascent mountain regiment had barely begun to develop the technique and organization necessary for military mountaineering. Rolfe saw the challenge as less about technique and more about personnel. It was possible to train a military skier or mountaineer in seven weeks, if the man had the aptitude and physical ability. But Rolfe lamented, "We have found that you cannot take just any trained infantryman and make him a skier or mountaineer." McLane, on his way to officer training in July 1942, echoed his commanding officer stating, "We found it possible to make skiers, but not skiers who were qualified to fight hard and fast under winter conditions."[17]

Mountain Testing

The second of Lieutenant Colonel Rolfe's tasks for the new mountain troops in the late fall of 1941 was to test equipment and transport. While the latter required testing in the mountains, it was not a complete unknown since transport for mountain units meant mules. Although Rolfe knew nothing of skiing or snowshoes or maneuvering in the mountains, he and many of his regular army officers and NCOs knew a lot about mules. In 1941 the army had two cavalry divisions, two (mule) pack artillery regiments, and two (mule) pack transport regiments on its rolls and a complete field manual dedicated to animal transport. As the companies trained on Mt Rainier through the winter and into the spring of 1942, back at Fort Lewis the battalion's one hundred mule-skinners and mounted orderlies, under the stable sergeant, constructed stables, feeding and watering troughs, blacksmith and harness shops, and corrals. Over the entrance to the corrals, Rolfe ordered a sign posted: "Through these portals pass the most beautiful mules in the world." The ninety-nine authorized mules arrived in the spring—Missouri mules, three to six years old. Rolfe named the lead bell mare "Minnie," in honor of Dole, who had recruited so many of his men—an honor Dole accepted in good humor.[18]

Come summer the companies received intensive pack training under the supervision of the muleskinners, learning to saddle, pack and unpack, and care for the mules. They then conducted long-distance route marches into the mountains with the mules. These tests determined that mules were dependable, albeit stubborn, in the mountains, able to climb slopes up to 45°, and careful with their own safety. Since proposed mountain infantry regiments had no assigned motorized vehicles, they would be completely reliant on mules to transport equipment and supplies. As the companies tested mule transport, Rolfe also ordered the officers to learn horsemanship. Some of the officers believed this was Rolfe's revenge for having to learn how to ski, but a mountain infantry battalion had twenty-two riding horses and an entire mountain infantry regiment nearly two hundred. So many mountain troopers could expect to ride.[19]

To test equipment, Rolfe presided over the Mountain and Winter Warfare Board, with Capt Albert Jackman, who had accompanied Bob Bates's Yukon expedition in the summer of 1941, as testing officer. Lt John Jay of the Signal Corps joined for photography, and Maj Robert Tillotson, just transferred from Alaska, served as the liaison to the quartermaster general. Drawing on the experiences of the divisional ski patrols in the winter of 1940–41, Robinson's tests in the Sierra Nevada, and Bates's Alaskan expedition, the OQMG developed, procured, and supplied the 1st Battalion, 87th Mountain Infantry, an issue of minimum equipment for skiing, snowshoeing, and winter camping. However, the specifications, which had been hurriedly prepared and were more ideal for civilian sportsmen than mountain soldiers, required testing and revision. Further, there were no mountain climbing items on the list, so specifications for those would also have to be developed and tested.[20]

The new mountain troopers conducted tests on equipment and clothing under the auspices of Captain Jackman's board. The men tested boots, determining that the ski boot developed and purchased based on civilian downhill skiing models was unsuitable and that a general-purpose mountain boot, for use with skis and snowshoes and on snow, ice, and rock slopes, was needed. They tested ski trousers, made of heavy woolen serge, which proved to collect snow. They tested long, gauntlet mittens made of lambskin, but an opening in the right palm for a trigger finger let in snow. The board studied goggles and glasses at length, before determining specifications for a "Ski-Mountain Goggle."[21]

Troops tested both hickory and laminated skis at Paradise Lodge, and neither proved to be superior, so both were procured. The troops tested several bindings, before settling on a cable binding with a coiled "Bildstein" spring. Seal and mohair climbers, or skins, to allow for uphill travel, were tested, with mohair found to be generally superior. The troops tested waxes and an emergency ski repair kit. And troops tested snowshoes, a larger oval "bearpaw" type and a smaller "emergency" snowshoe, to be carried for use when skis were impractical. The board also conducted tests on equipment for camping on the snow. A mummy sleeping bag with an inner and outer shell and an attached head canopy designed in 1941 was found to be too complicated. Troops experimented with one-, two-, and four-man sectional tents, but the board found none satisfactory. The initial stove designed by the quartermaster general proved to be a little heavy and bulky, and troops needed a leakproof fuel container and waterproof food bag. The rucksack developed in the summer of 1941, based on a commercial design, underwent examination by the battalion and the NSA's winter equipment committee, which found it poorly suited for military use and recommended improvements. The packboard, based on the well-established civilian Yukon model, tested as generally satisfactory, despite its weight.[22]

By April 1942 the board and 87th Mountain Infantry believed the equipment and techniques for winter and skiing were developed and tested enough to dispatch Lt John Jay with a detail of five enlisted men and two officers, Captain Lafferty and Lieutenant Woodward, to Sun Valley, Idaho. There they filmed what became a series of seven ski and winter training films running a total of three hours and twenty minutes. All the films contained a caution that equipment was constantly improving and what was issued could differ from what was shown. The first film, *Ski Equipment*, covered the details of clothing and equipment, such as how they should be used to ensure survival, and gave a complete list of equipment issued to each trooper. The next two, *Snow Camping above Timberline* and *Snow Camping in Timber*, demonstrated the selection of camp locations concealed from the enemy, particularly the need to obscure tracks when approaching a campsite, the duties of leveling the site and pitching tents, lighting, cooking, and sleeping facilities, and transporting, storing, and preparing food and obtaining water.[23]

Ski Safety, film four, discussed adjusting ski bindings and heel springs, determining the type of wax needed, the adjustment of the rucksack, and the wearing of snow goggles. It went on to show how to treat snow blindness, how to use sunburn preventative, and the need to remove excess clothing items while traveling and add extra clothing when resting. *Ski Safety—First Aid and Emergency Repair of Equipment* showed first aid for treating various types of accidents, the handling and removal of the injured, and the emergency repair of equipment. *Ski Sled* demonstrated the use, rigging, and hauling of a sled. The final training film, *Ski Mountaineering*, which drew heavily on *Manual of Ski Mountaineering*, discussed individual equipment, route, objectives, concealment, safety precautions, the use of compass and map, maintaining contact, the use of ski poles and ski touring technique, the pacing of movement, and the proper gradients for climbing. It continued with techniques for moving through dense timber and across streams, climbing rock or ice slopes, avalanche precautions and techniques, and the means of transporting equipment.[24]

The lack of highly specialized mountain climbing gear hampered the board's tests. Most of these items were of European origin, and it took time for American manufacturers to produce their own versions. Not until the spring of 1942 did some of the required items—ice axes, ropes, crampons—reach the field. The board's executive, Captain Jackman, organized a climb of Mt Rainier in May to test these items at high altitude and in glacier terrain, along with much of the standard mountain trooper ski kit. On May 8 Jackman led nine men, including Jay and Swiss mountaineer Cpl Peter Gabriel, onto Rainier on skis. The party established two intermediate camps, then set off from Camp 2 at 12,300 feet on May 16 for the summit. Led by Gabriel, they roped up, with crampons and ice axes. The climbing party tested all the army's skiing and mountaineering gear along the way up and back down. They learned the sectional tent was a disaster, however, with zippers icing up and condensation raining down. The four-man cook set proved to be a "waste of time." The ice axe, fuel container, gaiters, and ski mittens were "definitely unsatisfactory," while crampon teeth bent and broke off. But not all their gear performed badly. The test expedition found the new model of "trousers, mountain, windproof" better than the "trousers, ski, wool." And the standard issue army olive drab flannel wool shirt was "very satisfactory."[25]

As Jackman and his party skied back down Mt Rainier, another test expedition was in the works. By early 1942 Capt Bob Bates realized many of the prototypes to be tested would not be available until spring. He convinced his superior in the Office of the Quartermaster General to attend the April meeting of the American Alpine Club to ask for assistance in testing equipment. Brad Washburn, now a civilian consultant for the Army Air Forces, also attended the meeting. When the AAC agreed to help and a locale had to be determined, Washburn, in the words of mountaineering author David Roberts, promoted "a boondoggle of a mountaineering expedition" to the upper reaches of Mount McKinley, Alaska, as Denali was then known. His rationale was that conditions were very cold, near-arctic, even in the summer, on Denali. A party of seventeen assembled in Alaska, including four members of the AAC, Canadian representatives, Captain Jackman, and now-Sergeant Gabriel, who had climbed with Washburn before. The "Alaskan Test Expedition of 1942" set off on June 20, climbing to the Harper Glacier at 18,000 feet, just below Denali Pass, by early July. For three weeks the expedition tested over thirty items of clothing and equipment, rations, and experimental hygiene items, such as lip balm and paper underwear. Parties reached the summit of Denali on July 22 and 23, including Washburn, Bates, and Jackman. With their evaluations written up and submitted to Washington, DC, by radio, the expedition returned by early August.[26]

Members of the Special Forces Section of the OQMG, the NSA, and the AAC also conducted tests during the year. With all the test reports in hand by the late summer of 1942, the Standardization Branch of the OQMG proceeded to issue specifications for the procurement of the myriad of items the mountain troops would require.[27] This, combined with the dispatch of the 87th Mountain Infantry for maneuvers in central California, ended the technical development and equipment testing for mountain troops. Whole units could now be raised, equipped, and trained.

Mountain Training Center

By the middle of 1942, the question of where to do this had occupied the army G-3 for over eighteen months. The December 1940 meeting with the American Alpine Club impressed the challenges of surviving, let alone fighting under, conditions of high altitude, snow, and cold. So the G-3 began to consider sites suitable for mountain training. A site had to be at elevation, have an area suitable to house 20,000 men, be accessible by road and railroad, have adequate fuel and water, and contain sufficient space for maneuver and artillery ranges. The G-3 initially surveyed the West Yellowstone area of Idaho and Montana. Then, on March 7 and 8, 1941, four colonels from the G-3 toured the central Rocky Mountains of Colorado with the local forest supervisor, looking for sites that possessed all the necessary requirements, including an elevation of 9,000 feet.[28]

The 9,000-foot requirement would later create consternation among the mountain troopers, and even later among scholars, for no potential theater of employment was so high. Colonel Twaddle, the G-3, stated that a mountain camp needed "high altitudes, snow, and low temperatures" so that troops could live and train under these conditions year-round. American mountaineers knew at that time that elevations over 8,000 feet required acclimatization to the altitude, lest an individual succumb to "mountain sickness." Further, being at 9,000 feet would also ensure ample cold, as temperatures would be 50°F lower than at sea level. But it was the need for adequate snow cover for skiing on at least part of the ground for most of the year that truly drove the necessity for such a high mountain camp.[29]

The G-3's team surveyed the Aspen area, nearby Ashcroft, and Wheeler and Pando, both near Leadville. The Aspen area had a good spot for a divisional camp, but all the land was privately owned, and training terrain was too far away. Ashcroft had good terrain but was too small for a camp. Wheeler was too remote, eighteen road miles from the nearest rail hub in Leadville. Pando, which was seventeen miles from Leadville, was a railroad depot, and sat in a wide valley floor with road and rail lines, offered the best potential site in Colorado. On April 2, 1941, the G-3 submitted a memo to the chief of staff requesting funds to establish a camp for a division in high mountain terrain, either West Yellowstone or Pando. One response to the proposal, by Col Orlando Ward, suggested simply moving divisions already based near mountains into the mountains for short periods of training, such as those at Fort Lewis, Washington, Fort Ord, California, and San Luis Obispo, California. Twaddle's response rejected this proposal as the mountains were too far away from those camps and lacked adequate training areas.[30]

General Marshall turned down the G-3's request for funding on May 5, 1941, but did order full surveys for a mountain division camp at West Yellowstone and Pando to be ready for when the army received authorization to expand. As preparations for the full surveys were being made, the G-3 learned that use of West Yellowstone was denied because it was a breeding ground for the nearly extinct trumpeter swan. The Wildlife Conservation Committee carried out a campaign, led by Frederic Delano, uncle of the president, to block the army. In early June five officers—one staff officer, one medical officer, and three engineers—from the Eighth Corps Area headquarters thus closely investigated the Pando area. Their report found it suitable for a cantonment site as it had a railroad station, snowfall that began in October and lasted until June, and sat in a natural bowl giving protection from wind. There were many slopes adequate for ski training and nearly unlimited maneuver and training areas, including artillery and small arms ranges. However, the lack of a social outlet was a disadvantage, as the report held "the morals of Leadville are said to be on a rather low plane."[31]

The Eighth Corps forwarded the report to the War Department on June 27, 1941, where it sat for eight months. By early 1942 it was increasingly clear that Fort Lewis was not suitable for mountain training as the mountains were a half day away and there was no adequate housing on Mt Rainier. Further, the demands of the Western Defense Command, the higher headquarters in the area, were interfering with training. The army G-3 recommended designation of a separate area for mountain training at the end of January. Lieutenant Colonel Rolfe thus inspected Pando on February 6 with two feet of snow on the ground, finding the area suitable for a camp and for training. He recommended that barracks be insulated down to −20°F, that a recreational center with a sports center and indoor arena be built, that stables have sliding doors, ten-foot aisles, and hard surface floors to be used by animals or vehicles, and that each regiment have a 2,500-square-foot supply room for all the extra mountain equipment.[32]

Construction at Pando began on April 10, 1942, with a targeted completion date of November 15. The civilian constructors had to first straighten the meandering Eagle Creek, drain the willow-covered marshy ground, remove two hundred beavers, and bring in two million yards of fill dirt. By May 1 they could lay out roads and begin to construct buildings to deal with snow and ice with strengthened walls, steeper roofs, shorter eaves, and no gutters. The builders added a ski room to each barracks for troops to maintain and store equipment and dry out clothing. On June 23 the growing cantonment received the name Camp Hale, after Brig Gen Irving Hale (1861–1930) of the Colorado National Guard. Construction continued through the summer and fall, and was not completed until mid-December, by which time Camp Hale could hold a mountain division's worth of men and animals.[33]

In January 1942 the army G-3 recommended forming a mountain corps of three divisions plus corps troops. The War Plans Division disagreed as a lack of shipping would make it very difficult to transport a division with all its mules, let alone a corps. Instead, in March 1942, the G-3 planned for two mountain divisions to be activated during the year, with the third division and corps troops deferred. The first mountain division was to be the 100th, designated a special type mountain division to be activated at Pando in November. The commanding general of the 100th Mountain Division would also be commander of a Mountain Command for training. A special command was necessary as mountain units had to acclimate to elevation, had to learn to conduct supply with manpower, aircraft, and pack animals, and needed specialist climbers and skiers. By early April the army rethought its plan, particularly about activating and conducting basic military training of a division in the Colorado Rockies in winter. Instead, the 89th Division would be designated as a mountain division and activated in July 1942 at Camp Carson, Colorado, 150 road miles away from Pando. Upon completion of basic training and construction at Pando, the 89th Mountain Division would move up into the mountains to conduct its specialized training, while the 100th would activate at Camp Carson and include low mountain operations in its training.[34]

An obstacle soon arose to this plan. As noted above, all the necessary equipment and transport for a mountain division had yet to be fully tested, and specifications released, by the spring of 1942 so likely could not be procured in the coming year in sufficient quantities to support an entire division for the winter of 1942–43. It would thus be "unwise" to attempt to train a mountain division during the coming winter. The 89th Division would therefore be activated as a standard "flatland" infantry division at Camp Carson that summer and another experimental unit based on the 87th Mountain Infantry would occupy the mountain camp at Pando in November. The commanding general of the 89th would supervise this experimental mountain force and, once the issues of equipment and transportation were solved, would oversee the conversion of his division to a mountain division in the spring of 1943. By the end of April 1942, it was to be the 89th Mountain Division in Colorado, but not for another year.[35]

Expansion of the 87th Mountain Infantry from a single battalion to an overstrength regiment was at the heart of the army's plans to activate a full mountain division. This would entail continuing to utilize the services of the National Ski Patrol "to comb the mountain regions for specially qualified personnel" who could then be sent to Fort Lewis to receive their basic training. This complicated the regiment's ongoing mountain training, but the G-3 believed it was "worth it in view of the fine men to be procured quickly." The NSP issued Bulletin #12, stating the mountain infantry now needed another three thousand men of "the best material available from the men of the outdoors," not just skiers. By the summer of 1942, "gradually, then with a rush, the 87th Mountain Infantry filled up."[36]

The American Alpine Club played a key role in providing qualified mountain officers to the growing mountain regiment. In March 1942 the AAC's defense committee proposed staffing a mountain school for the army and enlisting "competent mountaineers." The army, facing the basic training challenges of expanding the 87th into an entire regiment, rejected the AAC's plan. But the AAC persisted, continuing to encourage the War Department to accept its proposals, including by writing directly to Secretary of War Stimson, who had been elected as an honorary member of the AAC the previous December. The club finally convinced the army to ask for its aid in recruiting men that could "best serve the nation as junior officers with the mountain troops." The adjutant general, responsible for personnel, on July 7 agreed to enlist qualified mountaineers as determined by the AAC. After basic training and upon passing an examination board, they would be sent to Officers Candidate School (OCS), after which they would be assigned to the mountain troops. The AAC ultimately enlisted twenty-eight men to serve as mountain officers, including David Brower of the Sierra Club, by the end of 1942. Rolfe, however, facing the need to officer two more mountain infantry battalions and potentially an entire mountain division, seized on the adjutant general's authority to begin to send qualified enlisted men, including Charlie McLane, to OCS in the summer of 1942 and returning them to the 87th.[37]

But plans for an eventual mountain division bogged down due to strategic developments and a looming lack of manpower. During the summer of 1942, the United States and the United Kingdom negotiated where and when their combined forces would enter into combat against Germany. The options ranged from a cross-Channel invasion in 1943, an emergency invasion in 1942, or a landing in North Africa in 1942. None of the prospective theaters were seen to require the employment of specialized mountain units. In July 1942 President Roosevelt directed US forces to join the British in North Africa by the end of October. At the same time, the US Army faced a manpower crisis, being some 162,505 men short in the Army Ground Forces in June. This shortage increased to over 300,000 men, leading to a postponement of unit activations, including the mountain unit. At the end of July 1942, the AGF recommended relieving the 89th Division of its mountain mission and organizing a mountain training center at Camp Carson, Colorado, to facilitate the activation of a complete mountain division in early 1943.[38]

Colonel Rolfe, soon promoted to brigadier general, arrived at Camp Carson in August and activated and took command of the Mountain Training Center (MTC) on September 3. A number of officers and men from the 87th Mountain Infantry and Mountain and Winter Warfare Board served as the headquarters cadre. A signal company, medical battalion, quartermaster battalion, and engineer battalion were all activated under the MTC within days, along with an ordnance company, antitank and antiaircraft company, and a military police platoon. Four battalions of pack artillery, with mules and muleskinners, arrived at Camp Carson in October. Rolfe spent six weeks acclimating his command at the lower elevations of Colorado Springs, before moving them to the barely completed Camp Hale, 158 road miles and three thousand feet higher, on November 16. A few days later a cavalry reconnaissance troop arrived from South Dakota.[39]

To staff the MTC and to fill the next regiment of mountain infantry, the army, having suspended the NSP's recruitment efforts in July, attempted to have replacement training centers locate any "rugged outdoor types" such as mountaineers, trappers, woodsmen, lumberjacks, skiers, mule packers, geologists, teamsters, hunting guides, or horseshoers among their recruits and send them directly to the MTC. While the replacement centers did find enough men to activate the 1st Battalion of the 86th Mountain Infantry on November 26, with a cadre provided by the 87th, there were not enough for an entire regiment. A month later, as the rest of the 87th Mountain Infantry rolled into Camp Hale from the central California maneuvers, the army again called on Minnie Dole and the NSP to ask for assistance in recruiting two thousand men in ninety days. A flood of questionnaires went out, a flow of completed applications returned, and many approved NSP applicants were in Camp Hale within ten days of applying to join the growing 86th Mountain Infantry.[40]

As 1942 had been a year of experimentation by mountain troops, the end of the year showed the results. The National Ski Patrol proved it could muster thousands of volunteers within a few months, providing excellent personnel to fill out two mountain infantry regiments. The techniques of military skiing were becoming well developed, while those of rock climbing were less so, but still progressing. Equipment specifications were determined, and procurement authorized, with gear flowing into warehouses. While the army understood mule transport, oversnow transport was still in a nascent stage, though improving. And the Mountain Training Center now existed to train mountain troops and activate an entire division in the coming year.

CHAPTER 3

MOUNTAIN TRAINING, 1943

Snow and Ice

By 1943 the US Army was training divisions through an assembly-line process. The divisional commander and his staff arrived at the division camp thirty-seven days ahead of activation, followed a week later by a cadre of officers and enlisted men. The remaining 452 officers arrived over the next few days, and the full complement of over 13,000 enlisted men flowed in from reception centers two weeks after activation. The new division then conducted thirteen weeks of basic training, eleven weeks of unit training, and another eleven weeks of combined training. Finally, the division moved to a large-scale maneuver area to participate in several months of division-on-division exercises before heading overseas.[1]

None of this applied to what would become the 10th Mountain Division. The cadre at Camp Hale was to staff the Mountain Training Center, not activate a division. Officers and men experienced in the mountains were quite few in number. Enlisted men arrived throughout the year, requiring regular rounds of basic training, in lieu of one period, which interfered with unit training. And the seasonal mountain training that had to accompany all the basic and unit training took time and required specialized instructors. And still, the army had yet to realize a firm requirement for mountain warfare capabilities, just some glimmers in the Aleutian campaign. Meanwhile, the nascent mountain division had to deal with several other challenges.

Issues

The initial issue for the US Army's mountain troops was personnel. At first it was hoped that units could be raised from volunteers—skiers or other "outdoor types" who could be turned into soldiers. The recruiting campaigns run by Minnie Dole and the National Ski Patrol served as the primary source of these

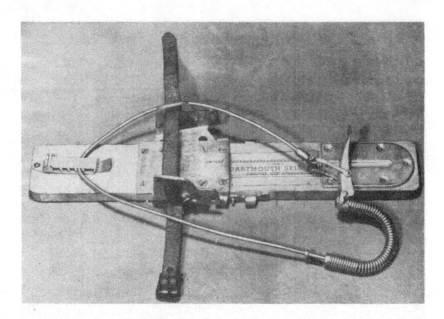

Ski Binding, Open

Ski Binding, Closed

Ski binding, from OQMG, *Equipment for Special Forces*, 94.

volunteers. From December 1941 until 1945 the NSP, in several episodic efforts in response to army requests, took in 12,055 applications. Of these, 7,914 were eventually selected for service with the mountain troops. Other volunteers, often already serving, took advantage of periodic army directives to transfer men with required skills and experiences to the mountain troops. Many of the volunteers were skilled skiers, with mountain experience, or were experienced mountaineers. They were motivated to serve and were highly intelligent. Most of the volunteers had the Army General Classification Test scores to qualify as potential officers, while the rest were potential noncommissioned officers. The more volunteers in an outfit, the better the training, and the higher the morale. The American Alpine Club sought to recruit its members, but its membership was small, and most were over military age. Many who could serve were already in uniform, such as Bob Bates. The US Forest Service and National Park Service contributed some of their rangers, packers, and guides, including Paul Petzoldt. Yet there were never enough volunteers for an entire mountain division. By one estimate volunteers made up only 20 percent of the ultimate division, concentrated in the infantry regiments.[2]

The army made up the shortfall by transferring men to Camp Hale. At the start of 1943, to fill up the supporting signal, medical, artillery, and quartermaster battalions and to replace the men assigned to the MTC staff and to the forming 86th Regiment from the 87th Mountain Infantry, the army transferred men in from three divisions—30th, 31st, and 33rd—based in Tennessee and Louisiana, who were soon referred to as "flatlanders." Despite instruction to "select enlisted men for these cadres who are suited for rigorous service in the mountains," the "flatlanders" proved to be almost "entirely unsuited to the rigors of mountain living," as there was no physical fitness standard for mountain troops, despite repeated requests for such from the Mountain Training Center. So those among the cadres who could not adapt to the mountains had to be weeded out, which required more cadres to replace them, resulting in further weeding out. While many of the cadres did catch the enthusiasm of the volunteers and came to embrace the training and the mountains, others did not want to be in the mountains and were uninterested in the training. Even some of the volunteers, expecting a ski vacation and discovering they were in the army, expressed a "spirit of dissension." Most of the men of what would become the 10th Mountain Division had little experience in the mountains, meaning they would have to be trained.[3]

Both the cadres and the volunteers received the full issue of mountain equipment, which was often bewildering to the former and disappointing to the latter. The army followed what the mountaineers of the American Alpine Club and the (backcountry) skiers of the National Ski Association had been

Mountain Clothing and Equipment Issue, Camp Hale, 1943

Item	Quantity
Individual Clothing	
Boots, mukluk (w/2 felt insoles)	1 pr
Boots, ski-mountain, with rubber cleated soles (w/2 felt insoles)	1 pr
Cap, ski	1
Cap, wool, knit	1
Drawers, wool	4
Gaiters, ski	1 pr
Jacket, mountain (w/sweater, sleeveless)	1
Mittens, insert, trigger finger	2 pr
Mittens, over, white	1 pr
Mittens, shell, trigger finger	1 pr
Muffler, wool, od[a]	1
Parka, reversible, ski	1
Shirt, flannel, od, coat-style	2
Socks, wool, ski	4 pr
Suspenders, trousers	1
Sweater, high neck	1
Trousers, field, over, white	1
Trousers, wool ski or trousers, mountain	1
Undershirt, wool	4
Individual Equipment	
Bag, food, waterproof	1
Bag, sleeping, mountain	1
Box, match, waterproof	1
Brush, mountain	1
Case, water repellent, bag, sleeping	1
Cover, pack, white	1
Goggles, ski, mountain	1
Knife, pocket, mountain	1
Pad, insulated, sleeping	1
Rucksack	1
Tent, mountain, two-man, complete	1/2 men
Thong, emergency	1

Source: WD, T/E No. 21 (1943).
[a] olive drab

advising for several years. The clothing consisted of several lighter layers, to better create insulating air space. Wool garments were worn against the skin and for warmth, as wool kept some insulating properties when damp. The outer layers were weather-resistant, not weatherproof, as they had to breathe, allowing heat and moisture to escape. These layers were made of tightly woven cotton fabrics. And each man had to have a suite of individual equipment.[4]

The new mountain troopers stuffed long-sleeved undershirts and full drawers, both made of a fifty/fifty wool/cotton blend, and wool ski socks into their increasingly bulging barracks bags for their base layer. For additional insulation they had their regular issue olive drab wool flannel shirt, a wool knit cap, and a wool muffler or scarf. The warehouse also issued two wool sweaters, one sleeveless and one with five buttons and a high neck. The base and insulating layers were to be worn beneath an outer layer and removed to lose heat and to dry or added to ensure warmth. At the top of this outer layer, the men wore a ski cap, patterned after civilian models. It was windproof and water-repellent with eyelets near the top for ventilation and ear flaps secured on the outside by a strap and buckle in the front in earlier models and folded inside in later ones. For the winter the men were issued a pullover reversible ski parka made of two layers of windproof, water-repellent cotton poplin, one layer white and the other olive drab, reaching to midthigh. It had a fur-trimmed hood and button closures. For summer wear the men drew a hooded mountain jacket, windproof and water-repellent, with a full zipper closure and the hood folded up under the collar. The mountain jacket had four large cargo pockets and a larger pocket across the back with internal suspenders, making it possible to carry equipment when not carrying a rucksack.[5] The ski cap, ski parka, and mountain jacket made up the most readily recognizable uniform of the mountain troops.

For wear below the ski parka or mountain jacket, regimental warehouses issued a pair of ski trousers, replaced during the year by a pair of mountain trousers with suspenders. The mountain trousers, referred to as a "ski type," were made of wind-resistant and water-repellent cotton sateen, had an elastic stirrup under the foot to keep the cuff tucked into the boot, zippered hand and rear pockets, and large cargo pockets. With the suspenders the trousers could be worn loose around the waist to allow for air flow, while carrying heavy loads in the pockets. The troopers also had a pair of white ski trousers made of light, water-repellent cotton poplin. Held up by a drawstring and without pockets, the white ski trousers were worn over the mountain trousers for snow camouflage and for additional warmth and wind protection. For the hands supply sergeants issued a fingerless knit wristlet, two pairs of wool insert mittens with trigger fingers (so when one pair was wet it could be dried), a pair of windproof poplin mittens with a leather palm and trigger fingers, and white covers for snow camouflage to be worn over the mittens. The first model of mittens and inserts had the trigger finger on the palm, while the later one had the trigger finger on the back of the mitten, making the palm more snow-resistant.[6]

The men at Camp Hale drew a pair of ski-mountain boots, as fine a piece of mountain equipment that could be developed at the time. The leather boot had a stiff sole, square toes, and grooved heels for ski bindings, but with a rocker bottom to allow for walking and climbing, improved by the addition of mountain boot nails on the edges, center, and heels of the sole. The nails, however, collected snow when skiing and placed the foot too high in the binding. Thanks to the efforts of the mountaineers assigned to the OQMG, by 1943 a rubber sole developed by the Italian mountaineer Vitale Bramani in the mid-1930s was increasingly available with 3/16-inch molded cleats, V-shaped in the middle of the sole and square U-shaped on the edges. This gave the boot a good grip on almost every surface, except smooth ice, and eliminated the snow buildup when in ski bindings. A pair of ski gaiters, reversible with white on one side, kept snow or debris from entering the boots and provided extra warmth in the cold. The boots were to be worn with two pairs of socks and felt insoles for insulation and to absorb moisture. When the socks and insoles were wet, they were to be replaced with dry pairs. Many men at Camp Hale also were issued mukluk boots, the warmest footwear the army had with a leather bottom and a fabric top to allow perspiration to evaporate rather than freeze on the feet. These were only worn on cold days in bivouac to allow the feet to dry.[7]

To prevent snow blindness, the men received ski-mountain goggles with green glass lenses and slits in the top and bottom of the eye cup to reduce fogging. Also included in the standard issue for each man were a plastic waterproof matchbox to have an emergency supply, a mountain pocketknife for emergency repairs with two cutting blades—one for food and the other to use on the wooden skis—a can opener, a leather punch, and a Phillips screwdriver. Finally, the soldiers carried a long, leather thong for emergency repairs on every piece of equipment. These items were typically carried in the pockets, for everything else the mountain troopers needed was carried in a large rucksack.[8]

The government-issue rucksack was similar in design to the well-known civilian mountaineering Bergen rucksack. Made of canvas, it closed at the top with a drawstring and a covering flap and had three external pockets. Attached to a tubular steel frame, which moved much of the weight to the hips and allowed some ventilation of the back, it had web shoulder straps and a waist belt. To the pack would be attached those items typically carried on the cartridge belt—first aid pouch, canteen, bayonet, entrenching tool—and the rifle to allow the mountain trooper to ski or climb with legs uninhibited and hands free.

For snow camouflage, the men received a white rucksack cover. A waterproof food bag went into the rucksack, along with a mountain sleeping bag—a down- and feather-filled mummy bag with a half opening. In winter the canteen was placed inside the rolls of the sleeping bag to prevent freezing. The bag could be enclosed in a water-repellent outer case for additional protection and warmth. A sleeping pad was issued to provide insulation and prevent transmission of moisture to the bag.[9]

Every two men drew a two-man mountain tent, with pins, poles, and guy-lines, with the expectation that one man would carry the tent with the lines attached and the other the twelve pole sections and six pins or stakes. Attempts at individual sectional tents that could be combined into larger shelters proved unsatisfactory as they were too small for the troopers and all their equipment. The OQMG developed a new tent, modeled after civilian Everest tents. Made of waterproof balloon cloth (the designers wanted nylon but not enough was available), the mountain tent was reversible—white and olive drab. It had a floor with a tunnel entrance and large front and rear ventilators for drying clothes and using a stove. Erected with four collapsible three-section poles, run through sleeves at the corners, forming an inverted "V" front and back, with guylines at the front, rear, and along the sides, held down by stakes, the tent was quite stable. Each trooper also received a stiff mountain brush to remove snow from clothing and equipment before entering the tent and to sweep snow out of the tent.[10]

Many mountain troops had problems handling the issued mountain equipment. The transferred cadres, the flatlanders, did not know how to wear and use all that was issued to them. The volunteers had different issues. Since many had experience with civilian kit, which was often better made in small batches and by hand, they had their own, strong personal preferences and brought those to military service. Many thus found fault with the government-issued gear made by manufacturers who had never produced such equipment in such quantities before. The ski-mountain boots were said not to fit into the bindings and were issued in too large of sizes, the new style ski cap was criticized as unsuitable for the winter, and the ski gaiter fitted badly. Lt Col Bestor Robinson, now with the OQMG, determined that experience, experimentation, and issuance of newer models would deal with many of these complaints, though they never went away completely.[11]

While some of the men had issues with their equipment, all had issues with the environment at Camp Hale. The altitude of the camp, selected to ensure a lengthy cold and snow season for training, physically wore many men out. Mountaineers understood that acclimatization was necessary for such eleva-tions; it was preferable to slowly move up over weeks to the highest altitude.

This option was not available at Camp Hale, where many men who had arrived from sea level were put to work within a few days at physical labor. The elevation meant not only a lack of oxygen, but also very dry air. This was made worse by Camp Hale's location in a sheltered basin. Without the wind to move the air, soot from hundreds of coal stoves and several trains a day hung around the camp, settling on every surface. This led to the "Pando hack" or "Pando-monia," a severe cough and sore throat, combined with exhaustion from the elevation.[12]

All these issues—personnel, equipment, environment—came to a head in the Homestake Peak exercise of early February 1943. In preparation for activation of a full mountain division later that year, Army Ground Forces directed the Mountain Training Center to test a battalion in the field under winter conditions. The 2nd Battalion, 87th Mountain Infantry Regiment, reinforced by a mule-carried battery of 75 mm pack howitzers of the 99th Field Artillery (Pack) and detachments from medical, quartermaster (pack mule), signal, antiaircraft-antitank, and engineer units, made up the exercise force. It was to move northwest of Camp Hale to an area east of Homestake Peak at 11,000 feet. There it would hold a defensive position below the peak and repel raids by a platoon of aggressor ski troops, made up of the MTC's and 87th's best skiers. The primary objective of the exercise was to test training, clothing, equipment, and supply. The AGF, OQMG, and NSP all sent observers, including William House and Minnie Dole. While Brigadier General Rolfe, commander of the MTC, realized that training was not yet advanced enough—many of the men had yet to even complete their basic training—he felt compelled to conduct the exercise anyway.[13]

Due to the lack of training, the exercise became what mountaineers and backcountry skiers today call a "suffer-fest." Trucks dropped the force off along the Leadville–Tennessee Pass Road (today US Highway 24) on the morning of February 4, into blizzard conditions of high winds, heavy snow, and temperatures of −10°F. Most of the men were recent transfers or new recruits and were not acclimated mentally or physically to the altitude and cold. They stood for two hours, putting on all their warm clothing. However, when they finally moved out, not having been instructed in the use of their specialized clothing, they failed to "delayer"—that is, take clothes off so as not to overheat. As a result, they moved out too fast, rapidly becoming sweat-soaked; things were only made worse when their skis began to slip as the road grew steep, as they had not been trained to use wax for cross-country grip or their mohair climbers, or skins. And they were not trained in the use of most of the specialized items they carried in nearly eighty-pound packs, many of which were not actually needed for the exercise. As the short winter day came to an end, many fell out of the formation from exhaustion and fear of the unknown.[14]

Once in the bivouac site, it became apparent most of the men had received no instruction in snow camping—the use of their sleeping bags, tents, and stoves, which many of the men had only been issued the day prior. The MTC thus canceled the tactical elements of the exercise and spent the next week focusing on methods of snow camping, including the use of snow caves, and generally learning how to survive and move in the mountains under winter conditions. This was only partially successful because nearly one-third of the exercise force became a casualty of frostbite, exhaustion, or sickness. Casualties could have been even higher had not Maj Walter Wood, an experienced mountaineer and AAC member observing the exercise for the AGF, stopped a platoon from going into avalanche terrain—east facing, 35–45° slope, beneath an overhanging cornice—to retrieve airdropped supplies. Equally oblivious to the consequences, artillery fired on the cornice, setting off an avalanche that nearly swept into the bivouac site. The test was finally ended on February 12, and the return to Camp Hale by the bedraggled exercise force went down in mountain trooper lore as the "Retreat from Moscow."[15]

The observers submitted their reports, all agreeing with Rolfe's assessment that more training was required. It was not enough to simply recruit skiers or other outdoor types or transfer any soldier to Camp Hale and provide them with military mountaineering clothing and equipment. Men, whether volunteers or assigned, had to be physically capable of being in the mountains. All required mountain training in winter and summer at both the individual and collective level, in addition to basic and unit training. The skills for such training had to be pooled from the enlisted and junior officers who had mountaineering and skiing experience. This group in particular lost confidence when they saw their senior officers, who were learning winter mountaineering on the job, floundering in situations they had long ago mastered. The problem, as Minnie Dole put it, was the mountain troops had "rank at the top and brains at the bottom."[16] Mountain troops required mountain training for which they would need qualified mountain instructors. And to take full advantage of their training, mountain troops also needed mountain officers.

Mountain Training

The mission of the Mountain Training Center was unclear. It was initially conceived as the headquarters for a reinforced regiment acting as a test force to determine the best equipment, training, and organization for a future mountain division. But, organized as a protodivisional headquarters, it faced the need to conduct basic and specialized mountain training for a division's worth of units during winter, before there was a division. The MTC came to understand its mission as "learning how to fight in the mountains." The staff of the MTC, organized as a regular infantry division headquarters with around two hundred officers and men, was not large enough for the simultaneous, dual job of supervising specialized mountain training and regular infantry training. While the MTC had billets for four captains—specialists in skiing, rock climbing, dog management, and mule packing, to supervise specialized training—they were never filled. The MTC simply forged ahead with a "confusing counter-pattern of basic training in the midst of a highly specialized mountain fighting program."[17]

As a mountain division had not been activated at Camp Hale and experienced men were hard to find, even with the best efforts of the National Ski Patrol, recruits trickled in during the first half of 1943 at a rate of as few as three a week or as many as one hundred. Basic training thus had to be done in echelons, or else combined with mountain training. Neither approach, as it was noted at the time, was acceptable. The MTC had to modify the Army Ground Forces directives intended for a standard infantry flatland division that did not cover skiing, mountaineering, cold weather camping, clothing care, or cold weather equipment maintenance. Any winter training event in the mountains took several times longer than standard directives planned for due to altitude and snow. Acclimatization and cold weather complicated basic training. Standard plans called for movement to training areas via motorized vehicles, which the MTC did not possess, thus adding three hours a day. Bivouacking at the training area would save time, but this required men acclimated and trained in cold weather camping, something the Homestake Peak experience vividly demonstrated.[18]

The companies of what would become the 2nd Battalion, 86th Mountain Infantry, illustrated the "confusing counter-pattern" of simultaneous individual basic and mountain training. In April 1943, in the two weeks before the battalion was activated on the 26th, Company E conducted winter bivouacs, while Company F fired on the rifle range in a snowstorm, Company G received ski training, and Company H was just beginning its basic training learning close-order drill, viewing training films, and attending lectures on military courtesy and discipline. Ultimately the MTC determined that basic training for a mountain trooper would take seventeen rather than thirteen weeks, to allow for additional individual mountain training: acclimatization, skiing, rock climbing, cold weather camping, and animal handling.[19]

The MTC realized that much of this additional mountain training required specially qualified instructors. The MTC, like the 1st Battalion, 87th Mountain Infantry, a year prior, looked to experienced civilian skiers and mountaineers who were willing and able to volunteer for the mountain troops to serve as instructors. Of the many experienced civilian skiers at the MTC, most could only instruct skiing, not all the other skills and techniques required for mobility and survival in the mountains in summer and winter. "Paradoxically," as one of the instructors later put it, "the mountain troops lacked mountaineers." There were comparatively few civilian mountaineers in the United States, and many of these were too old for military service or had already entered military service in other branches or services. Nor were there any qualified mountain guides in the United States to draw on. Paul Petzoldt ran one of the few guiding companies in the nation, but Petzoldt was initially only assigned to Camp Hale as an enlisted medic. The MTC managed to assemble some twenty experienced mountaineers at Camp Hale by the spring of 1943, who would train a cadre of over one hundred instructors, especially drawing on the ski instructors.[20]

Having gotten these instructors to conduct mountain training, the MTC faced another problem. Organized as a divisional headquarters, the MTC had no lines on its table of organization for an additional 150 instructors. Without lines on a T/O, the MTC's instructors would be part of other units with the center having no control over them. A unique solution was soon found. The original plans for a mountain division included a horse-mounted reconnaissance unit, the 10th Cavalry Reconnaissance Troop. However, the cavalrymen and their horses proved unsuitable for mountain scouting. Army Ground Forces directed the transfer of the cavalrymen to the QM pack companies, or out of Camp Hale completely, on April 25, 1943, and their replacement with "skilled mountaineers and skiers." The MTC thus "harvested" the reconnaissance troop's seven officer and 142 enlisted billets for its mountain and winter warfare instructors. The mission of the new "10th Recon" was now to teach standard military mountaineering techniques.[21]

The activation of a division in July 1943 complicated an already complicated situation. The Mountain Training Center's mission was now complete, and most of the officers and men transferred into the new divisional headquarters, leaving over one hundred experienced mountain and winter warfare instructors. On October 23, 1943, the MTC disbanded, and the remaining personnel transferred to a Mountain Training Group (MTG) that was activated to serve as a pool for mountain training instructor teams, soon augmented by two hundred men from the 87th Mountain Infantry. This put a further strain on the T/O, with over thirty second lieutenants assigned to the MTG, but no second lieutenant billets authorized, for example. The MTG, for administrative purposes, reported to Second Army, and as the new division was not authorized a cavalry reconnaissance troop, the 10th Recon also reported to Second Army. Finally, in March 1944, the Second Army transferred the 10th Cavalry Reconnaissance Troop without equipment or personnel to Fort Knox, Kentucky. Most of the men in the 10th Recon and MTG were then transferred to the infantry regiments of the 10th Division. The remaining thirty-four officers and 102 enlisted instructors joined a reorganized MTG that included skiing, snowshoeing, rock climbing, equipment, and medical evacuation sections. The instructors of this new MTG could thus train a new mountain division, if one was to be activated.[22]

One problem never resolved was how to identify and promote the skiing and mountaineering instructors, who were often privates. The Mountain Training Center in October 1942 requested an allotment of technical ratings for "climbing and skiing guides" in mountain units. Such a rating would allow instructors to be promoted based on their skills, not on their billet within a unit. After seven months of back-and-forth with AGF, the MTC's request for mountain guide technical ratings were dropped with no action. The army never grasped the technical skill required of a mountain warfare instructor (MWI). Many instructors at Camp Hale thus never advanced beyond the grade of private first class, despite the fact they had the ability to be a platoon sergeant or even a platoon commander, with nothing but "a narrow white band of adhesive tape on their jackets and parkas to show for their skill and experience."[23]

Even with experienced instructors teaching mountain skills to individual soldiers, the use of the techniques in the field had to be supervised by experienced officers. After the Homestake Peak fiasco, at Minnie Dole's urging, the War Department expanded the plan agreed to with the AAC the prior summer and allowed enlisted men in the mountain troops, experienced in skiing and the mountains and with qualifying test scores, to attend Officers Candidate School and then return to Camp Hale as second lieutenants. This was an exception to army policy, which was to send newly commissioned lieutenants to different units to avoid fraternization issues. For this reason, many of the qualified enlisted men—and there were many, given the greater number of college graduates among the volunteers—had refused to apply to OCS for they did not wish to leave the mountain troops. With the change to policy, during the spring and summer of 1943, over two hundred mountain troopers made their way to Georgia and then back to Colorado as second lieutenants, more than a full divisional complement. Almost half of the junior officers in the mountain troops would come from the ranks.[24]

The initial tranche of new lieutenants reported back to the MTC in early May 1943, some assigned to their previous unit, others to new units. Former staff sergeant Stennett M. Shepherd, a veteran of the 87th from the Mt Rainier days and a graduate of Stanford and the University of California Law School, was assigned to the headquarters detachment, 2nd Battalion, 87th Mountain Infantry. Lt Arthur M. Gustafson, a former sergeant in Company F of the 87th, reported to the 10th Quartermaster Battalion. Company I, 86th Mountain

Infantry, received four new officers, all former members of the 87th. The 86th also received two officers back from its ranks, Donald C. Lane and Henry C. Knowlton. The trip back from OCS to Hale did not always go smoothly. In August 1943 eight new lieutenants from the 10th Division were sent to Alabama. But most did return to the mountain troops, where their friends and ski partners were still enlisted men. Despite orders to the contrary, many enlisted men visited officers' quarters and many lieutenants went into the enlisted clubs, albeit as circumspectly as possible. Ultimately, the men and officers of what would become the 10th Mountain Division shared a deep bond over their shared mountain training.[25]

Mobility

Much like the year prior at Fort Lewis while in command of the 1st Battalion of the 87th Mountain Infantry, Colonel Rolfe at Camp Hale, now in command of the MTC, in January 1943 started training in the middle of winter, which meant skiing. Unlike the year before, Rolfe and his command had far more information and experience at hand. The months on Mt Rainier gave a season's worth of insight into military ski training and provided the basis for a chapter on military ski technique for an *Experimental Ski Manual.* Newly arrived at Camp Hale in the late fall of 1942, the staff of the MTC reworked the experimental manual's chapter on military skiing for a *Proposed Manual for Mountain Troops.* The chapter was to "give the instruction needed to enable a soldier who has not skied before to travel safely, with a pack and in a unit of men, over rugged, snow-covered mountain terrain." The MTC kept the basic progression system of the Arlberg technique but added a simplified system of drill with skis to allow units of skiers to "move without disorder" and brought in elements from other skiing techniques. In particular they added the sideslip, keeping the skis parallel and placing them across the fall line, a technique most associated with the French, Alpine, or parallel school.[26]

This effort at a unified system was something American civilian skiers embraced. German-Swiss immigrant Frank Harper published the *Military Ski Manual* in early 1943. Harper argued for a unification of the best skiing techniques from the existing schools, building on the Arlberg's focus on the snowplow, adding in the Swiss school's emphasis on evenly weighted skis, and then the parallel method, which prepared a skier for more advanced turns. The MTC knew of Harper's work, in large part because it was heavily illustrated with photos from their Mt Rainier experience. John S. Holden, one of the first American professional ski instructors, also argued for getting the Swiss, Arlberg, and parallel systems together. A beginning skier would learn to walk, climb, go straight, traverse, and then sideslip. This would allow the skier to execute a turn by driving with their hips and steering with their feet, vice swinging the shoulder.[27]

John Woodward, now a captain and director of the MTC ski school, personally preferred the Swiss ski technique as it "relied on stemming, unweighting, and weight transfer to make turns" instead of shoulder rotation, but he did not have many instructors who knew the technique and no time to teach the rest. He thus laid out a ski school schedule in January 1943 with twenty basic and twenty advanced three-hour lessons that taught a "Swiss-French-Arlberg mashup." The first lesson began with the basic explanation of equipment, taught use of snow goggles and sunburn cream, and introduced ski drill. Woodward kept the standard progression of walk, downhill, stop, traverse, and turn, though the basic lessons only taught the snowplow turn, initiated from the snowplow position down the fall line, and the stem turn, a snowplow turn initiated a from a traverse across the fall line. Woodward added the sideslip to the Arlberg techniques, introducing it with the snowplow in lesson four to brake or check speed, particularly at the top or bottom of a turn. Instructors could use the sideslip to emphasize even weight and a stable, quiet upper body while making turns.[28]

However, the basic lessons focused more on using skis for oversnow mobility than downhill skiing. Cross-country techniques, closer to today's ski touring than to Nordic skiing, took up one hour of every three-hour lesson from the fifth lesson. Initial instruction included the proper use of waxes and of climbers (skins in current parlance). The basic lessons continually emphasized climbing and mobility techniques, including the herringbone step, sidesteps, and traversing, uphill and downhill. The instructors also taught careful skiing over bumps and "bushwhacking," or tree skiing. Three of the twenty basic lessons were fully devoted to ski touring including course setting and navigation, breaking trail and setting a skin track, pacing, and proper layering of clothing to avoid overheating or to conserve body heat, as necessary. Students wore a light rucksack of ten pounds for the first ten basic lessons, increased to twenty pounds for the last ten.[29]

The MTC Ski School's twenty advanced lessons concentrated on turns additional cross-country techniques. Advanced turns taught included the uphill christie, or "hockey stop," used to stop when traversing; the advanced stem turn with a narrower snowplow turn; and the lifted stem christie, a low-speed, short-radius turn that requires the inside ski to be lifted to complete. The stem christie—in which the skier initiates the turn from traverse, into a snowplow turn, but brings the skis back together in parallel in the middle of the turn, and then skids or sideslips the skis back into a traverse—was the most advanced turn taught, as MTC did not teach the telemark turn. Again, one-third of each lesson concentrated on cross-country techniques, with three full lessons devoted completely to cross-country. Now the soldiers were to ski with a thirty-pound field pack for the first ten advanced lessons and with a forty-pound pack and ten-pound rifle for the last ten lessons. This included skiing on variable snow, breakable crust, and variable terrain, using poles to check speed by pole riding or jump turns. Many troopers learned it was best to ski slowly under these conditions and often left their climbers on their skis to act as brakes, engaging in what today is called "downhill skinning."[30]

Not everyone at Camp Hale was to receive ski training. Tables of equipment only authorized skis for just over one-third of any unit assigned to the mountains. In January 1943 the MTC planned to conduct ski training for the infantry units, the signal company (who would be responsible for stringing phone lines cross-country), but only 10 percent of the supporting artillery, quartermaster, antitank and antiaircraft artillery, ordnance, and military police units. Skiers drew a pair of skis, laminated or increasingly hickory, with steel edges, uniformly 3½ inches (89 mm) at the tip, 3 inches (76 mm) at the waist, and 3¼ inches (83 mm) at the tail. Length varied by skier height from six feet nine (206 mm), to seven feet (213 mm), to seven three (221 mm), to seven six (228 mm). Poles were either steel or laminated bamboo cane, and bindings were of the Kandahar type with a cross-country or touring setting and two downhill settings. A ski safety strap fastened the binding loosely to the boot to prevent the ski from being lost in case it came out of the binding. Each skier also received three tubes of color-coded waxes: blue for dry snow, red for speed, and orange for wet snow. When waxes were not enough to ensure the skis would not slip while climbing, soldiers would put on mohair climbers, or skins, looped over the tips and attached to the skis with straps. These were initially issued in brown, but those were soon superseded by white-colored climbers.[31]

Several other ski accessories were unit issue, typically about one per squad. These included ski adaptors and contraction bands, two pairs of which could be combined with two rucksack frames and two thongs to make an emergency sled to move supplies or evacuate a wounded soldier. The most common ski breakage was at the tip, so an emergency repair ski tip, of aluminum, predrilled with four holes and screws, was also issued. The contraction bands could also be used to clamp the repair tip onto a broken ski. For all other emergency repairs, there was a ski repair kit with a combination file and countersink, a scraper, a multitool with pliers, wire cutter, screwdrivers, and wrenches, and an assortment of wood screws, bolts, wire, leather laces and thongs, steel edge pieces, and white adhesive tape.[32]

The mountain troopers in the winter of 1943 took their skis initially to one of four slopes, lettered A, B, C, and D, around Camp Hale, each with a

Ski Equipment Issue, Camp Hale, 1943

Item	Quantity
Individual	
Bindings, ski	1 pr
Climbers, ski, mohair	1 pr
Poles, ski	1 pr
Skis, Type 1, laminated or hickory	1 pr
Strap, ski, safety	1 pr
Unit	
Adaptors, ski	1 pr/12 men
Bands, contraction, ski	1 pr/12 men
Kit, repair, ski	1/12 men
Tip, ski, emergency, repair	1/12 men

Source: WD, T/E No. 21 (1943).

five-hundred-foot rope tow, though B Slope with its northerly exposure and spruce cover generally held the best snow. After a few initial lessons, likely taking a week or two, the troopers mustered on a Monday morning and marched with their packs, camping kit, and skis to Cooper Hill about seven miles to the south on the Continental Divide. Here the army built by the end of 1942 beginner, intermediate, and expert slopes—all served by a T-bar six thousand feet in length and gaining over one thousand feet of elevation. While the company practiced their snow camping, the instructors lived in a barracks. For a week the soldiers skied all day, every day, sometimes into the evening on moonlit nights, returning to Camp Hale on Friday and then back to Cooper Hill for another week of ski training.[33]

While only one-third of the troops at Camp Hale in the winter of 1943 learned to ski, all the troops assigned to the MTC were taught snowshoeing, in six two-hour periods. The infantry units carried emergency snowshoes—small, lightweight, 10½inch-wide by 20inch-long ovals—to be used when operating in deep snow where skis could not be used, such as close combat. The rest of the support units, and the infantry weapons platoons, were issued "bear-paw" snowshoes, 13-inch by 28-inch ovals, which were found to be handier in woods, underbrush, and rough terrain, though the standard trail snowshoe, a longer and narrower design for Alaskan use, was also available. All the snowshoes were constructed with wooden frames and rawhide webbing. Then, as now, skiers were biased against snowshoes, but snowshoes did provide individual mobility in support units such as pack artillery. Instructors emphasized the mobility and freedom on snowshoes, their nomenclature and care, and walking technique, lifting the foot just high enough to clear the snow, then throwing the foot forward with an "easy, casual motion." Snowshoers had to learn to be careful with their clothing as well, not wearing too much as they perspired, but keeping a layer available to put on at halts.[34]

For mobility on the snow and ice of glaciers or permanent snowfields, the "higher craft of mountaineering," according to one well-respected mountaineer, required other techniques besides skiing and snowshoeing. The problem was that there were few glaciers in the continental United States, outside of the coastal Pacific Northwest, especially deep inland in the central Rocky Mountains of Colorado. The solution at Camp Hale was to build an artificial glacier. At the start of 1943, on a slope in the lower Resolution Creek training area just east of camp, engineers cut logs and stacked them up to form crevasses and seracs. Water was then poured over the logs until it froze, and snow was packed on top of that. Unfortunately, the slope chosen was south-facing, and the fake glacier melted in the winter sun. In March 1943 engineers built a second artificial glacier, this time higher up in the Resolution Creek drainage and on a north-facing, shaded slope, which lasted until mid-May and allowed for training on ice.[35]

The ice axe, a wooden shaft with a steel point on the bottom and a combination of pick and adze on the top, was the most iconic piece of mountaineering equipment. But ice axes, like most of the mountaineering kit used by the mountain troops, were not manufactured in the United States before the war. The quartermaster general's Cold Climate Unit had to select just one model to allow for mass production. They settled on a basic design for a heavier axe based on the design by Austrian alpinist Alfred Horeschowsky, which had been used in the 1941 Alaska expedition. As lighter ash wood was unavailable, heavier hickory had to be used for the shaft, and it took a while for manufacturers to produce acceptable models. The result was a good ice axe, by mountaineering standards of the time, but heavy. William House, head of the Mountain Unit in the OQMG, stated after the war that they should have chosen to procure a lighter, shorter, handier version of the ice axe.[36]

Crampons were another crucial piece of ice equipment. A set of metal points in a frame and attached to the boot sole, crampons allowed walking on ice slopes. The quartermaster general quickly settled on the relatively light ten-point crampon (four points each under the toe and heel, and two points under the instep). Again, before the war crampons were imported items, so there were no domestic manufacturers. The teeth of the first versions, made of stamped metal, bent and broke during field tests in 1942. The American Fork and Hoe Company of Wellingford, Vermont, proposed using steel straps,

½-inch wide and 1/8-inch thick, riveted together. This allowed the uprights to be made of softer steel, with harder points. The design proved satisfactory and the resulting version, with 1½-inch long points secured by three straps, went into production.[37]

So that troops could learn how to use ice axes and crampons, the Mountain Training Center in January 1943 planned for twenty-two hours of glacier travel instruction. The loss of the first artificial glacier disrupted these plans, but ultimately the 87th and 86th Mountain Infantry Regiments did receive two days of instruction on the second artificial glacier. This may have been enough as the training was likely intended just to provide familiarization with the basics of glacier travel. Not every mountain trooper was to be equipped with crampons and an ice axe. The proposed T/E for mountain units contained only eighteen ice axes and pairs of crampons for a company, for example. Along with three ropes, this allowance allowed each rifle platoon to form a single rope team of six men to prepare a trail across a glacier or snowfield, which they marked by three-foot dowels painted orange or black. For such personnel, almost 150 from each of the three infantry regiments at Camp Hale, the MTC held another round of advanced ice training on Mt Rainier's glaciers and snowfields in September 1943.[38]

Ice techniques began with climbing deep snow by kicking in steps and placing the ice axe ahead as an anchor. To descend the same could be done backward, or the men could slide downhill on their heels or feet, glissading, using the axe as a rudder. Steeper, icy slopes required the use of crampons, with the ankles flexed to ensure all the points bit and the point of the ice axe kept uphill for balance. For parties without crampons, the pick end of the ice axe was used to cut steps into the ice large enough for boot nails or cleats to find purchase. The simplest method was to cut steps upward and diagonally, as cutting steps downward was more difficult. The ice axe could also be used to self-arrest in a fall. The falling climber had to roll onto his face as digging in his heels could cause him to start rolling uncontrollably. The trooper grasped the top of the axe with both hands and gradually dug the pick into the surface to stop. To avoid self-arrests, the ice axe also could serve as an anchor for several types of rope belays, using the pick or shaft, with the addition of the belayer's shoulder. Climbers also hammered in ice pitons, hollow tubes with a ring at one end, to serve as anchors. Rescuing a climber after a fall into a crevasse, the greatest danger on a glacier, required specialized techniques. The party could haul them up using a rope with single or double stirrups, anchored by ice axes. Or the fallen climber could employ Prusik knots on two stirrups and a chest loop. The climber being rescued would lift his legs, slide the stirrup knots up, stand up, slide the chest loop up, and repeat.[39]

Survival

The MTC went beyond mobility—beyond skiing, snowshoeing, snow climbing, and glacier travel—to train for survival in the mountains in winter. Relying on notes assembled for a mountain troop manual and the *Manual of Ski Mountaineering*, with further demonstrations by Paul Petzoldt, the MTC instructed soldiers that in the cold they had to be comfortable with being slightly uncomfortable. Individual warmth in the mountains in winter came from physical activity, held in by clothing. The acronym C-O-L-D served as a mnemonic for the care and use of clothing: Keep it Clean, Avoid Overheating, Wear it Loose in layers, and Keep it Dry. The base layer clothing worn against the body—underwear, socks, mittens—required the most frequent cleaning, along with the camouflaging white outer layers. So as not to soak the clothing with sweat, leading to freezing, outer layers were to be worn loose and ventilated at the neck, wrists, and waist. Insulating layers had to be removed before physical exertion, which would cause perspiration. Troopers had to always be drying damp clothes, particularly their socks, whenever the opportunity presented. Socks or mittens could be placed between inner layers, held by a safety pin, or placed in the sleeping bag to dry. Wet weather gear was only to be donned when it was raining or when the troops were immobile, lest they be soaked from the inside.[40]

Winter bivouacking or camping occupied thirty nights of training, often combined with ski training. Twenty-four of those nights were in tents, primarily the two-man mountain tent. This was pitched with a back corner to the wind, to prevent snow drifts from blocking the entrance. Pitching the tent on snow required using skis or ski poles to secure the guy ropes or using tent pegs buried horizontally in the snow. All snow had to be brushed off clothing and equipment before entering the tent, and the men slept head to foot. When striking the tent, care had to be taken in case the floor froze into the snow. Such mountain tents, as mountaineer William House noted, "proved to be a tough problem all along." They were heavy, weighing nearly thirteen pounds. The resin-treated cotton cloth, used to make a tent waterproof, did not breathe; as a result, condensed moisture tended to cascade onto the inhabitants. Had the waterproofing been removed, tents would have been lighter, but they would have soaked up their weight in moisture when in use, making them even heavier and less protective. Efforts were made to improve the mountain tent, and by 1944 a lighter version in nylon, weighing eight pounds, eleven ounces, with two doors to increase ventilation, was in the supply system, though this was too late for the men at Camp Hale.[41]

The unsatisfactory nature of the mountain tent meant most mountain troopers relied on improvised shelters. Training required them to spend four nights in a brush or timber shelter with a fire and two nights above tree line in a snow shelter with a mountain stove. Official doctrine was a bit light on the matter, with the 1941 *Operations in Snow and Extreme Cold* manual devoting just two descriptive pages; instructors therefore turned to outside expertise and materials. These described brush shelters, such as lean-tos, and tree shelters beneath fallen or standing trees. Snow trenches, snow caves, and igloos offered the most effective shelter in the winter. In shelters the mountain sleeping bag was placed into its water-repellent cover and needed some form of insulation beneath it, whether sleeping pad, spare clothes, pack, or pine boughs.[42]

Units also had to learn how to transport supplies in the winter cold and snow. Mules, as pack artillery battalions quickly learned, would go until the snow reached their bellies and then no further. Motorized oversnow vehicles were in their infancy in early 1943, though the Studebaker Corporation did provide ten hours of driver instruction for the experimental T15 tracked vehicle. Experiments with dog sleds found them impractical, as Bestor Robinson had foreseen two years before, as they could only operate on packed trails and there were not enough sled dogs available to keep a tactical unit supplied. Oversnow transport thus fell to the troopers using a variety of toboggans and sleds. A two-week course in the Homestake Peak training area taught 160 men from the supply and ammunition sections of the infantry regiments the basics of loading, lashing, hauling, and trail breaking with snowshoes. They utilized a standard military toboggan, with a flat bottom and upturned front, and a sled-toboggan, a toboggan to which runners were attached. Neither model proved entirely successful in deep snow or on steep slopes, and, as on Mt Rainier the previous winter, it was found more practicable to break up loads and man-pack them.[43]

Avalanches were the greatest potential threat to survival in the snow and ice, beyond the cold, exposure, or lack of supplies. It is estimated that on the Alpine front durin World War I, avalanches killed more soldiers than enemy fire. To deal with this threat, the MTC drafted a chapter on snow avalanches for the proposed mountain troop manual. In doing so, it used several sources, including the primary work in English on avalanches at the time, Gerald Seligman's 1936 *Snow Structures and Ski Fields*. Seligman, drawing on field research in the Alps, discussed snow structure and the changes that took place in snow-fields, aspects of avalanche development, and measures to avoid avalanches. The *Manual for Ski Mountaineering* provided the basis for the avalanche chapter, quoted verbatim at times, since the *Manual*'s editor, David Brower, was now Private Brower, assigned to Camp Hale. Brower had been brought to the MTC headquarters by Captain Woodward to "work on a mountain-training manual." The chapter on "Snow Formation and Avalanches" in the

Manual of Ski Mountaineering cited Seligman, discussing snow, stratification, effects of slope and ground, avalanche types, detection of snow conditions, precautions in avalanche terrain, actions if caught in an avalanche, and rescue techniques.[44]

"Snow Avalanches" in the proposed manual noted that avalanches were caused when "the snow structure is so changed or modified that there is not enough bond between the snow crystals, or the snow layers, or between the snow and the ground." But there was "no short cut, no easy rule of thumb, to determine whether a snow slop is in danger of avalanching"; rather, "an accurate knowledge is required of the internal structure of the snow." The chapter identified five types of avalanches: dry snow, wet snow, wind slab, cornice break, and ice. Dry-snow avalanches occurred when snow crystals rounded, reducing the bonds between them. Wet-snow avalanches happened when the snowpack got wet, from melting, rain, or humidity, lubricating the bonds between layers. Wind slab avalanches threatened where wind-packed snow bonded poorly to the underlying snow and could avalanche in large blocks. The danger of these could be detected by a "hollow thud," referred to today as "whumpfing," as the slab settled under foot or ski. Cornices formed snow drifting over ridges on the downwind side. These could break off and cause avalanches below, so it was best to avoid travel over or under them. If a cornice had to be crossed, then it could be cut through to reduce the chance of an avalanche. Ice avalanches were a threat in glaciated mountains.[45]

To gain the "accurate knowledge" of the snowpack to determine the probability of an avalanche required an understanding of layers and anchors. To know if the layers of snow were bonded together, especially where there were several deep layers that could result in large, destructive avalanches, the chapter recommended checking by pushing the handle of the ski pole down into the snow, feeling for the resistance, or lack thereof, of the layers. The chapter held that slopes over 22° were more likely to avalanche, but if a slope had anchors for the snow to hold onto—rocks, trees, terraces—it was less likely to slide. Snow on concave slopes was less likely to slide while convex slopes were more likely to run, especially wind slab avalanches. Detection of conditions was the basis of the accurate knowledge, derived from listening to the snow react underfoot, probing with a ski pole, and being aware of temperature changes and wind directions. The most thorough method was to dig a hole, today referred to as a pit, and "examine the textures of the various layers." The quartermaster general did develop and test "devices for testing the quality of the snow and determining the likelihood of snow slides," but it is unknown what those devices were and if any made it to Camp Hale. Ultimately the probability of an avalanche depended on the steepness of the slope, slope shape, anchors and bonds between layers, recent weather, presence of wind slabs or cornices, evidence of prior avalanches, and snow depth.[46]

Preferably any slopes that might avalanche should be avoided, but if that was not possible then the least dangerous route should be taken. Slopes were to be "crossed as near the top as possible" and it was "always safer to travel along ridges than in gullies." Troops had to consider snow conditions and avalanche dangers both above and below them as they traveled. It was best to keep an interval between men, so that an avalanche would not catch the whole unit. The snow science of the time held that it was best to go either straight up or down a dangerous slope, on foot. Before crossing a suspect slope, ski bindings had to be loosened so they would come off, ski pole straps removed, and the waist belt of the pack unfastened. A sentinel should be posted to alert the rest of the party to an avalanche and silence was to be maintained to hear the warning or the avalanche itself. A rope could be attached to one man crossing at a time, anchored on the near side by the rest of the party. Mittens were to be worn to prevent hands from freezing if caught in an avalanche, and a thirty-foot avalanche cord was trailed behind, to increase one's chances of being found if buried. Finally, the chapter, following a Swiss army article translated by Ad Carter, called for a dangerous slope that had to be crossed to be avalanched using mortar fire just below the crest of the ridge.[47]

Ultimately all mountain units had to be instructed in rescue procedures in case an avalanche occurred. If caught in an avalanche, the trooper had to fight to keep his head uphill, feet downhill, and "maintain a powerful swimming motion" to try to stay as close to the surface of the snow as possible. Skis, ski poles, and packs had to be ditched, if possible, as they would be caught by the snow and drag the trooper deeper. If caught under the snow, the trooper had to try to create space around his head and chest before the snow froze. If possible, a trooper could grab a tree or rock and hold on, letting the avalanche pass over and by. If not caught in the avalanche, the rest of the unit had to watch those swept away to know where to search. A rescue party would then probe that area with poles at least ten feet long; searchers three to four feet apart would probe left to right at one-foot intervals. Once a probe struck a body, the victim could be dug out. The quartermaster general procured aluminum snow or avalanche shovels and avalanche probes for rescues. While victims rarely survived more than several hours, a thorough and persistent search was crucial.[48]

Despite the dangers and complexities of avalanches, no separate block of training was dedicated to them, however. Avalanche instruction was incorporated into the cross-country lessons of ski training, during ski marches, and at snow bivouacs. The focus was thus on the precautions to be taken in avalanche terrain, particularly avoidance, not on the detection of snow conditions, and there was no effort to forecast avalanche dangers. Yet, while the mountain troops did occasionally trigger avalanches, they never suffered any losses. In part this was unquestionably due to the emphasis on avalanche avoidance, but also to simple luck. The MTC's and then 10th Division's main training areas were in less avalanche prone areas. The areas along Resolution Creek, Vail Pass, and Chicago Ridge are generally west- or south-facing and low-angle, most slopes being less than 30°. Such terrain is generally considered less likely to avalanche. In the Homestake Peak and Gold Park areas, which have a more easterly aspect, most of the terrain is also low-angle, with avalanche-prone terrain easily identifiable.[49]

As winter turned to spring in the high Rockies, the avalanche danger lessened, as did the pace of mountain training on the steadily melting ice and snow. There was also a thawing in the army's attitude toward mountain and cold weather training, a realization that it could be crucial. The landing force on Attu Island in the Aleutians in May 1943 suffered more casualties from the climate, particularly trench foot, than from Japanese attacks. General Marshall, the chief of staff of the army, realized that trained mountain or alpine troops should have been sent to Attu, as they would have better withstood the conditions. He "personally gave orders" that the 87th Mountain Infantry Regiment was to go for the next landing on Kiska. The 87th departed Camp Hale in June 1943 and took part in the landing on Kiska in August, unopposed as the Japanese had withdrawn. Of the over five thousand men in the 87th Mountain Combat Team, only seven suffered trench foot.[50] As the value of mountain training slowly became clear to the army, instruction at Camp Hale turned to mobility and survival in rock and alpine, above tree line, terrain.

CHAPTER 4

Mountain Training, 1943

Rock and Alpine

As spring took hold in the Colorado high country in 1943, something was missing at Camp Hale. The plan, articulated the previous summer, had been to activate a mountain division at Camp Hale in the spring of 1943. In preparation the army approved a full mountain division table of organization, T/O 70, on August 1, 1942. On January 1, 1943, Brigadier General Rolfe, with a full year of experience and experimentation, recommended changes to this T/O, emphasizing flexibility and the ability of small units to operate independently in the mountains. He proposed increasing the use of quarter-ton trucks or jeeps and reducing the number of animals in the division by nearly half. The cavalry troop would be mounted in jeeps, the number of riding animals reduced, and the mules in the artillery battalions cut from 803 to 550. Oversnow vehicles would replace trucks and mules in the winter. Rolfe also recommended reducing the number of battalions in the mountain infantry regiments from three to two, increasing maneuverability and easing supply. Yet, at the start of summer, no mountain division had been activated or even ordered to activate. A few days later, on June 26, 1943, Lt Gen Leslie McNair, commander of Army Ground Forces, inspected the Mountain Training Center, after which all became clear. There was to be no mountain division at Camp Hale. Instead, the MTC received the tables of organization, tables of equipment, and details to activate the 10th Light Division.[1]

10th Light Division (Alpine)

Not long after approving the mountain division T/O in 1942, the War Department began to question the need for special type divisions: airborne, jungle, amphibious, and mountain. For such operational environments it now appeared better to raise divisions with less manpower and equipment, particularly

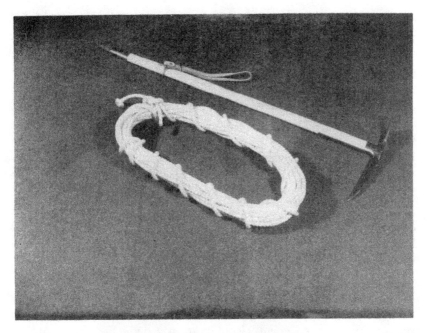

Ice Axe And Mountain Climbing Rope

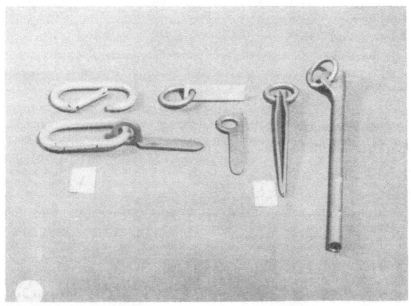

Mountaineering equipment, from OQMG, *Equipment for Special Forces*, 89.

transport, in the United States and then give them the specialized training and equipment required once deployed in theater. Such divisions would ease a series of critical shortages that came to the fore during that year in shipping, manpower, and production. A smaller division, with one-third less manpower and with less heavy equipment, especially heavy vehicles, would be easier to transport overseas. But no theater commanders wanted such a light division as it would be too light for combat. Regardless, the AGF, which spent six months developing new tables of organization for a light division, won approval in June 1943 to form three light divisions as experimental units. The 89th Infantry Division would transition to a light division with primarily jeep or light truck transport. The 71st Light Division was to be activated at Camp Carson, Colorado, formed from two existing, jungle-trained regiments, with handcart and pack mule transport. And the 10th Light Division would be a potential high-mountain or alpine division, also with handcarts and mules, in addition to toboggans for the snow.[2]

On July 15, 1943, the 10th Light Division was activated at Camp Hale. (The "Alpine" designation was never used by the division staff, which increasingly referred to the division as the 10th Infantry Division.) Given the administrative and reorganizational demands placed on the new outfit, the division did not hold an activation ceremony until October 16. The army, which had begun to realize the requirements for at least cold weather warfare, did assign commanders to the new division who had some experience in the Aleutians campaign. Brig Gen Lloyd E. Jones, soon promoted to major general, led the occupation of Amchitka and was the new divisional commanding general. Brig Gen Frank L. Culin commanded a regiment during the fighting on Kiska and was the assistant division commander (ADC). Brig Gen David L. Ruffner, previously on the Mountain Training Center staff, took command of division artillery. Brigadier General Rolfe, as a noted expert on mule transport, turned over command of the MTC and reported as the ADC, 71st Light Division (Pack), which was activated the same date at Camp Carson, Colorado. Most of the MTC staff became the 10th Light Division staff.[3]

The 10th Light Division consisted of a headquarters supported by signals, military police, and ordnance platoons; three infantry regiments; division artillery with an antitank battery, an antiaircraft artillery battalion, and three field artillery battalions; an engineer battalion; a medical battalion; and three pack (mule) companies. Authorized 9,022 personnel and 2,016 animals, the light division had nearly 5,000 men and 6,000 animals less than the planned-for 1942 mountain division. Across the division units were smaller, with less firepower, and with less transportation for supplies than had previously been intended for mountain operations. The infantry battalions lost their weapons companies,

10th Light Division, July 15, 1943

Headquarters, 10th Light Division
Headquarters Company, 10th Light Division
110th Signal Platoon
Military Police Platoon, 10th Light Division
710th Ordnance Light Maintenance Platoon
85th Infantry Regiment
86th Infantry Regiment
90th Infantry Regiment
Headquarters, 10th Light Division Artillery
Headquarters Detachment, 10th Light Division Artillery
576th Anti-Tank Battery
727th Anti-Aircraft Artillery Machinegun Battalion
604th Field Artillery Battalion
606th Field Artillery Battalion
616th Field Artillery Battalion
126th Engineer Light Combat Battalion
10th Medical Battalion, Light
255th Quartermaster Pack Company
256th Quartermaster Pack Company
257th Quartermaster Pack Company

Source: HQ, 10th Light Division, Camp Hale, CO, General Order No. 1, 15 July 1943, TMD, Box 5.

but the light division organization assigned a 60 mm mortar squad to each rifle platoon, increased the number of machine guns in the rifle company weapons platoons to four, and added a section of two 81 mm mortars to the battalion headquarters. Each light infantry regiment now had only 103 mules, vice the nearly 800 under the mountain infantry T/O, though they did also get seven handcarts. The artillery still manned forty-eight 75 mm howitzers, now with only 753 pack mules, down from 1,898, but with the addition of seventeen jeeps. The light division also lacked a quartermaster battalion and cavalry reconnaissance troop. However, it was authorized special alpine equipment including five hundred M29 Weasel light-tracked cargo carriers, twenty-four bulldozers, two V-type snowplows, two rotary snowplows, and three tramways.[4]

Camp Hale was thus busy organizing and reorganizing the new division after July 15. The reorganizing and redesignating of units already at the Mountain Training Center provided personnel for the signals, military police, ordnance, antitank, engineer, and medical units. Antiaircraft Command assigned the 727th Anti-Aircraft Artillery Machinegun Battalion with thirty-six .50-caliber heavy machine guns to the division. Two of the three artillery battalions, the 604th and 605th, activated and trained the third battalion, the 616th, with personnel distributed uniformly across the three battalions. The 86th Infantry Regiment was the only one present at Camp Hale in July, as the 87th was in the Aleutians. Two new regiments, the 85th and 90th, had to be created by redistributing the 86th's mainly National Ski Patrol–recruited volunteers across all three regiments, joined by two regimental cadres from Hawaii, who were quickly named "pineapple boys" by the volunteers.[5]

But to fill out the three artillery battalions and three infantry regiments, the 10th Light Division needed more personnel. Minnie Dole and the NSP were able to recruit another two thousand volunteers. While almost eight hundred went straight to Camp Hale, the remainder completed basic training at artillery and infantry replacement centers before joining the division. As before, the National Ski Patrol would not be able to recruit enough volunteers for a division. On August 6, 1943, almost five hundred men and officers from the reorganizing 89th Infantry Division reported to Camp Hale to fill the ranks. In October, the II Armored Corps sent 1,333 enlisted men to the division from inactivated armored infantry units. And in December 409 enlisted men reported from reorganized tank destroyer battalions. None of these were volunteers for the mountain troops and required "considerable" mountain training.[6]

There was also a steady flow of men out of Camp Hale. Given the quality of the volunteers and a growing sense that they were missing out on the war, many, perhaps one-half, transferred to other outfits, such as the Army Air Forces or Airborne Command. Many of the fillers were found medically unsuited for service in the mountains and were transferred to other units. After many months of trying, the Mountain Training Center finally received authority to transfer men who could not acclimate to altitude or cold weather, could not carry the heavy mountain pack, or could not for whatever reason adjust to the mountains. From June 1943 to February 1944, the division medically reassigned nearly one thousand men. The division also regularly furnished officer replacements, particularly infantry and artillery officers. Even with volunteers continuing to come in, along with periodic requests for fillers, the division did not reach full strength for eight months.[7]

For three weeks from July 26, the new division prepared for unit training. Infantry units ensured all their personnel had completed basic training and were ready to conduct unit training. They practiced rifle marksmanship and acclimated through field training and marches with increasing pack weights and distances. In preparation for movement to unit training on August 16, all necessary equipment was requisitioned, and commanders and staffs made the necessary reconnaissance of the training areas. The field artillery units continued basic training necessary after their redistribution of personnel, while the rest of the divisional units carried on with their unit training.[8]

The division also received training directions from higher headquarters, addressed to the "10th Light Division (Alpine)." Unit training, progressing from platoon to company to battalion to regiment, would take place from August 15, 1943, to January 8, 1944. The division would then execute combined training with all its elements in exercises and maneuvers to accomplish its assigned training mission from January 10 to March 31, 1944. The training mission had two parts. The 10th Light Division (Alpine) was to train to operate in mountains and terrain where roads were poor or nonexistent and under adverse and extreme weather conditions. This would support the second part of the mission, to test the organization and equipment best suited for mountain warfare. Like the activation of the 1st Battalion, 87th Mountain Infantry Regiment, in November 1941 and the MTC in September 1942, the 10th Light Division (Alpine) in July 1943 was an experimental organization, not a unit forming for combat.[9]

Mobility: Rock

In pursuit of its training mission, the division thus ordered mountaineering training, including rock climbing and techniques for alpine terrain, as one its first events. In April and May 1943, the MTC conducted a series of four-day rock-climbing courses on the cliffs at the east end of camp. It trained fifteen men from each company in the 87th Mountain Infantry and the entire 10th Medical Battalion in free-climbing, knots, belays, fixed ropes, party climbing, rappels, and an introduction to pitons. Further, all the officers assigned to the MTC took the course. As many of these officers became the 10th Division Staff, the MTC then provided a half-day rock-climbing course for the rest of the staff during the afternoons of July 26–28. From this experience the division then tasked the MTC to develop a mountaineering school for the infantry battalions.[10]

The division mountaineering school under Lt Col Robert Cook of the MTC took place north of Camp Hale at the entrance to the Homestake Valley (just north of the intersection of Highway 24 and Forest Road 703). The MTC designated three rock areas: AA and B were on the west side of Homestake Creek, while C was on the east, just off the highway. For nine weeks, starting the week of August 30, 1943, an infantry battalion with selected officers from an artillery battalion marched north out of camp on Monday morning at 0730. The battalion's three companies, organized into eight-man squads for training, bivouacked near a rocky area for the next six days. The men brought just mountain tents and the inner sleeping bag in rucksacks and wore mountain jackets and trousers. They wore helmet liners for head protection from falling debris and rocks (this innovation predated civilian use by decades). Troopers climbed in either mountain boots with nailed or rubber cleated soles or the standard service shoe (a midheight boot) whose composite rubber sole "was found to have surprisingly adequate qualities" for rock climbing. The MTC provided the specialized climbing equipment of ropes, pitons, and carabiners.[11]

Mountaineering equipment proved difficult to procure. Before the war most had been made in Europe. To get the quantities required, American companies had to be trained to make modified European types. The Office of the Quartermaster General found that the development of army climbing gear "involved a disproportionate amount of research, testing and experimentation," but sufficient amounts were being fielded by the spring of 1943. After the ice axe discussed in the previous chapter, the rope was the most iconic piece of climbing equipment. Climbing ropes had long been made of high-grade Manila hemp, but Japanese conquests caused a shortage of that material. The Plymouth Cordage Company of Massachusetts experimented with nylon, which proved to be stronger. A Manila rope could only stretch 13 percent of its length before it broke, but a nylon rope stretched to 39 percent before breaking. Nylon ropes proved to be resistant to abrasion, held knots better, and absorbed less moisture. Procurement of a thinner and thus lighter nylon rope was considered, but there were concerns it would be difficult to handle. The army adopted a 7/16-inch-diameter rope, 120 feet long, with a strength of 3,400 pounds, and weighing 6½ pounds, though this was often cut into two 60-foot ropes. Mountaineer William House later stated that the nylon rope was the quartermaster general's "greatest single contribution to mountaineering."[12]

House also sought out manufacturers for pitons and carabiners, or snap links, to fix a rope to the rock where there were no natural belay points. While many firms were reluctant, enough were found to develop and produce carabiners on a large scale. The resulting "Snaplinks, Mountain" were steel, four-inch oval keylock carabiners, with a strength of two thousand pounds, and could be operated one-handed. The carabiners were to be attached to pitons, flat soft iron spikes, which were hammered into crevices. Because no pitons were being manufactured in the United States, the Mountaineers' Exchange of San Francisco, an importer of European climbing equipment, assisted in the design of several different shapes of piton, which the Ames, Baldwin, Wyoming Company of West Virginia mass-produced. While making pitons by machine proved initially difficult and there were shortages of materials, pitons that met standard were finally manufactured.[13]

The army procured four types of "Pitons, Mountain." A Type I piton was a blunt spike or "spatulate" for horizontal cracks with an eyehole at the end to attach the carabiner. Type II was also spatulate with an eyehole but was used for vertical cracks. Piton Type III was rectangular to be placed in very small cracks either way as it had a ring at one end for attachment. The Type V (there was no Type IV), which had a ring as well, was an angle of folded iron that allowed for maximum deformation when driven into rock. Compared to carabiners and pitons, piton hammers proved quite easy to procure. And the quartermaster general also acquired rope-soled climbing shoes, following the European trend of *kletterschüle* (climbing shoe), and it is possible that the MTC's climbing instructors used them.[14]

Rock climbing and mountaineering were rare activities in 1940s America, even more so than snow skiing, so finding enough instructors was a challenge for the MTC. As noted in the previous chapter, there were only twenty men at Camp Hale in the spring of 1943 who could qualify as rock-climbing instructors. This core group was able to train around one hundred men as additional instructors, many of whom had never climbed before. Instructor training sought to establish a uniform set of standards, likely drawing on the *Handbook of American Mountaineering* and presented in a series of lectures, notes, checklists, and outlines. This knowledge was imparted to the troopers by the experienced climbers who served as rock-climbing instructors. These included such European expatriates as Swiss mountain guide Peter Gabriel and Austrian ski instructor and mountain guide Friedl Pfeifer, as well as David Brower, now a lieutenant back from OCS and assigned to the 10th Recon along with Gabriel and Pfeifer.[15]

Once bivouacked along Homestake Creek, each company met up with its instructors, one or two enlisted instructors for each squad and a company supervisor officer, who trained the officers separately on the "Officers' Rocks" between the A and B rock areas. The supervisor officer then gave each company an orientation lecture. The mountains, he began, had many dangers for a mountain soldier, but with training they could be a friend. The mountaineering school was to teach "the fundamentals of leading troops safely across rocky and precipitous mountain terrain." These basics would allow units to secure and utilize the advantages heights and higher elevations presented. It would fundamentally be individual skill training: how to move through mountains using the least energy and how to install fixed ropes at dangerous places. Soldiers would learn how to survive in the alpine terrain, to select bivouac and tent sites, to operate a mountain stove and prepare mountain rations, to "maintain an even body temperature," and to preserve strength and health. While one week was not enough to make anyone an expert climber or alpinist, the principles presented in the course would be applied in upcoming unit maneuvers.[16]

The mountaineering school devoted roughly half of its time to rock-climbing techniques for mobility on near-vertical or vertical slopes. First the students climbed unroped and unbelayed—that is, free-climbing—close to the ground, learning the various types of holds: pull, push, finger, arm, and leg. Instructors placed emphasis on maintaining a steady rhythm, planning the route several

10th Light Division Mountaineering School Schedule, 1943

1st Day	March to and Establish Bivouac Area	4 hours
	Orientation Lecture	1 hour
	Free Climbing	2 hours
	Knot Tying	1 hour
2nd Day	Continuous Climbing	1 hour
	Belay Practice	3 hours
	Mountain Walking, Individual and Group	2 hours
	Mountain March Formations	2 hours
	Night Climbing on Fixed Ropes	3 hours
3rd Day	Upper Belay Climbing	2 hours
	Roped Party Climbing	4 hours
	Rappelling	2 hours
	Advanced Free Climbing	1½ hours
4th Day	Piton Demonstration	1 hour
	Mountain Stoves and Rations	2 hours
	Mountain March Route Selection and Navigation	½ hour
	Mountain March on Fixed Ropes and Equipment Lines	4 hours
5th Day	Mountain March Formations and Route Selection	9 hours
6th Day	Written Examination	1 hour
	Mountain Assault Demonstration	1 hour
	March to Camp Hale	4 hours

Source: HQ, 10th Light Division, TM#7, 28 August 1943, TMD, Box 5.

moves ahead. The students then followed their instructor, copying the hold demonstrated, and included five minutes of handless climbing, just using legs, to learn the importance of footwork and balance. The soldiers then learned the basic knots required for rock climbing: overhand, square, bowline, bowline on a bight, butterfly, bowline on a coil, and Prusik. The overhand was the first step in typing all knots. Square knots tied two ropes together. A bowline was the standard knot to tie the rope around the upper chest of a climber, while a bowline on a bight added a shoulder loop for extra safety. The butterfly knot was used to tie in to the middle of a rope and secure a fixed rope. The bowline on a coil took up excess rope not required for climbing, and the Prusik knot could make stirrups for climbing but was more often used in ice climbing.[17]

After knots came continuous climbing, where three men were roped together at terrain-dependent intervals and all three moved at the same time. It was a technique mainly used on glaciers, on moderate terrain with high consequences of injury if a fall occurred, and on easy pitches between difficult pitches of climbing. Rock-climbing instruction then turned to belays from best to poorest: sitting, standing hip, and shoulder. The belayer had to be well braced in the direction of a potential fall, taking in slack with the left hand, running the rope low around the hips or over the shoulder, with the right hand as a brake. A belayer had to hold his position, inform the climber how much rope was left, not allow any slack to accumulate, and be prepared to use a hand-hold anchor in case of a fall, braking with one hand. The soldiers learned the signals by voice or rope tugs for "Test" (pull on the rope), "Climb," "Rope" (feed out more rope), "Slack" (take in rope), and "Off Belay." Each man practiced breaking the fall of a log or similar weight at twelve feet in a sitting belay, eight feet in standing belay, and three feet in a shoulder belay. They also practiced falling—calling out "Falling," then keeping their feet toward the rock, holding the rope in their hands, and looking down for their landing area.[18]

The rock-climbing schedule also dedicated three hours to climbing fixed ropes at night to demonstrate their use in getting equipment and men over difficult terrain in a minimum amount of time. Lines would be left free to haul up equipment and the men climbed on ropes fixed to the rock with pitons, properly tied in so several men could climb at once. Speed of action and dispersion of men at the top and bottom of the ropes were crucial. Then, having learned how to free-climb, belay, and fall, the men moved to upper belay climbing, where one student belayed another from above as he climbed. This allowed the soldiers to climb difficult pitches and practice techniques with greater safety. The instructors encouraged men to climb pitches they believed they would fall from, then when they usually would not fall, the experience gave them a greater margin of safety. This experiential knowledge of when they probably would fall and when they probably would not, proved more important than faith in rope and belays.[19]

The training moved to roped party climbing in "ropes" of three or two climbers. Instructors explained the order of men on the rope and the knots required. The first man, with a bowline knot behind his back or on his side if carrying a pack, was the lead climber. The second man was the belayer, tied in with a bowline on a rope of two and butterfly on a rope of three. The third man on a rope of three, tied in with a bowline, provided security. Once the lead climber completed a pitch, he would belay the second man up. In a rope of three, the first man would then provide security for the second man as he belayed the third man up. A three-man climbing party allowed for continuous security, but it was slower, so the two-man party was preferred for speed. Two ropes of two combined speed and mutual support, with the leader of the second rope following the second man of the first rope as closely as possible.[20]

Having learned to ascend the rock safely, students were now ready to learn how to descend by rappelling. Instructors demonstrated a seat rappel, utilizing a sling around the upper legs and the rope passing through a carabiner, but trained the soldiers on the "Dülfer" method. This technique passed the rope between the legs, around a hip, across the chest, over the opposite shoulder, and down the back. Typically, this was the left hip and right shoulder with the uphill rope in the rappeler's relaxed right hand and the downhill in their left as a brake. They kept the rope hip and leg downhill and leaned out just far enough to make the feet hold against the rock as they walked down. Rock climbing finished with a session of advanced free-climbing without ropes on moderate terrain to practice route selection and increase confidence. Finally, the men received one hour of demonstration on pitons. This was not enough time to teach the men to use pitons, which would require almost sixteen hours. But they were shown the type and use of each piton, the placing of pitons, and rope use through pitons, including belaying using carabiners.[21]

Survival and Mobility: Alpine

The MTC reduced the amount of time spent on piton training in the mountaineering school schedule to gain more time to train soldiers for mobility in alpine terrain. This is the near-barren landscape near or above tree line at the highest mountain elevations. In the winter this meant skiing; in the summer it meant mountain walking. Adding the techniques of mountain walking to those of rock climbing equipped units to cross mountainous terrain, especially terrain the enemy might consider impassable. Soldiers learned of the hazards mountains created for mobility: cliffs and steep terrain, rock falls, fields of small and large rocks (scree and talus), and sudden weather changes. Troops had to be conditioned to walk in the mountains, had to have the necessary equipment, and had to have a plan. Instructors taught soldiers to walk uphill, along trails, or cross-country with a slow, easy gait, a rhythmic pace, adjusting their breathing to the rhythm. Talking was to be avoided and each step had to be deliberate, placing the feet flat against the terrain to avoid slippages, and using footholds where available. Soldiers learned that walking downhill was often more difficult, as it was easier to fall. They had to again keep their feet flat, lengthen the step, keep the body forward, and absorb the shock of each footfall with their knees. Walking across talus was to be avoided but, if necessary, a route had to be carefully selected and men had to step from rock to rock, not jump. Walking across the small rocks of a scree field was also to be avoided, as ascending was very hard to do, while descending could be accomplished via glissading techniques, as on ice and snow.[22]

The mountain troopers learned never to touch or go under a log when they could go over or around and to not jump from log to log. Walking through woods or brush required consideration of men following, not letting branches swing back and strike them. Crossing ledges or climbing or descending small cliffs was best done via free-climbing techniques—hand- and footholds, foot-work—as roping up was time-consuming. Men had to learn to rest before fatigue set in, taking short rests on their feet, usually in cold weather, while during longer rests they would remove equipment, get off their feet, and seek to stay warm as their sweat cooled by adding clothing. Mountain walking in a unit put more requirements on leaders to ensure uniformity of gear and keeping weight to a minimum, to ensure proper pace, dispersion, breaks, discipline, and rest. Ultimately, mountain walking training was to ensure the soldier could walk up and down steep slopes safely and with a minimum expenditure of energy, so that he would arrive at his destination in good condition and able to fight.[23]

After soldiers received instruction on mountain walking, the squads assembled for training on mountain marching. Leaders were instructed in setting a pace appropriate for the terrain and selecting an efficient route. The men had to learn to absorb the "accordion effect" of a unit's spreading out and then coming back together by maintaining a proper interval between themselves. The squads then trained on mountain marching formations. These were necessary for control and speed, for security from enemy fire or observation, for maneuverability to launch an attack, and to minimize casualties from exhaustion, getting lost, or injury. The terrain, ground cover, number of men, mission, and enemy situation determined the formation. Mountainous terrain was too constricted and rough for the field manual's generally preferred formation of two subunits forward—squads or platoons—and one in reserve.[24]

Mountain march formations were either square for maximum compactness or in columns of files for minimum compactness. A square formation was best for control and required the least amount of terrain, but security could be poor in the woods or on flat, even ground. A column gave least control but allowed for the best use of the terrain, with good security on trails and in rough terrain. There were possible variables on these two formations. Several columns could march forward on adjacent routes, which put a premium on route selection, trail breaking, speed, and security. At bottlenecks a column could break down into files of twos and threes, temporarily to allow the obstacle to be crossed. Given the generally limited choice of formations, mountain marches required more security efforts. Units on the march in the mountains needed flank guards, possibly many and very far out, where they would have trouble with communication. More scouts would be needed, operating at a greater distance from the main force. And more patrols would be necessary, particularly reconnaissance and security patrols. All such efforts in the mountains—whether by flank guards, scouts, or patrols—required men who were self-sufficient with increased equipment, strong climbers, expert observers, and capable of selecting routes and taking independent action.[25]

Given these challenges of mountain marching, the mountaineering school devoted a day and a half for the squads to apply what they had learned in the field. The field training began in the afternoon with route selection and navigation instruction, applied as each squad marched to fixed ropes and equipment lines, ascending and then descending. They then boarded trucks for Tigwon Road to the north of Red Cliff, where they would hike to Lake Constantine below the Mount of the Holy Cross. There they bivouacked, applying what they had learned about their mountain rations and stoves (see below). The MTC devoted the entire next day to a mountain march problem including the utilization of formations, marching techniques, roped and unroped climbing, and route selection as each squad moved over the ridge between Lake Constantine and the training site on Homestake Creek. During this time the unit's officers acted as observers, allowing the enlisted men to execute on their own.[26]

Since being mobile in alpine terrain would be meaningless if troops could not survive, MTC's mountaineering school also included lectures and demonstrations on the use of the mountain stove and cook set, the preparation of mountain rations, and the packing of the rucksack. Initially mountaineer and skier Bestor Robinson, serving with the quartermaster general, worked with the Kansas-based Coleman Company to develop a Primus-style stove, long used by mountaineers, as such stoves had only been previously manufactured in Europe. The resulting M1941 model proved a bit heavy, at two pounds, six ounces, and a bit bulky. In 1942 Aladdin Industries of Indiana developed a new design, adopted by the army as the "Stove, cooking, gasoline, M1942, 1 burner." The M1942 mountain stove weighed one pound, one ounce, with folding tripod legs and brackets on top and a pump combined with the filler cap and a kit of spare parts. Its half-pint fuel tank held enough gasoline to burn for two hours, and the whole stove fit into a straight-sided pot for transport. It required training to maintain and trouble-shoot. The stoves were to be issued on a one per four men basis, with two one-quart fuel cans per stove, enough for eight hours of operation. Mountain cook sets were also issued one per four men, consisting of two nested aluminum pots, as recommended by mountaineers and ski mountaineers, with a lid that could also serve as a frying pan. The stove could also be placed into the cook set when carried in the rucksack.[27]

The quartermaster general developed mountain cook sets since it was expected that mountain troops would have to operate in small, widely dispersed groups, making the company mess, with its kitchen and cooks, impractical. For the same reason the quartermaster general also developed mountain rations. Mountaineers held that at least 4,000 calories a day, perhaps as many as 5,000, were necessary to keep a man healthy and whole in the high alpine in winter and summer. The food had to be light, with many dehydrated items. It had to be a balanced diet of fats, proteins, and carbohydrates. The food had to be easily cooked, with much of it precooked, so it could also be eaten cold. And it needed to be organized into simple menus yet avoiding monotony.[28]

In November 1941 the quartermaster general issued specifications for a mountain ration. One ration was to feed one man for one day, weigh no more than 2½ pounds, and come packed with five or more other rations to provide variety. It had to be easily cooked at altitude, contain as many precooked foods as possible, and provide at least 4,800 calories. The standard army emergency ration, the K ration, could not be used as the mountain ration because it did not provide enough calories, was too heavy, and lacked variety. Throughout 1942 and into the first quarter of 1943, food items for the mountain ration underwent tests on Mt Rainier and Denali and in Canada and Colorado. By March 1943 the standardized mountain ration had three menus of differing items, packed four to a carton. It emphasized dry cereal, dehydrated cheese, vegetables, fruit, soup, and precooked canned meats. It weighed just over three pounds and provided 4,300 calories.[29]

The MTC learned from its winter experience that the mountain stove and the mountain ration were both highly specialized items and required instruction in their use. As no more than one-third of any unit, and likely a lot less, had been through the winter training, the mountaineering school devoted nearly two hours of lecture and demonstration to the stove and ration "to enable the soldier to maintain his health and efficiency in the field." Instructors showed the men how the ration items combined to form meals. The dried fruit, cereal and milk, biscuits and butter, and coffee were for breakfast. For dinner the men placed dried fruit, cheese, crackers, chocolate, and lemonade into their pockets to eat and drink during the day. (As mountaineers say, lunch starts after breakfast and continues to supper.) Supper was soup, meat, vegetables, the remaining biscuits or crackers with butter, hard candy, and tea.[30]

When four men divided the ration, one carried the cereal and milk, one the soup and butter, one the meat, and one the vegetables to spread the weight and speed preparation. The MTC instructors emphasized the need for water to use the ration. In the summer the men were to use running water to save fuel, with no treatment. In winter, getting water would be a challenge, and they would have to melt snow, being careful not to burn the bottom of the pot. Water for breakfast needed to be prepared the night prior and kept in canteens in the sleeping bag to prevent freezing. The MTC found that one stove and cook set per two men, instead of one per four, proved to be the most efficient and instructed the men on how to fill, light, operate, extinguish, and repair the stove. And instructors suggested ways to prepare the items in each ration, to increase variety and make the food more palatable, such as making jam from the dried

Mountain Ration, 1943

No.	Weight	Package	Component
1	16 oz	Lined wax carton	Cereal (Ralston, Maltex, or Gen Mills)
1	4½ oz	Can	Dry whole milk
3	24 oz	Lined carton	Sugar
8	16 oz	Cellophane	Dried fruit (apricots, peaches, or raisins)
8	16 oz	Cellophane	Crackers or biscuits
1	10 oz	Can	Butter
1	1 oz	Can	Soluble coffee
8	16 oz	Greaseproof paper	Chocolate
1	5 oz	Carton	Dehydrated cheese
2	2¾ oz	Waxed paper	Candy
4	1 oz	Paper	Lemonade powder
1	6 oz	Bag in carton	Dehydrated soup (tomato, onion, or pea)
1	12 oz	Can	Meat (luncheon meat, corned beef, or pork sausage)
1	8 oz	Carton	Dehydrated vegetables (baked beans, potatoes, or precooked rice)
4	½ oz	Paper bag	Tea
12	½ oz	Carton	Gum
40	1 oz	Cellophane	Cigarettes
100	1 oz	Paper	Toilet paper
1	2 oz	Fiber container	Salt

Source: OQMG, *Development of Special Rations*, 71–72.

fruit, using the chocolate bars to make hot chocolate, frying the luncheon meat (Spam), or using the rice and cheese to make cheesecakes.[31]

As the rucksack was also a new piece of equipment for many of the men, mountaineering school instructors spent about thirty minutes reviewing how to pack it efficiently before donning it for the day-and-a-half mountain march. Heavier items, such as food, were placed in the bottom and sides of the rucksack, along the back and nearer the hips. Spare clothing, carefully rolled and tied, and then the tent went into the pack next. The stove or cook set, depending on what each man carried, was placed on top of the tent. The sleeping bag, tightly rolled, with the canteen inside it in cold weather, filled out the main compartment of the rucksack, with the over white trousers tucked alongside in winter. In the summer the canteen was attached to the outside of the pack along with the first aid kit. The fuel canister went into the large outside pocket on the rear of the pack, while small items were placed inside the canteen cup and packed into one side pocket, and spare socks, with extra mittens, white rifle cover, and white pack cover in winter went into the other side pocket. Ropes, repair kits, or other unit gear went on top of the sleeping bag just under the lid of the pack, which also functioned as a map case.[32]

Mountaineering School's final event on Saturday morning was the mountain assault demonstration. With the battalion undergoing training watching, a squad of attacking instructors supported by a machine gun firing live ammunition over their heads approached the base of a cliff. The top of the cliff was defended by a few instructors, sheltering in a trench from the machine-gun fire with a life-size rag dummy in uniform and triggering quarter-pound sticks of dynamite to simulate grenades. Once the attackers reached the top, they engaged the defenders in mock hand-to-hand combat, culminating in the dummy being tossed over the cliff, accompanied by a "blood-curdling shriek." It was great entertainment for the battalion observing, who applauded as the instructors bowed from the top of the cliff, but it also impressed on the men that rock-climbing mobility in the mountains could become an attack, a mountain maneuver.[33] However, all the rock and alpine techniques acquired in the school setting still required weeks of application in unit training.

Mountain Unit Training

From mid-August to mid-September 1943, the 10th Light Division focused on unit training. Companies, battalions, and regiments moved into the mountains around Camp Hale. There they bivouacked near tree line, for weeks at a time, on Tennessee Pass, at Gold Park along Homestake Creek, on Shrine Pass, on Ptarmigan Hill, and along Resolution Creek, to conduct maneuvers in alpine terrain. The 90th Infantry spent three weeks in August bivouacked at Gold Park, shooting mortars in the vicinity of the Holy Cross City ghost town and firing light machine guns. It then ran tactical schools for officers and NCOs to develop and execute attacks and defenses. The 86th Regiment at the same time was on Tennessee Pass, running company-on-company night infiltration and attack problems. Once it had completed mountaineering school, the 85th Infantry spent most of September camped on Ptarmigan Hill, as the 86th and then the 90th rotated battalions through the cliffs above Homestake Creek. Returning to Camp Hale, units fired on the various rifle ranges, threw hand grenades, and ran through a series of battle courses, including attacking pillboxes, reducing barbed wire emplacements, and the infiltration course, where machine guns fired over the soldiers' heads and dynamite blew up around them.[34]

The 604th and 605th Field Artillery Battalions began their unit training back in July with a 170-mile march by foot and mule from Camp Carson to Camp Hale, traversing up Old Stage Road to Cripple Creek, then on to Hartsel

and Fairplay in South Park, over Mosquito Pass to Leadville, then across Tennessee Pass. Artillery battalions bivouacked at Ptarmigan Hill as well but conducted most of their live-fire training west of the railroad, west of Camp Hale,
in the vicinity of Mitchell Creek. The 126th Engineer Battalion trained in the
Resolution Creek area, working with equipment transport by mule and setting
equipment lines over cliff faces. One company of the battalion, the 226th Engineers, conducted quite different training. Equipped with vehicles and other
motorized equipment, the company built trails, roads, bridges, cableways, and
tramways. Once Turquoise Lake west of Leadville froze, the company built a
landing strip on it. In early October, the 226th bivouacked at Officer's Gulch off
US Highway 6 (today I-70) in Summit County and built a motorized tramway
up Tenmile Peak.[35]

The division also conducted training, including specialized schools. A division intelligence school ran for twelve days in August with approximately 150
officers and enlisted men. It taught compass and map reading, observation
techniques, sketching, and reporting. The MTC provided a lesson on scouting and patrolling in the mountains, emphasizing the need for patrols to carry
increased equipment in order to be self-sufficient. Gaining elevation over the
enemy would aid in observation, and knowledge of mountain terrain aided
patrol movement. A division communication school also took place in August,
training over 500 officers and men on field phone emplacement and use, use
of radios, and messages, including company-level runners. To allow units to
conduct unit training without having to carry out basic training, the 10th Light
Division established a recruit school in September. Any infantry replacement
arriving at Camp Hale without having completed basic training after September 20 attended the recruit school. Staffed by over 150 officers and men from
all three infantry regiments, the school compressed basic training into just six
and a half weeks.[36]

Starting at the end of September, the division ran a series of command post
exercises (CPX). These were map-based with no actual troops in the field, the
purpose of which was to "give instruction and practice in staff procedure, to
develop coordination between staff sections and to furnish practice in the issuing of orders." The first two CPX, on September 23 and October 7, 1943, involved
just the division staff with a scenario that the division was in the vicinity of
Red Cliff, Colorado, at the junction of Homestake Creek and Eagle River. It
was to attack to the northeast, seize Shrine Pass, Vail Pass, and the mouth
of Tenmile Creek near present-day Copper Ski Area. The principal problem
revealed in these exercises was "the computation of time and space," as units
made marches in a command post exercise that later proved to be impossible
in actual experience.[37]

The division staff did take away lessons from the September and October CPX, ones long held by the MTC staff. First was the need for the division to have a dedicated reconnaissance capability. A light division had no cavalry reconnaissance troop, so the 10th Division established a reconnaissance echelon "on call" from the 1st Battalion, 86th Infantry Regiment. Initially the reconnaissance echelon consisted of two rifle companies with a small headquarters section of three officers, a nine-man signals detachment from the 110th Signal Platoon with an SCR-284 radio on the division radio net, and a six-man demolition squad from Company B, 126th Engineer Battalion. However, in December, after another command post exercise, the entire battalion with its communication section reinforced by four radio operators with an SCR-284, the demolition squad, and necessary animal or tracked cargo carrier transport made up the divisional reconnaissance echelon. To carry out their divisional mission, the 1st Battalion, 86th Infantry, received extra training in reconnaissance, intelligence, skiing, and rock climbing.[38]

The CPX also reinforced the need for units in the mountains to be self-sufficient and capable of operating independently. The division thus organized three combat teams (CTs) comprising an infantry regiment reinforced by a field artillery battalion, a medical company, an engineer company, and a signal platoon. Additional assets, such as the divisional antitank battery, could also be attached to a CT. The 10th Division combat teams mirrored what was an increasingly common practice in US Army divisions at the time, the organizing of the three regiments into reinforced regimental combat teams (RCTs). However, while an RCT generally had minimal logistic assets assigned, a 10th Division CT also included a quartermaster pack company with several hundred pack and riding mules.[39]

On October 14 the division held its third command post exercise, to include not just the division commander and staff, but also the commanders and staffs of the division artillery and the 85th, 86th, and 90th Infantry Regiments just organized into Combat Team 85, CT 86, and CT 90. Again, the purpose of the exercise was to train staff procedures, practice issuing orders, and test the distribution of orders. Still a map-based exercise, the problem was now to advance the division from Tennessee Pass northward to Minturn and then west to Dotsero. Movement rates now appeared more realistic. On roads and trails, men on foot and animals would move at 2.5 miles per hour, plus an additional hour for every one thousand feet ascended. Cross-country movement reduced the rate to 1.5 miles per hour, along with an hour per one thousand feet.[40]

To further "determine logistical data, and to make use of the division supply system," the division conducted a field exercise on October 25–27. The entire division participated; the only men excused were those who had not had two weeks to acclimate. The division marched in a single column along the road from Camp Hale to a bivouac site in Gold Park with CT 86 as the advance guard, followed by CT 85, and then CT 90. This was about seven miles with two thousand feet of elevation gain. The engineers established a truck head for Class I (rations and water) and Class V (ammunition) supply a mile and a half below the bivouac with sufficient space to unload trucks and load mules. The march was planned to take only six hours, but it took eighteen hours for the entire division to close on the bivouac. Early season snow showers made the road treacherous for mules, who slipped and fell. They had to be recovered, reloaded, and reorganized before the march could resume. The supply of rations proved slow but satisfactory, as each man carried a mountain ration, but transportation was insufficient to conduct an ammunition supply.[41]

As the 10th Division experienced the challenges of simply moving and surviving in the mountains, it also tested the unit training for maneuvering in the mountains. Divisional leadership tests of selected infantry platoon and rifle squad leaders took place in October. For the platoon leadership the test was an advance guard problem. The platoon leader had to "render prompt decisions; issue clear and concise orders to carry out his plans; maintain contact with the point by connecting files; and keep the support commander informed of the situation." The platoon leader, "through aggressive leadership, controls the action of his platoon in carrying out the assigned mission." The rifle squad leadership problem was a reconnaissance patrol. The squad leader as a patrol leader was to select a suitable route, designate an alternate leader, and inform the patrol of the mission, terrain to be crossed, individual tasks, and an assembly point in case the patrol was forced to separate. At dangerous areas, the patrol leader sent a scout ahead. And the patrol leader had to decide when information gained was to be sent back by messenger or by the return of the entire patrol.[42]

From November 22 to December 11, 1943, the division carried out firing proficiency tests for all rifle and weapons platoons and 81 mm mortar sections. The rifle platoons fired sixteen rounds per rifle and ten rounds per 60 mm mortar, the weapons platoons shot one hundred rounds per light machine gun, and the 81 mm mortar sections also fired ten rounds per tube. Any unit that failed would be retested after December 13. Rifle company proficiency tests took place starting on December 27 and ran to the end of the month. Division staff selected one rifle company from each infantry battalion and the engineer battalion to test. The test area was at the south end of camp, between the highway and the railroad, with the rest of the battalion watching from the high ground to the west of the tracks. The problem was an approach march, occupation of an assembly area, and an attack. It was to test the company leadership and the state of troop training of the tested company, while instructing the watching companies on fire plans, infantry action, and teamwork. Ten men, likely from the 10th Recon, provided the enemy. Loaded with ten blank rounds per rifle and one hundred per light machine gun, the company attacked and captured the high ground running from the railroad to Highway 24 across from Rule Gulch. Umpires scored the attacking companies on their tactics and technique. The time required to make decisions, formulate a plan, and issue orders by the company commander and the use of maneuver, assault, and reorganization heavily weighted the tactics score. The technique score emphasized the use of cover and concealment and fire control and distribution across the company objective.[43]

Mountain Training Detachments

By 1943 the rock and alpine training of the 10th Division at Camp Hale was the War Department's third mountain and winter warfare priority. The priority was the winter training of standard infantry divisions, with low mountain training of such units second. The Mountain Training Center and, after October 1943, the Mountain Training Group supported these efforts with training detachments of officer supervisors and enlisted instructors. From November 1942 thirty officers and ninety-six enlisted men from the MTC trained the 2nd Infantry Division at Camp McCoy, Wisconsin. The detachment split into small teams and trained small groups of the 2nd Division at old Civilian Conservation Corps camps in Wisconsin and Michigan in cross-country skiing, snowshoeing, and winter camping. After six weeks, the groups reassembled for divisional maneuvers lasting until April 1943. The training proved to be a success. The infantrymen, many of whom had never seen snow before, learned to ski twenty miles a day with heavy packs and sleep out in −30°F temperatures. The rolling wooded terrain allowed for more use of oversnow and wheeled vehicles to transport supplies, so the troops did not have to carry as much equipment. A platoon cook set, smaller rucksack, lighter ski with simpler bindings, and larger four-man tent were all considered by the quartermaster general for winter operations.[44]

Given the success of this winter training, another training detachment of thirty officers and one hundred enlisted men from the MTG left Camp Hale in late October 1943, bound again for Camp McCoy. This time, rather than training an entire division, the detachment trained about one thousand officers and NCOs from the 76th Infantry Division for six weeks. Again, instruction focused on cross-country skiing, snowshoeing, and winter bivouacking, though the lack of snow that winter hampered the detachment's efforts. These students then instructed their own men, under the supervision of the MTG members, before embarking on divisional maneuvers that lasted until March 1944. Captain Woodward led another MTG detachment to Pine Camp, New York, in early November 1943. He was to provide winter training for the 5th Armored Division, focusing on snowshoeing and winter camping. After a week of instruction, the division received orders to deploy overseas, ending the training and sending the detachment back to Colorado.[45]

The requirement for low mountain training came about in early 1943 as Army Ground Forces were preparing the 36th and 45th Infantry Divisions for the invasion of Sicily. This necessitated training in amphibious landings and subsequent operations in mountain terrain with a primitive road network. The AGF selected a training area in the Blue Ridge Mountains of Virginia, roughly one hundred miles west of Richmond, naming it the Buena Vista Maneuver Area after a town at its edge. The MTC provided a training detachment for the Blue Ridge Mountains to "familiarize the units with operations in mountains and primitive terrain." Each division sent a regimental combat team to the maneuver area with MTC officers serving as technical advisers. The program consisted of five days of marches and acclimatization followed by ten days of force-on-force maneuvers. Approximately five to ten men per rifle company, one liaison detail per artillery battalion, and five men from the regimental intelligence platoon also attended an assault rock-climbing school at Balcony Falls, staffed by MTC instructors.[46]

From March 1 to April 15, 1943, the 36th and 45th Divisions rotated RCTs through the Buena Vista Maneuver Area. The AGF determined that standard infantry divisions could operate in low mountains, under certain conditions. Division personnel had to be in good physical shape since moving off-road meant all heavy equipment had to be carried on packboards. There had to be some sort of road network, however primitive, to allow the 2.5-ton trucks and 105 mm howitzers to move forward in support of attacks, though the MTC advisers strongly recommended the quarter-ton jeep as the only reliable vehicle in mountainous terrain. And command and control had to be decentralized with task-organized, self-sufficient, battalion, company, and even platoon combat teams. The 36th and 45th benefited from their low mountain training in Sicily, so the AGF continued the effort, moving the maneuver area into the Allegheny Mountains of the West Virginia Maneuver Area, headquartered in Elkins, West Virginia.[47]

Ultimately RCTs from five divisions—the 28th, 31st, 35th, 77th, and 95th— and one medical group underwent low mountain training in the West Virginia Maneuver Area from August 1, 1943, to July 1, 1944. Each RCT spent one week in physical conditioning and acclimatization, ending with squad, platoon, and company exercises. The second week saw two battalion and two RCT problems against a notional enemy, allowing for live fire. Upward of thirteen MTC officers accompanied each RCT, but as umpires at the battalion and regimental level, not technical advisers. The West Virginia Maneuver Area mountain training detachment also ran an assault climbers school at Seneca Rocks and Champe Rocks. Each RCT assigned around two hundred officers and men to the school, which ran for the whole two weeks. The first week covered ropes, knots, and belays on wooden towers, based on those built at Fort Lewis in Washington during the summer of 1942. In the second week the instructors selected the best men and trained them on cliff faces in hand- and footholds, rappelling, pitons, and night climbing. The goal was for each company to have five to six men trained as assault climbers.[48]

Three to five officer supervisors and thirty to thirty-five enlisted instructors from the MTC/MTG staffed the assault climbers school. After the 10th Division completed its mountaineering school in mid-October, many of those supervisors and instructors went east to Seneca Rocks in relief, including Lieutenant Brower. Before turning the school over to the new detachment, the outgoing officers encapsulated their training program into a "Handbook for Assault Climbers." While none of the units who underwent training at Seneca Rocks ever carried out a cliff assault, they did learn valuable lessons from their low mountain training in the Allegheny Mountains. Weather was unpredictable, even in the low mountains, running the gamut from subzero temperatures and blizzards in the winter and floods from melting snow and rainstorms in the spring. Simply moving in the mountains was a challenge as the few roads rapidly became packed with vehicles. Moving off-road required training in and use of mules and packboards.[49]

Most unit commanders simply found that the greatest value of low mountain training was the physical conditioning and mental hardening solders gained. Yet many also reported their men needed more food in the mountains, but higher authorities always rejected requests for increased rations. In general, the low mountain training did benefit the divisions that underwent it. The commander of the 45th Infantry Division in Sicily reported that low mountain training was "'the best substitute' for actual combat in the mountains." However, with the number of divisions in the United States declining in the summer of 1944, reducing the army's ability to support division-level maneuvers, the West Virginia Maneuver Area closed on July 1, 1944. The members of the mountain training detachment, which had been transferred to the control of the maneuver area in March, received individual reassignment orders that would, in the words of Dave Brower, scatter them "all over the compass."

Brower got on the phone. He called Minnie Dole of the NSP and his climbing friends Dick Leonard and Bestor Robinson in the Office of the Quartermaster General, trying to get the detachment sent back to the 10th. It worked; the orders were changed.[50]

Given the success of low mountain training for standard units in the United States, the Fifth Army fighting in Italy decided to continue mountain training for units in theater. While the British military was willing to share training facilities, the British mission to the War Department requested that the US Army send a detachment of instructors. The AGF therefore selected five officers and fifteen enlisted men from among the most experienced instructors in the Mountain Training Group at Camp Hale for the 2662 Mountain Warfare Detachment. Many had just returned from the Aleutians, others had taught on Cooper Hill or in the Virginia and West Virginia maneuver areas, and a few had just returned from the canceled training at Pine Camp.[51]

They left Camp Hale on December 15, 1943, originally bound for the British Middle East Mountain School in Lebanon but redirected to the Snow Warfare School at Sepino, Italy, arriving on January 19, 1944. The mission of the school "was not to train large scale formations, but to train instructors who could take the skills back to their units." For the next nine months, in conjunction with the British instructors, the 2662 taught rock climbing, line hauling, mountain marching, and mule packing to cadres of instructors from British, Indian, Polish, and US divisions. The detachment also sent small training teams to forward units to provide instruction, as well as function as a mountain warfare cadre, leading patrols and reconnaissance missions or organizing mule trains to move supplies forward in combat. After a short hiatus awaiting return to the United States, which was countermanded, 2662 Detachment rejoined the British school, now known as the Mountain School, at Terminillo, high in the mountains sixty-five miles from Rome, in November 1944. Here they ran a monthlong winter mobility course, including rock, snow, and ice climbing, skiing, and winter bivouacking for US and Allied troops. They also continued to provide cadres to forward units.[52]

The deployment of mountain training detachments, particularly to the West Virginia Maneuver Area, and the ongoing deployment of the 87th Regiment to the Aleutians campaign at the end of 1943 showed that the army had begun to recognize the need for units trained to operate in mountainous terrain with poor road networks and under extreme winter conditions. But the army's primary mountain and cold weather warfare capability resided in the 10th Light Division at Camp Hale, which was neither ready for deployment nor preparing for deployment, as it was at that time an experimental unit. Indeed, by the middle of December 1943 it was clear that the division could not complete its unit training phase by January 10, 1944, as originally planned. This was owing to an influenza epidemic in November and December, the slow arrival of personnel, and a lack of snow. While mountaineering training had been accomplished, specialized individual and unit preparations for winter operations, skiing, and oversnow transportation still had to be carried out. Unit training was thus extended to February 5.[53] The next year would see many mountain maneuvers.

CHAPTER 5

Mountain Maneuvers, 1944

January 1944 found US mountain troops amid their third winter, their second in the Colorado mountains. Their numbers grew in that time from a single battalion to a pair of regiments to an entire division. Their training matured from hastily adapted civilian techniques to military-specific methods. And by the start of the year, the snowpack was enough to train in winter operations and skiing. Yet the American mountain troops still needed to execute their combined training phase of regimental and divisional mountain maneuvers, after which they could then expect to participate in larger division-on-division exercises. And they were still an experimental unit for which no theater of deployment had yet been identified or could be until a report of results was compiled. After three years of experimentation, the US military still did not require a specialized mountain warfare capability or unit.

Military Ski Mountaineers

Winter 1944 showed the men at Camp Hale as increasingly competent military ski mountaineers, able to survive and move in the high mountains, in the alpine terrain above tree line, under the harshest of winter conditions. No one showed this better than the instructors and specialists of the Mountain Training Group and the 10th Reconnaissance Troop. On December 28, 1943, fifty-one men from both units, eight on snowshoes, the rest on skis, set off along Herrington Creek southwest of Leadville in temperatures around −5°F. Following the creek bed west, the men bushwhacked through thickets, trees, and scrub, continually losing their mohair climbers, especially at the front and back, as they were held on only by straps. The troopers identified the need for a notch at the end of the ski to better tighten the climber straps. Carrying heavy packs on narrow skis in a snow-filled gulch meant the men had to take turns breaking trail in the loose snow, but no longer than five minutes each.[1]

A column of pack mules of HQ, Det 10th Division Artillery, Camp Hale, Colorado, moves up the trail (March 17, 1944). National Archives Local ID: 111-SC-240545, https://catalog.archives.gov/id/100310536.

After two and a half hours, the party intersected the Main Range Trail (today's Colorado Trail) at 10,350 feet. They dropped packs and set off for the summit of Mount Elbert at 14,440 feet, the highest point in Colorado. They climbed along a ridge through thick forests for an hour and a half before reaching tree line at around 12,000 feet. Temperatures were in the teens with winds around twenty miles per hour. Under these conditions the party shortened the usual hourly ten-minute break to just three or four minutes, to avoid cooling down too much. After climbing another thousand feet, they cached their skis and snowshoes, as the wind had blown the rocky ridge clean of snow. The rubber-cleated mountain boots proved better in this terrain than the older ski boots. Twenty men returned to camp, suffering from the altitude, and another nineteen turned back four hundred feet below the summit as they were running out of daylight. Only twelve men made the summit. The skiing back to camp encountered every possible snow condition, but all made it before dark.[2]

The expedition then erected tents, built fires, and ate, finding the white felt mukluks to be excellent camp wear. The night was clear and cold, and the tents frosted up badly from condensation. The next morning proved to be cloudy and warmer with snow flurries. The party set off north along the Colorado Trail rotating trailbreakers every few minutes. By midday, they descended into Half Moon Creek, the men riding their ski poles to make it down the narrow, steep, rocky trail. One man broke his ski tip, but soon repaired it. The snowsho-ers descended about thirty minutes behind the skiers. They continued along the trail, increasingly following just the tree blazes, reaching a bivouac site on Willow Creek. The men used two old cabins on the site for shelter or selected tent sites among the trees and settled in for the night.[3]

December 30 dawned overcast with strong winds, gusting to forty miles per hour, so only twenty-two men attempted the summit. They climbed up the wind-packed snow to tree line around 12,000 feet where they again left their skis and proceeded on foot to the 14,429-foot summit of Mount Massive. The "face mask, chamois" proved to be invaluable in high winds above timberline, preventing frostbite, but the canvas and wool "mittens, shell, trigger finger" allowed wind to seep through, freezing the fingers. A full leather mitten was preferable. The men descended quickly to their skis and skied back to camp, within an hour of making the summit. The entire expedition skied back down a rarely used trail, which occasionally disappeared, to where a road crossed Willow Creek. This proved to be the hardest part of the trip, requiring bushwhacking over steep, rock-strewn slopes for two miles. Forest Service trails, they learned, were not to be considered ski trails. The skiers reached the "entrucking" point in an hour to two hours, but the snowshoers were again a half hour behind. The expedition returned to Camp Hale by six o'clock that evening. In summary the expedition covered ten miles on the first day to summit Elbert, then ten miles the second day to the slopes of Mount Massive, and twelve miles on the third day to sum-mit Massive and then return to the trucks. The thirty-two-mile trip in severe winter weather confirmed the ability of Camp Hale's military mountaineers to survive and be mobile in the high mountains in winter.[4]

On January 11, 1944, a party of seventeen men of the 10th Recon set off from the Climax town site on the south side of Fremont Pass with the mission to conduct a high-altitude bivouac. Skiing up the valley behind Climax for a few miles (today the pit of the Climax Mine), the party selected a 2,500-foot couloir to climb to the main ridge of the Mosquito Range. Below Mount Bartlett they established a bivouac at 13,200 feet, digging tent platforms into the snow. Tem-peratures at night dropped to −20°F, but the men suffered no ill consequences. The next day was clear, so the party split into two patrols, one to summit Mount Democrat to the south, the other to summit Bartlett and Traver Peak. These patrols triggered two avalanches, but no one was injured, due more to luck than to avalanche awareness. All returned by the late afternoon when temperatures in the sun had reached nearly 30°F. Some skied off the east side of the divide into the Clinton Creek basin, practicing "Eastern headwall skiing." The last day, January 13, the party descended and met up with their transportation back to Camp Hale.[5]

The 10th Recon further demonstrated its ability to move through and survive in winter mountains in a flurry of single-day backcountry ski touring trips or ski patrols from the middle of January. On the January 18 seven men departed the Mitchell town site on Highway 24 between Camp Hale and Tennessee Pass. They headed west up into the mountains, then descended Yoder Gulch to the main gate of the camp. Three days later eleven men unloaded from trucks just below Ptarmigan Pass at the head of Resolution Creek east of camp. They toured onto and along Wingle Ridge, then skied down to the road into the town of Red Cliff. On January 24 ten men skinned up Yoder Gulch and along the south ridge of Homestake Creek valley, following a logging road down into No Name Gulch north of Camp Hale. Two days later ten men trucked up the East Fork Eagle River southeast of camp, dismounting on the southwest slope of Sheep Mountain. Continuing on skins up the jeep road to the summit, the patrol skied down the north slope then skinned up North Sheep Mountain before descending into Cataract Creek. A patrol of eight men headed up Taylor Creek off Highway 24 south of camp on January 27, reaching Chicago Ridge and following it north back into Camp Hale.[6]

The MTG and 10th Recon conducted these ski mountaineering and ski tours as there were now enough experienced officers and men in the division to serve as unit instructors for ongoing winter operation and ski training. The division directed "individual instruction in snow and extreme cold" during November 1943 with "experienced officers" serving as instructors. The subjects were those determined to be required from the experience of the previous year and included bivouacs, care of animals, clothing, individual precautions against exposure, marches and route selection, preparation of the mountain ration, sanitation and first aid, shelters, snowshoes, and toboggans. The lessons were based on instructor experience and a number of text references. These included the manual on snow and extreme cold, the sections in the operations manual on mountain operations and snow and extreme cold, and two training circulars issued by the Office of the Quartermaster General in March 1943 on the basic principles and use of cold weather clothing. Instructors also utilized the snow camping, ski safety, first aid and emergency repair, and ski mountaineering training films.[7]

Also in November the division trained soldiers to operate and maintain the tracked, over-the-snow Light Cargo Carrier T15/M28, or Weasel. Each infantry regiment trained five mechanics and twenty-seven drivers, and each artillery battalion four mechanics and twenty-one drivers by the end of December 1943. Operated by one driver, the M28 Weasel had a small cargo compartment with room for one passenger. The division also received the improved M29 variant, with a larger cargo compartment, and trained drivers and mechanics for it in

January 1944. Camouflaged in mottled white paint, the Weasels transported supplies forward onboard or in towed toboggans and could evacuate casualties back to the rear. They could also be used to tow skiers, thus increasing their mobility. While their availability was limited, these oversnow vehicles finally gave the division transportation options when the mountain snow got too deep for mules.[8]

The 10th Division intended to begin a ski program in November 1943 "for the instruction of skiers in fundamentals only, with emphasis on cross-country movement." Instructors were to be trained over a ten-day period with division training commencing on November 19 and lasting four weeks. However, a lack of snowfall during the month resulted in a postponement until "the first Monday after suitable snow conditions exist." The division hoped to start ski training on December 27 but was not able to do so until January 3, 1944. The MTG prepared a detailed schedule for ski instructors, a refinement of the 1943 ski schedule. Instruction focused on individual mobility on skis and stressed controlled skiing and cross-country techniques. The schedule laid out twenty daily lessons of three hours, progressing from nomenclature, care, and waxing of skis to simple cross-country runs, to climbing steps, to the snowplow, to sideslipping, to the snowplow turn. As before, cross-country skiing occupied at least one-third of each lesson.[9]

There was no time for the twenty advanced skiing lessons, since the division needed to take up combined training, so in 1944 instructors introduced the lifted stem pole or lifted stem christie turn on Day 12. This was the most advanced turn taught in the ski program as it was the most useful turn in soft or heavy snow, or when the terrain required short turns, and when carrying a heavy pack. In a downhill traverse the skier braked by weighting the downhill ski, then pushed the uphill ski out with a wide stance to initiate the turn. The skier then placed the downhill pole at a point near the tip of the downhill ski and turned around the pole, lifting up the downhill ski and placing it alongside the other, completing the turn. Instruction also included climbing using climbing wax on Day 13 and with climbers, or skins, on Day 14. The ski program concluded with a six-mile cross-country patrol race.[10]

In 1944 the entire division participated in ski training. Skiers and instructors from the artillery battalions, medical battalion, engineer battalion, division staff, and headquarters utilized all the lettered slopes around Camp Hale, with the engineers using their own slope in McAlister Creek. The infantry regiments utilized the lettered slopes for two weeks, then cycled through Cooper Hill for two weeks. The 90th Regiment went first, and of the nearly one hundred instructors the regiment required, only three were from the MTG, which shows the progress made in developing military mountaineers. The 86th followed for two weeks, then the 85th Infantry Regiment. Even after the completion of the divisional ski program, many of the men continued to argue over the merits of the Arlberg or "parallel" techniques.[11]

The MTG and 10th Recon continued developing military mountaineering techniques and practices. On February 21 three officers, including Capt John Jay, and thirty men from the MTG and 10th Recon, along with Sgt Paul Petzoldt of the 10th Medical Battalion, set out on a ski mountaineering tour from Leadville to Aspen, across the Continental Divide. The route today is called the "Trooper Traverse." They carried mountain rations for several days, avalanche probes and shovels in case of a rescue, ropes, and ice axes. They also had experimental four-man tent flies, with no floor. Departing the Malta town site south of Leadville, the party skinned up Half Moon Creek and bivouacked near the Champion Mill. They melted snow to prepare their rations, six packed pans for each four-man mess. Many of the men also put hot water into their canteens and placed them in their sleeping bags. The tent flies, treated to make them water-resistant, did not breathe and thus rained frozen condensation down on the men as badly as the two-man mountain tent.[12]

The next day they climbed up the basin behind the mill, aiming for a saddle between Mount Champion and Deer Mountain, now called Darling Pass. Here Captain Jay and Sergeant Petzoldt disagreed on the route. Jay preferred a more direct ascent, but Petzoldt, who likely knew more about avalanches than anyone else, was concerned that the slope might slide. Petzoldt and twelve men thus took a safer, if longer, route to the saddle, while Jay and the rest took the more direct approach. In general, the men felt they were lucky to have avoided an avalanche. The first one thousand feet off the ridge proved to be too steep to ski, so the party glissaded down before putting their skis back on and crossing the Lake Creek drainage to a bivouac site on a shelf above the North Fork of the creek. On February 23 the group switchbacked their way up onto the Continental Divide, then contoured around a peak to ski down above Lost Man Lake. They skied down Lost Man Creek to the base of the Williams Range in the vicinity of South Fork Pass.[13]

In falling snow, increasing winds, and decreasing visibility, they followed a ridge up onto the range, locating a narrow couloir. The party carefully descended via sidesteps, traverses, and kick turns until the slope opened enough to ski down into the timber above Hunter Creek where they spent their last night. On the last day, February 24, the men skied down Hunter Creek, bypassing where the creek entered a canyon by climbing over Thimble Rock Ridge, and then into Aspen to the entrance of the Jerome Hotel. The innkeeper, Larry Elisha, provided the group two bottles of Seagram's Seven Crown whiskey and let them stay the night in the hotel. The next day the party returned to Camp Hale.[14]

Captain Jay with five officers and fifty men of the 10th Recon returned to Aspen on March 6, 1944, heading fifteen miles out of town to the ghost town of Ashcroft. Here they conducted winter survival and avalanche training; the latter proved necessary when Cpl Bill Bowes triggered an avalanche. Bowes followed his instruction and kept his feet downhill while swimming uphill, keeping his head above the snow, which allowed him to be dug out. Jay was caught at the edge of the slide and was carried to the foot of the slope as well. Ski tours into Montezuma Basin, Castle Park, Pearl Pass, and Pine Creek also observed several avalanches. The troop practiced building snow caves and igloos and setting game snares. The final day consisted of ski maneuvers with the troop splitting into two sections and trying to keep their ski tracks concealed by timber, terrain, and shadows. Both sections managed to unknowingly outflank the other.[15] As the MTG and 10th Recon were focusing on the specific skills and abilities for winter military mountaineering, the rest of the 10th Division completed unit training.

Combined Mountain Training

The division's combined, or combined arms, training was to run from February 7 to April 29. The purpose of this phase, per a February 1944 directive from Army Ground Forces, was "to weld the several units of the division into a division team capable of acting as a concerted whole and maintaining itself under any and all battle conditions." It consisted of three sets of exercise: regimental combat team exercises culminating in field maneuvers, division exercises and maneuvers, and command post exercises. The division held CPX for the RCT exercises on January 6 and the division exercise on February 29.[16] In combined training the individual mountain troopers and their primary units—squad, section, platoon, company—were no longer the training audience. They were now training aids or props for the battalion, regimental, and division commanders and staffs, who were trained and evaluated in the combined phase.

As combined training got underway, the division suffered more personnel perturbations. The 87th Mountain Infantry Regiment returned to Camp Carson, Colorado, from the Aleutians at the end of 1943 and was assigned to the 10th Division in February 1944, replacing the 90th Regiment. The 90th, before it left Camp Hale, reassigned those men who had volunteered via the National Ski Patrol to the 85th and 86th Regiments. The 87th, which still contained a good number of skiers and mountaineers, was reorganized as a light infantry regiment. At the end of March most of the men assigned to the 10th Recon and the MTG were transferred into the three infantry regiments. This allowed the division to finally reach its full strength of 9,358 officers and men.[17]

A series of six regimental combat team exercises took place between February 7 and March 25, each four to seven days in length. The three regiments—85th, 86th, and 87th—organized as combat teams (CTs) with artillery, signal, and logistic support, mules and Weasels, moved to the familiar training areas on Tennessee Pass, below Homestake Peak, and in Gold Park. While it was a mild winter—a weather station at the headwaters of the Eagle River above Camp Hale recorded one-third less snow than usual—there were still at least two feet of snow on the ground. Per FM 7-20 *Infantry Battalion* and FM 7-40 *Rifle Regiment*, RCT exercises focused on the actions and procedures of the regimental and battalion headquarters and staffs, troop movements and bivouacs, offensive and defensive operations, and retrograde movements. The culmination of the RCT phase was the two-day battalion combat firing test.[18]

On the first day the tested battalion organized a defensive position. Per the manual and training directives, the battalion commander took his S-3 operations officer and a messenger when reporting to the regimental commander to receive his order. He made a reconnaissance of the assigned area with the artillery liaison officer and S-3 before issuing a defensive order, which was to include "security, distribution, and missions of rifle companies and all weapons under battalion control, coordination of fire, use of the reserve (to include counterattack) . . . , ground organization, communication, and administration." In wooded, broken terrain such as mountains, a battalion occupied a frontage of one thousand yards with a main line of resistance on a reverse slope. Two companies were forward, with their organic machine guns assigned sectors of fire and platoon 60 mm mortars assigned targets in the many defiles, gullies, and bits of low ground that defined the mountainous terrain. The battalion reserve of one company defended the position in depth, protected the flanks and rear, counterattacked, or established a combat outpost. The battalion's two 81 mm mortars were emplaced together, in battery, and assigned primary and secondary targets, and the artillery recorded targets for close defensive fires.[19]

On day two of the battalion combat firing test, the tested battalion attacked an (unoccupied) defensive position prepared by another battalion. This was a live-fire attack with artillery support from all twelve guns of a field artillery battalion. The battalion commander made a reconnaissance of the position with his artillery liaison officer and ensured his company commanders and platoon leaders did the same. The battalion plan of attack assigned "company objectives; where and in what direction the main and secondary attacks are to be made; zones of action of the attacking rifle companies; formation of the battalion; composition, location, and employment of reserves; . . . security measures initially necessary; and the time of attack. Tentative plans for the defense of the objective, when taken, should also be made." The plan of attack had to be adapted to the terrain. One lesson learned during the 10th Division's unit training phase was that a frontal assault straight uphill would not work. It was simply too exhausting. Attacks had to outflank the enemy and come in from the sides or from an upslope attack position, which was advantageous on skis.[20]

During the attack the bulk of supporting fire was assigned to the battalion's main effort. As the attack advanced, the battalion's mortars and machine guns displaced forward to ensure continuous close fire support. This could lead to friendly fire incidents. During the attack by 3rd Battalion, 86th Infantry, on Tennessee Pass, likely in the gulch north of Cooper Hill, an errant 81 mm mortar round fell into Company L's command post, killing one man and wounding another. Because of this risk, the battalion established a battalion aid station to deal with casualties and advance it as the attack developed. Finally, upon seizure of the position, the battalion reorganized and dug in, in preparation for an enemy counterattack. The battalion combat firing test in the mountains concluded with a nine-mile ski test—seven miles for those with snowshoes— back to Camp Hale, to be completed in two hours.[21]

The 87th Infantry completed the last battalion test on March 24, 1944, ending the RCT phase of combined training. The entire division now prepared for division maneuvers. The men reviewed precautions to avoid avalanches, including choice of slope and route across a slope, and what to do if caught in an avalanche: loosen equipment prior, protect the mouth to prevent suffocation, keep feet downhill, and swim uphill. The 10th Recon's recent avalanche experiences at Ashcroft may have informed much of this instruction, as the troop was officially disbanded on March 21 and most of the officers and men were assigned to the infantry regiments. And they received a "Check List for Small Unit Leaders" that encapsulated much of what had been learned over the previous year since the disastrous Homestake maneuvers of February 1943.[22]

The checklist reveals the 10th Division as quite capable backcountry skiers and troopers, capable of surviving, moving, and maneuvering in the winter mountains. They set out with skis waxed, rucksacks adjusted, and ski goggles on. To avoid overheating on the move, many wore just their wool base layers, lightweight white trousers, and ski parka. They maintained their intervals and kept silent on the march, often moving at night to avoid observation. When halted they removed their packs and sat on them, to avoid sitting in the snow and freezing. They had learned not to drink out of ponds or streams. In a bivouac site or assembly area, they added clothing as necessary to prevent chilling, including new pile jackets, applied lip balm and sunburn cream, and maintained their dispersal.[23]

When advancing on skis, troopers slung their rifles around their necks or carried them single-handedly. The men learned to go prone on skis, falling forward onto their left side and spreading their skis out behind them in a V, creating a more stable firing position by using the rucksack as a rest and removing the left ski. To move under fire, they removed both skis and lay flat on them, crawling forward. At some point they abandoned the skis and moved on foot or on the smaller emergency bear-paw snowshoes, if they carried them. If not engaged tactically, the men dug in, cleaned rifles, waxed skis, or ate. Many dropped the cook set from their packs, using a lighter large fruit or vegetable can instead to melt snow and boil water. Every man had to eat at every meal. When moving into the line, the troopers left their tents with the company supply sergeant for use in the rear and built brush or snow shelters or often just dug a snow pit and lined it with pine boughs. They changed their socks and inner soles before going to sleep, drying the damp pairs out inside the sleeping bag. The boots, cleaned of ice and snow, were placed between the sleeping bag and the water-repellent case. And they learned not to drink anything after late afternoon, to avoid nature's call in the middle of a subzero night.[24]

For these distinct skills and abilities, the Camp Hale troopers finally were allowed distinct insignia and uniform. In January 1944 the army approved the now familiar distinctive shoulder insignia of two bright scarlet bayonets bordered in white on a brilliant blue, white-bordered powder keg background. The blue of the powder keg signified an infantry division, while the crossed bayonets represented the numerical designation of the division. Many in the division had wanted an insignia of crossed skis, not bayonets, and some thought the powder keg resembled a pickle barrel. The camp newspaper "accidentally" displayed the patch upside down, something it corrected in the next edition, but many men wore the patch that way in tacit protest. More important for trooper self-prestige was division approval in February 1944 to wear the distinctive mountain trousers, ski-mountain boots, ski gaiters, and ski cap off base while on pass, furlough, or leave. As these were items issued to no other unit in the continental United States at the time, they showed the public that the wearer was a mountain trooper.[25]

The division learned much from the RCT phase about mountain and winter warfare. Rifle battalions avoided attacks where they would be exposed for considerable time and space to enemy fire, such as a frontal attack uphill or across wide snow-covered flats. Instead, they sought to use their ski mobility and the mountains as cover and concealment—gullies, ridges, woods—to approach the enemy position as closely as possible. Since the artillery had fewer guns and less ammunition in the mountains, the infantry called for fire at the last possible moment. It then immediately took advantage of the short barrage to advance to within 150 to 200 yards, when the guns had to shift.[26]

Battalion commanders built up a substantial base of fire using their battalion mortars and one or even two rifle companies, in lieu of keeping one in reserve. These provided covering fire for the advance of the third rifle company. However, deep snow minimized the effect of much of this fire. Snow absorbed most of the splinters and shock from artillery shells, and mortars had practically no effect when the snow was deeper than four feet. More than five feet of snow would stop a rifle or machine-gun bullet. A daylight attack uphill in snow could not be done without heavy air and artillery bombardment and a large infantry force, conditions that were difficult to attain in the mountains at any time of the year. Enemy positions with a height advantage had to be taken in a night attack, or in fog, or in a snowstorm, or by complete surprise, advancing from an unexpected direction.[27]

Frontal attacks were thus to be avoided in mountain and winter warfare. Attacks by regimental combat teams and the division "should principally be conceived as offensive *out-maneuvering.*" This consisted of using relatively weak forces to hold the enemy with limited attacks. The main strength of the attack would be a single or double outflanking maneuver by units on skis, aiming for the enemy's rear and supply lines. With his supplies cut and rear areas occupied, the enemy would have to resort to frontal attacks and "take the dirty job of the last 200 yards and heavy losses." Such deep thrusts could now be supplied by motorized oversnow vehicles, the M29 Weasels, supplemented by pack mules and man packs.[28] The officers of the 10th Division passed much of this hard-earned knowledge on to the umpires from the army's XVI Corps, who arrived in Camp Hale in late March 1944 to conduct a series of divisional maneuvers.

D-Series

The D-Series was initially intended to consist of a two-week maneuver followed by a three-week maneuver, during which the division was to be in the field the entire time. These five weeks were designed, in the words of XVI Corps maneuver director Lt Col Lucien E. Bolduc, to "tackle the problems that have arisen in the mountain fighting of World War II." The D-Series exercises would be a far cry from the more relaxed unit maneuvers. They were force-on-force with a battalion or an entire CT of the division serving as the enemy, instead of a squad or two. Explosives would simulate artillery and mortar fire or land mines. Prisoners would be taken; casualties would be assessed. Maj Gen Lloyd Jones, the division commanding general, believed the maneuvers would be a test of morale, of the "confidence of each man in himself, his equipment, and his fellow soldiers." Over 8,600 men, two thousand mules, and several hundred M29 Weasels moved to the field on March 26, 1944, for the first week of the exercise, right into the teeth of a strong spring storm. While the winter had been mild in the Colorado Rockies, the spring proved to be anything but—a classic La Niña weather pattern. During the week of March 27, temperatures dropped to −20°F at night and four to five feet of snow fell, drifting up to eight feet deep in spots.[29]

The D-Series tested 10th Division's ability to execute its main tasks as laid down in FM 100-5 *Operations*: troop movement, offensive combat, defensive combat, and retrograde movements. Troop movement placed "troops at their destination at the proper time and in effective condition for combat." The first event of the exercise was thus the movement of the division out of Camp Hale, south over Tennessee Pass, to favorable positions north of Leadville, likely in the vicinity of Missouri Hill, to meet an enemy attack. In the snow-covered mountains the advance used all available roads and trails, some rebuilt by the divisional engineers, and the CTs marched in separate terrain corridors. Movement rates were slow in the snow and high altitude, and marching units needed advance and flank guard patrols on skis. Despite all this "the infantry and artillery got to where their commanders wanted them."[30]

During the night of March 27, the division learned that the enemy was advancing in greater strength than expected and that the 10th was thus to fall back to defensive positions along Tennessee Pass. According to the manual defensive combat was to gain time until more favorable conditions existed for the offense. In the mountains, heights that observed and allowed fire on approaching enemy forces had to be defended, particularly those heights on the flanks of passes and defiles. The 10th dug snow trenches, as the ground was too frozen to dig into, and prepared heated shelters to the rear. Reserve units on skis were placed along the main routes of movement behind the defensive position. After withdrawing to Tennessee Pass and occupying their battle positions, the 10th Division troopers returned to Camp Hale at the end of the week, where they bivouacked in their tents, in the snow, in rest areas within sight of their barracks.[31]

The weather cleared over the weekend, and on Monday, April 3, they set off on the first of two offensive combat problems. Offensive combat, according to FM 100-5, seized a physical objective that would destroy the enemy position and facilitate future operations. In mountains these objectives were typically terrain features, such as passes or heights, which controlled lines of communication, both friendly and enemy. And there was an enemy: the exercise director trucked the 87th Infantry to Vail Pass to serve as an opposing force for the week. For the first problem the 87th defended east of Shrine and Ptarmigan

Passes, while the 10th Division advanced with the 85th Infantry on the left up Wearyman Creek and the 86th on the right along Resolution and Pearl Creeks, with both regiments organized into combat teams. This was in line with FM 100-5's statement that attacks in the mountains would be conducted by several tactical groups "operating in adjacent terrain compartments or corridors." In clear but cold and windy weather, the division seized the ridges above Vail Pass and, after patrols determined the enemy's position on April 4, attacked the next day in columns of skiers over Sugarloaf on the right and Wingle Ridge on the left, triggering a small avalanche. This maneuver outflanked the enemy at the mouths of the passes. At this point, on Wednesday afternoon, the umpires ended the problem and sent the division to a rest area north of Camp Hale and the "enemy" back to its bivouac on Vail Pass.[32]

After spending a day and night in the rest area, the division conducted a second attack on Vail Pass. This time the 87th defended the heights including Wingle and Machinegun Ridges, placed a battalion on Hornsilver Mountain as a combat outpost, and launched skiborne raids into the division rear. The 10th attacked on Good Friday, April 7, again with Combat Team 85 on the left and CT 86 on the right, but this time maneuvering along the heights. CT 85 climbed up Hornsilver and drove in the enemy outpost, while the 86th climbed the ridges above Resolution and Pearl Creeks. On April 8 CT 86 took Resolution Mountain, Ptarmigan Hill, and Machinegun Ridge. The latter only fell after the attacking battalion commander placed all twelve light machine guns and all nine 60 mm mortars in the battalion in battery with his two 81 mm mortars on the north slope of Sugarloaf Peak to cover the advance of the rifle companies. This allowed CT 86 to seize Ptarmigan Pass in a rising blizzard. Despite Easter Sunday being cold, windy, and snowy, CT 85 was able to pass over Ptarmigan Pass and continue the attack. This ended the second offensive combat problem of the D-Series.[33]

At this point, sometime around Easter Sunday, the maneuver director, Lieutenant Colonel Bolduc, decided to expand the two-week exercise into a third week and cancel the follow-on three-week exercise. The division thus moved into a rest area north of Pando on Monday and spent the next day recovering from their high alpine exposure. The weather grew sunny and warmer, reaching 39°F by Thursday. The last problem of the D-Series started on Wednesday, April 12, and was to be a retrograde movement under enemy pressure into a defensive position. CT 85, with its field artillery, engineer, medical, antiaircraft, and antitank attachments, played the enemy force attacking down Homestake Creek. CT 87, with antiaircraft, engineer, and medical attachments, sought to delay this enemy two miles east of Gold Park, with CT 86 in reserve. The enemy was able to infiltrate CT 87's positions during the night of April 12.[34]

The next day the umpires reported the constructive division on the 10th Division's left flank had fallen back. The 10th had to conduct retrograde movements that, as the manual noted, "in the face of the enemy are difficult maneuvers and require constant control and supervision by all leaders." 1st Battalion, 87th Infantry, was to act as a delaying force, but CT 85 pushed them back within four hours, nearly capturing the 87th's regimental command post. However, CT 86 was able to establish a new defensive position, which it held for the rest of the day and into the night. A raid led by the 86th's intelligence officer, Maj Donald Alan, on the night of April 13–14, recovered the notebook of the CT 85 commander with all unit locations, greatly aiding the defense. The problem and the D-exercise finally ended at 1000 on Friday, April 14.[35]

For the men of the 10th Division, the D-Series was a "suffer-fest," a bout of prolonged misery. They froze, particularly during the first week. Their feet were blistered raw by marches, both day and night, skiing, snowshoeing, or "postholing" many miles and climbing many thousands of vertical feet. They were exhausted, rarely getting more than a few hours' sleep a night. They were hungry and thirsty as they typically did not have enough time to melt water and prepare their mountain rations. They were often resupplied with canned standard army rations that did not have enough calories and water in jerry cans that froze. The 8,673 men in the division suffered 1,378 casualties requiring medical attention. Most of these (340) were physical injuries, followed by upper respiratory infections (197) and frostbite (195). The exercise plan did move men into nontactical rest areas every two to three days for a day or two, where they rested, recovered, dried out socks, ate hot food, and even got mail. While the 10th Division thus spent six of the twenty days of the D-Series in rest areas, most of the men remembered the time as one, long, continuous, brutal slog.[36]

By all accounts morale at Camp Hale hit rock bottom in the days and weeks following the D-Series. Many troopers questioned why they had done the maneuvers. Some men went AWOL during and even before, later arguing somewhat disingenuously that the conditions were much tougher than anything they could expect to see in combat. More pointed out that they had not learned anything in the maneuvers but had to carry them out so the "brass hats can get a bit of practice at handling a division in the field." But that was exactly what the D-Series was for. The army recognized that during division exercises enlisted men learned the least, while commanders and the staff learned the most. But divisions that had not carried out large-scale maneuvers did poorly when engaged in combat. The men of the 10th directed much of their ire at the division commander, General Jones, who should have been the one to explain this to his men. Jones, however, had chronic bronchitis, exacerbated by the altitude at Camp Hale. He was simply not a presence in the division, especially in the field, which left oversight of the training to his assistant division commander, Brig Gen Frank Culin. Culin took to skiing with enthusiasm and regularly visited units in the field, accompanied by his aide, Lt Monty Atwater, a skier as well as a "Harvard-trained mountaineer and forester."[37]

Mountain Test

But the deep root of the division's low morale appears to have been the fact that it had no deployment order. It was training simply to train, as best the men could tell, not to enter combat. But, again, that is exactly what the 10th Light Division (Alpine) was activated to do. It was "organized to test the organization and equipment best suited to the employment of a division in high mountain warfare." At the conclusion of its combined training, the division had orders to submit a report covering organization, weapons, equipment, communication, engineering, cooking, supply, transport, and time and space data, with any recommended changes. Therefore, after the D-Series, the division staff set to and completed the "Report on Tests of Organization and Equipment" by May 15. General Jones went back to Washington, DC, to brief General McNair, commander of AGF, on the findings.[38]

McNair was already in receipt of a report on the two other light divisions, the 71st and 89th, which carried out divisional exercises against each other in California from February to March 1944. This report confirmed the 10th's report: that the light division was too light. The light division organization did not have enough infantry, it did not have enough support weapons or artillery, it did not have a reconnaissance capability, it did not have enough engineer, medical, communication, or supply capabilities, it did not have a large enough staff to operate twenty-four hours a day, and it could not sustain itself in combat. The 10th's report found the specialized mountain equipment and clothing issued to be satisfactory, though men equipped with snowshoes needed suitable footwear for temperatures below 20°F. The mountain ration was also found to be satisfactory, as were the combat ration, or C ration, and the daily ration, or K ration, but some sort of hot drink had to be provided.[39]

For communication, a large amount of wire had to be laid, often in deep snow, which required more messengers and field wiremen, and there were not enough phones in the tables of equipment. SCR-195 infantry and SCR-511 cavalry radios proved unsatisfactory for communications in the mountains. Authorization and issue of SCR-300 FM sets improved radio communications within the battalions, but the SCR-284 AM radios were unreliable for communications between the division and its subordinates. There were not enough administrative and supply personnel in the division for efficient performance. In particular, the 10th's report concluded that "a division operating in high mountainous territory requires a greater number of supply personnel than a normal lowland division."[40]

But the major problem for operating in the high mountains was that of transportation of equipment and of basic and resupply loads of rations and ammunition. The light division tables of equipment provided handcarts to transport equipment, augmented by toboggans for oversnow use. Neither proved of any use. Again, the 10th Division learned that men hauling carts or toboggans expended more energy than if they simply carried the loads on their backs. The division's allowance of mules was insufficient for carrying its organic equipment in one load, thus requiring two or more shuttle trips. Nor were there enough mule packers to efficiently and quickly pack and unpack the mule trains. This meant the foot elements of the division could advance farther and faster than their support. The need for the mule trains to make multiple trips left the division without any transportation for resupply of ammunition and rations. The M29 Weasel cargo carriers assigned to the division had excellent mobility for oversnow transport and in any terrain that was not heavily wooded. The Weasel was able to carry 1,200 pounds, the equivalent of six pack mules, which increased the division's mobility. Cargo carrier sleds that required towing by the cargo carriers proved impractical in the mountains, as they often rolled over, but could be useful in level or gently rolling terrain. Finally, to keep the weight of each man's rucksack to the minimum required, sufficient transport had to be provided to the infantry to carry much of their heavier equipment, such as tents.[41]

The AGF had already decided to reconvert the 71st and the 89th back to standard infantry divisions in April and recommended doing the same to the 10th Light Division in May. After all, General McNair wrote to General Marshall, "the personnel and equipment necessary to correct deficiencies would approximate that necessary for conversion to a standard division." Reports from Italy suggested that standard divisions could be adapted to mountainous terrain and that maintaining a special type division could cause undesirable personnel, equipment, and supply complications. According to an AGF study, Marshall demurred. While he acknowledged that there was "no firm overseas requirement" for a division adapted to mountain operations, Marshall was "favorably impressed 'with the organization and potential capabilities'" of the 10th. Instead of agreeing to convert the division to a standard infantry division, Marshall directed the AGF to make detailed recommendations to reorganize the 10th to better carry out its mission of high-altitude combat.[42]

Meanwhile, the 10th Division continued to train at Camp Hale. The men conducted attacks on fortified positions, with flamethrowers and explosives, along Homestake Creek in April. They attended a mine school in May where anyone who made a mistake that would have killed them was "buried" in a faux graveyard outside the classroom. Officers attended an Air Ground School to learn the techniques of employing close air support. During the first week of June, the division artillery HQ held a forward observer school for infantry officers. Experience showed that the rugged terrain in the mountains limited the ability of artillery forward observers to observe targets. Infantry lieutenants thus learned an abbreviated call for fire procedure to assist them.[43]

Taking advantage of the spring snow, longer days, and warmer temperatures, the division also conducted a basic ski school for the trickle of men still reporting to the division and an advanced course of fifteen lessons of forty total hours in two weeks for the rest, again bivouacking at Cooper Hill. The advanced skiing was the final expression of military skiing at Camp Hale. It focused on cross-country or ski touring techniques, beginning with the basics of waxing and control of skis and uphill techniques, including use of climbers. The course introduced the telemark position—one foot slightly forward, knees slightly bent, even weight on both feet—as downhill trail technique for greater stability, ability to absorb bumps, and usefulness under varying snow conditions. Much of the instruction focused on squad drills. Squads would break trail, serve as a point patrol, secure a high point, and practice flank security along a ridge. The last drill was a military ski competition with the squads competing along a course by delivering messages, observing and sketching targets, making a report, and firing on targets. Tactical problems—platoon attacks, providing all-round security for a bivouac site—took up several afternoons. The last four lessons were two ten-mile, one fifteen-mile, and one twenty-mile cross-country ski tours.[44]

As the snow melted, the division also opened up a rock-climbing school on May 29 under Maj John Woodward, at the Homestake Creek training area used the year prior. This was a streamlined course, teaching two battalions at a time in one week on free-climbing, knots, belaying, rappelling, and night climbing. The intent was to provide confidence to the men that they could operate in rocky terrain. Reports from Italy showed that troops without rock-climbing training were "afraid of vertical terrain." Troops at Camp Hale without rock-climbing experience were also afraid of the terrain, calling the instructors (with tongue firmly in cheek) "sadists" for their constant insistence they were not in danger. But these men quickly learned how many hand- and footholds a seemingly unclimbable rock face actually had. Progress in skiing and rock climbing had a positive effect on morale, something Minnie Dole learned from a letter he received from a trooper in the 87th Regiment in May.[45]

10th Mountain Division

Dole had been paying attention to the efforts at Camp Hale, beyond carrying out recruiting via the National Ski Patrol system. He visited the 10th Division in early March for three days, meeting with General Culin, observing the 87th on Cooper Hill, and touring the training areas in an M29. Dole apparently went back in early April, for he wrote General Marshall on April 11 that "I have just returned from a visit to Camp Hale" and offered to give a brief report to the chief of staff, "knowing your personal interest in the training of mountain troops." Dole met with Marshall, now in the Pentagon, on April 19. After Marshall reviewed a memorandum prepared by Dole that focused primarily on the assignment of physically unqualified men to the 10th and the lack of a senior officer who understood mountain warfare to champion the division to the War Department. In the memo Dole asked Marshall directly what the division was being trained for.[46]

Marshall's response demonstrated that he did value mountain training, particularly for winter operations. Marshall had personally intervened to send the 87th Mountain Infantry Regiment to participate in the Aleutians campaign in 1943. He admitted to Dole that, had the army had a mountain division in Italy in the winter 1943, the entire campaign might have proceeded more favorably, bypassing the German strongpoint at Monte Cassino. But with only one mountain-capable division and limited shipping capability, were the 10th to be committed to one theater, it could not move to another if a requirement arose. The division was in reserve for now. Dole ended the meeting with a request that the men of the 10th be issued a special insignia to signify their expertise, to help with their morale. Perhaps a tab with *MOUNTAIN* worn above the division insignia? Marshall agreed to take it under consideration.[47]

Having directed the AGF to recommend ways to reorganize the 10th to better fight in the mountains, Marshall offered the division to his overseas commanders during a meeting in July 1944. Dwight D. Eisenhower in the European theater was willing to take the division, but only if it was made into a standard infantry division, for he had no requirement for fighting in mountains. It was a different story at Marshall's next stop in Italy. Lt Gen Mark Clark's Fifth US Army had been engaged in mountain warfare along the flanks of the Apennines since October 1943. Clark's primary mountain troops, the mountain-trained US and Canadian First Special Service Force (FSSF), a roughly regimental-sized formation of 2,600 men, and the Moroccan mountain division and group of mountain irregulars in the *Corps Expéditionnaire Français* (French Expeditionary Corps), were all withdrawn from Italy in the summer of 1944 to participate in the invasion of southern France. Clark needed mountain troops, as he faced another season of campaigning across the North Apennines to the Po River Valley, with the Alps looming beyond. Learning of the 10th's availability from Marshall, he readily accepted the division. Clark, who had been in the AGF G-3 in 1941 when the discussion of mountain warfare training and organization had first arisen, recollected in his memoirs that the division "was ideally suited for the high Apennines."[48]

As General Marshall set off for Europe at the end of June 1944, the 10th Light Division headed out of the Rockies for Camp Swift, outside of Austin, Texas. The division was slated to participate in a multidivision exercise in the Louisiana Maneuver Area in September, and the army wanted to give it two months to acclimate to the heat and humidity. While such large-scale division-on-division maneuvers were critical in preparing commanders and their staffs for combat success, again, no one explained this to the men of the 10th. Morale, just starting to creep up, plummeted once again and more volunteers left the division. Paul Petzoldt accepted an assignment to Officers Candidate School to get away. The first detachment of the division left Hale on June 22, and the entire division arrived at Swift by July 1, where their mules attracted the attention of the base newspaper's reporters. The men quickly took to the camp's swimming pools, to deal with the heat. For the next two months they continued to train: foot marches, platoon combat firing, combat intelligence, stream crossings, air-ground coordination, and regimental and division field exercises. By September the army canceled the maneuvers as the demand for troops in Europe had taken most of the divisions in the United States.[49]

After returning from Europe, Marshall received the recommendation to strengthen the 10th into a full mountain division on July 22. The AGF modified the previously approved August 1942 T/O 70 Mountain Division. The War Department accepted the recommendation on September 6 and instructed the division to begin reorganizing as soon as practical. The 10th received these instructions and a tentative mountain T/O on September 16 and, with the cancellation of the Louisiana maneuvers, set to immediately. The new mountain organization corrected the light division's firepower deficiency by increasing the rifle squad to twelve men, moving the 60 mm mortars to the weapons platoon of each mountain rifle company, and adding a weapons company and antitank platoon to each mountain infantry battalion. This increased each battalion's supporting firepower to twelve light machine guns, nine 60 mm mortars, eight heavy machine guns, six 81 mm mortars, and three 37 mm guns. To correct the light division's transport problem, the mountain T/O added mules to the medical, signal, engineer, and infantry units. In the rifle companies, as an example, each mortar squad, machine-gun squad, and rifle platoon had a mule and mule packer to ensure their supply. Each infantry regiment ultimately had 953 horses and mules.[50]

The new mountain organization answered the lack of a divisional recon-naissance element with a 162-man cavalry reconnaissance troop. Mounted on 155 horses, it was among the last mounted units in the US Army. The division artillery remained at three battalions of twelve 75 mm pack howitzers, but now had 404 pack mules and riding horses. The new organization also included a motorized antitank battalion with eighteen 57 mm antitank guns. It also increased engineer, medical, communication, and supply capabilities. The mountain engineer battalion had three pack companies with 177 horses and mules and one motorized engineer company with twenty-two vehicles. The mountain medical battalion added a veterinary company and a clearing company to three collecting companies. A full signal company replaced the light division's platoon, with a construction or wire-laying platoon and opera-tions platoon. The three quartermaster pack companies, now with 298 horses and mules each, joined two truck companies with fifty vehicles each, in a new mountain quartermaster battalion. And the mountain division headquarters had fifty men more than the light division.[51]

The 1944 mountain division was 14,102 officers and men strong, nearly 1,000 men more than a standard infantry division, mainly due to the increased number of muleskinners for the 6,152 horses and mules, and had 425 motor vehicles. The reorganization of the 10th Light Division into the 10th Mountain Division proved to be a staggering task. The division began by reassigning men and mules from the division artillery and quartermaster companies to provide the new organic transportation for the infantry regiments and supporting battalions, as these men had been through mountain training. It then had to absorb an additional 3,500 men, mainly from the AGF for the infantry heavy weapons companies, and over 4,000 more mules and horses.[52]

All these reorganized units and new men had to train together. For the rest of October, the division conducted infantry platoon proficiency tests, battalion combat firing tests, defense training, and reviewed regimental combat team procedures. Starting on October 25, 1944, the division ran an animal transport school on Wednesday, Thursday, and Saturday afternoons. This covered the mule, the saddle, grooming, saddling, and unsaddling on Wednesday. The preparation of cargo by wrapping it in the six-foot-by-six-foot canvas cover, or manta, and securing it with the thirty-foot lash rope using a squaw hitch occupied the Thursday section. Saturday afternoon covered using the lash rope and the basket hitch and single and double diamond hitch to tie the cargo to the packsaddle.[53]

10th Mountain Division, November 6, 1944

Headquarters, 10th Mountain Division
Headquarters Company, 10th Mountain Division
10th Mountain Cavalry Reconnaissance Troop
Headquarters, Special Troops, 10th Mountain Division
126th Mountain Engineer Battalion
Military Police Platoon, 10th Mountain Division
110th Mountain Signal Company
710th Mountain Ordnance Maintenance Company
10th Mountain Medical Battalion
10th Mountain Quartermaster Battalion
85th Mountain Infantry Regiment
86th Mountain Infantry Regiment
87th Mountain Infantry Regiment
Headquarters and Headquarters Battery, 10th Mountain Division Artillery
604th Field Artillery Battalion
605th Field Artillery Battalion
616th Field Artillery Battalion
10th Mountain Infantry Antitank Battalion

Source: HQ 10th Light Division, Camp Swift, TX, General Order No. 37, 6 November 1944, TMD, Box 5.

Finally, on November 6, 1944, the 10th Light Division was redesignated the 10th Mountain Division. The new units were officially activated that day, and the existing units were designated as mountain units. In addition to its headquarters and headquarters company, the division included a headquarters, special troops, to oversee the engineer battalion, military police platoon, ordnance company, and signal company. The division artillery included a headquarters and headquarters battery and three pack field artillery battalions. Three mountain infantry regiments, now with separate service companies and three weapons companies, made up the bulk of the division. An antitank battalion was created from the previous antiaircraft machine-gun battalion and antitank battery. The medical and quartermaster battalion completed the division. Further, the division was specially designated as the "Mountain Division," to be known as "Mountaineers," and the *MOUNTAIN* tab was approved to be worn above the division emblem, though none were issued. Some of the men went ahead and purchased tabs on their own.[54]

The next day, November 7, 1944, the now-mountain division learned of its readiness date, the day it was to begin moving overseas. One regiment was to be ready to go on November 28, and the rest of the division in December. While the when was known, the where remained a secret. On November 11 the ADC,

Col Robinson E. Duff, reported to the War Department in Washington, DC, and learned the only mountain troops in the US Army were heading for the Mediterranean theater of operations. Duff alerted the 86th Mountain Infantry under Col Clarence Tomlinson that they would be the first to move, and then he caught a plane for Italy. The rest of the division completed its training, while learning how to conduct training during a sea voyage. The 10th Mountain Cavalry Reconnaissance Troop also completed its reconnaissance patrol tests, both mounted and dismounted, and platoon combat firing tests.[55]

On Thanksgiving Day, November 23, the division also learned it had a new commander. By October General Jones had clearly lost the support of the men, and his bronchial condition rendered him incapable of overseas service. Brig Gen George P. Hays, a Medal of Honor winner in World War I, replaced him. Hays was commanding the division artillery of the 2nd Infantry Division when General Marshall encountered him during a visit to Europe in October 1944. Remembering his friend from France twenty-six years earlier, Marshall determined Hays needed another assignment. On November 12 Hays received orders to report back to the War Department. Arriving four days later, Hays discovered he was to command the 10th Mountain Division and met with Minnie Dole, who happened to be visiting the Pentagon. Dole impressed upon Hays the challenges the division had faced and the value of its men. "Any prima donnas," Hays asked? "They are all prima donnas," Dole answered. "That is what makes them potentially great." Hays moved quickly to assume command of the division, visiting the men as they trained and addressing an assembly of officers and NCOs.[56]

Hays had only a few days or weeks with the division before its deployment got underway. The 86th left Camp Swift on November 28, spent a week at Camp Patrick Henry, Virginia, getting orientated to shipboard life, and boarded a troopship on December 10, setting sail at 0645. The 85th and 87th arrived at Camp Patrick Henry on December 25 and set sail on January 4, 1945. The rest of the division boarded ship and got underway on January 6. All the ships were bound for Naples, Italy, though only a few senior officers knew that. However, the 10th Mountain left a lot of its equipment dockside. Colonel Duff and the War Department made the decision to leave the division's horses and mules stateside for future shipment. Sending the animals would require several specialized ships.[57]

The greatest concern was that the specialized mountain equipment, developed and tested at great effort, was left behind. The division requested a minimum of personal equipment, based on three years of experience. This included down-filled sleeping bags, ski-mountain boots, mountain trousers, sweater, mountain jacket, gloves with wool inserts, and ski cap. They were only issued the new field uniform with a sweater and a field jacket. Sleeping bags were crucial for survival in cold temperatures. The boots were ideal even if the men never skied, as they were warm and prevented trench foot. The trousers had reinforced knees and seats and were more durable. And the ski cap, the distinctive piece of equipment, was important for morale.[58]

The equipment was available in stateside depots, the Mediterranean theater authorized its issue, but for reasons that the 10th could not determine, the quartermasters refused to release it. In desperation an officer sent a letter to Minnie Dole, who forwarded a typed copy to Marshall, asking him if he could find a way to ensure the issue of the necessary equipment. The reply to Dole came not from Marshall, but from Hays. He informed Dole that he was the division commander, he was responsible for its welfare, and he would "brook no interference whatsoever." Dole by one account took the rebuff "in good grace." He recognized that Hays was the commander and would be the one to take the division into combat.[59]

The beginning of the 10th Mountain Division's overseas movement in December 1944 culminated nearly four years of efforts by the army, the American Alpine Club, and the National Ski Patrol. The requirement for winter and mountain warfare had been recognized, including the need for a mountain camp. The specialized equipment and necessary training had been identified, determined, and procured. Many thousands of volunteers for the mountain troops had been recruited. The necessary mountain training in both winter and summer had been carried out, along with the requisite mountain maneuvers. And, while the organization of mountain units had been sidetracked into a series of experiments, a mountain division, organized and equipped along the lines best determined years before, had finally been designated. All this, at least in the eyes of army leadership, ended the need for cooperation with civilian skiers and mountaineers, as the 10th Mountain Division was bound for combat in the mountains of Italy.

CHAPTER 6

Mountain Operations, 1945

A t 0900 December 23, 1944, the 86th Mountain Infantry disembarked at Naples, Italy. Progressing through three staging areas, the regiment moved into a training area south of Livorno on December 31. There the division took its first casualties when a left-behind German mine exploded killing eight men and wounding four on January 6, 1945. The 86th departed the training area for the front line two days later. The 85th and 87th Mountain Infantry Regiments arrived in Italy on January 13, disembarking at Naples and Livorno, and the rest of the division unloaded at Naples on the 18th. Not long after the start of 1945, therefore, the 10th Mountain Division was ready for mountain operations.[1] The year also saw the issuance of mountain warfare and winter warfare doctrine, something that had been sorely lacking. It saw the conduct of decisive mountain operations by a specially designated, trained, and (somewhat) equipped mountain unit during the final phases of the Italian campaign. Ultimately, 1945 set the course for US mountain warfare efforts for the next two decades.

Mountain Warfare Doctrine

Much of the difficulty of the previous four years in establishing a mountain division could be traced to the lack of a "book" for the army to turn to, to determine how to train, equip, and employ units in winter and mountain warfare. The Mountain and Winter Warfare Board, upon its establishment in November 1941, received the task of formulating, developing, and recommending changes in mountain and winter warfare doctrine. The board was unable to devote much time to the creation of a manual in its first year, but it did gather materials, particularly the translations by Ad Carter. The greatest source of data for a mountain troop manual were two works produced by members of civilian ski and mountaineering organizations in 1942 specifically for the purpose of training mountain troops: the Sierra Club and National Ski

WAR DEPARTMENT FIELD MANUAL
FM 70-10

MOUNTAIN OPERATIONS

WAR DEPARTMENT • DECEMBER 1944

United States Government Printing Office
Washington: 1944

Title page to FM 70-10
Mountain Operations
(1944), from WD, FM
70-10 (1944).

Association's *Manual of Ski Mountaineering* and the American Alpine Club's *Handbook of American Mountaineering.* From these works, Carter's translations, and, later, the winter 1942 experience on Mt Rainier, the Mountain Training Center began work on a *Proposed Manual for Mountain Troops* in the fall of 1942 at Camp Carson and then Camp Hale. A number of individuals worked on the project, including David Brower on avalanches and rock climbing and John Woodward and Montgomery Atwater on military skiing. The MTC compiled chapters, some more detailed than others, on rock climbing, organizational equipment, mountain rations, mountain marches, military skiing, avalanches, first aid, transportation of casualties, mountain weather, and mountain medicine. The MTC sent these chapters on to AGF headquarters, where, following some confusion as to what exactly the MTC was doing, they seemingly disappeared into the AGF's files. By the summer of 1943, work had all but ceased on the mountain troop manual at Camp Hale.[2]

The MTC also recommended changes to the slim 1941 version of FM 31-15 *Operations in Snow and Extreme Cold*. In September 1942 the MTC suggested rewriting the manual "to cover the conditions in the many possible theatres of war." An outline listed the clothing, marches, transportation, and camping techniques in northern woods, northern plains, tundra, mountains below timberline, alpine terrain, and arctic conditions. The MTC further added a few revisions and changes from its experiences. These included not wearing mukluks until the temperature dropped below zero, the value of the whisk broom for removing snow from clothing and equipment, the warning that gasoline stoves should not be left burning inside a tent lest the occupants die from carbon monoxide poisoning, and keeping muzzle covers on rifles until in the presence of the enemy.[3]

In March 1943 the Office of the Quartermaster General issued Training Circular (TC) No. 36 covering the care and use of all the newly developed, procured, and issued mountain and cold weather clothing and equipment. The "mountaineer mafia" in the OQMG placed much of what they knew and had learned over test expeditions of the previous three years into the circular. The MTC, now drawing on the experience of two winters, submitted several suggestions to the quartermaster general in May, such as firmly securing the rifle to the body and pack to prevent it from causing injuries in a fall. The MTC also recommended using "traffic scouts" ahead of ski columns to guide troops around obstacles and breaking up long ski columns into shorter columns moving on parallel routes.[4]

Meanwhile, AAC member Ad Carter, officially assigned to the OQMG, continued his work inside the War Department. Carter translated nearly one hundred articles from foreign military journals, mainly German, Swiss, and French, on everything from aerial tramways to avalanches to machine guns to training. He also translated the Austrian 1917 instructions for mountain service and 1918 mountain warfare manual, a 1923 French guide for mountain officers, the 1935 German mountain troop training regulations, and the 1942 German handbook on winter warfare. The Military Intelligence Division published his work on German mountain and winter warfare and ski training and combat in 1944. Carter provided this translated foreign material to the War Department to assist in its drafting of US manuals on mountain warfare and operations in snow and extreme cold.[5] The army thus took Carter's work, MTC's chapters and recommendations, and the final report of the 10th Light Division to write mountain and winter warfare doctrine in 1944.

Initially the army issued a new version of FM 100-5 *Operations*, approved on June 15, 1944, with updates, additions, and changes to its sections on mountain operations and combat in cold and extreme cold. In some cases, these were simply updates to terminology, changing "bombardment" to "combat aviation" and "mechanized" to "armored." There were also additions. Now, mountainous terrain "not classified as Alpine" offered no insurmountable obstacle to operations, which required "the ability to carry heavy loads in long marches over rough trails." Light portable bridging equipment was "necessary in mountain operations," and the paragraphs on marching emphasized pacing and spacing between elements. In snow-covered conditions, the manual added, ridgelines might offer better avenues of approach as "the wind often sweeps the crest clear and allows more rapid movement"—exactly what the 10th Recon had learned in its ski patrols.[6]

The major revisions came in the paragraphs covering offensive combat in the mountain operations section. The 1941 version envisioned a mountain attack with "several tactical groups operating in adjacent terrain compartments" and "aimed at defiles in their zones of advance." In 1944 a mountain attack now consisted of a single "axis of advance" aimed at "key terrain features." To facilitate this type of attack the 1944 FM 100-5 eliminated the 1941 boundaries between tactical groups "along crests" and stated that "boundaries between tactical units are usually not designated" and "units are given axes of advance to their objectives, particularly when they operate at extended distances from each other."[7] These changes seem to echo the experiences of the two attacks on Vail Pass during the D-Series. The first attempted to move two regiments up two terrain compartments. The second attack saw one regiment seize a pass along an axis of advance, with the second regiment passing through.

Besides updating the operations manual, the War Department worked on three other manuals throughout most of 1944, including a new one on mountain operations, an update to the winter manual, and a formalization of the TC into a technical manual on clothing and equipment. The 10th Division at Camp Swift received at least the first two, and quite possibly the third, to review. The headquarters hastily reassembled members of the MTG and the training detachments to carry out the work, including Lt David Brower, now the intelligence officer (S-2) of the 3rd Battalion, 86th Regiment, and probably Maj John Woodward, now the executive officer of the 1st Battalion, 87th Regiment. Brower reviewed the mountain operations manual, working late into the night for ten days, reorganizing, reillustrating, and rewriting the chapter on military rock climbing.[8] Published in the fall of 1944 with the input from the members of the now–10th Mountain Division, these manuals—Technical Manual 10-275 *Principles of Cold Weather Clothing and Equipment* (October 26, 1944), FM 70-15 *Operations in Snow and Extreme Cold* (November 4, 1944), and FM 70-10 *Mountain Operations* (December 30, 1944)—provided the US Army with its first mountain warfare doctrine.

This doctrine laid out how forces would survive and be mobile in the mountains, in both summer and winter, to be able to maneuver on the enemy. Survival in the mountains required conditioning soldiers with daily marches and climbs. Two weeks of acclimatization was necessary if training at altitudes higher than eight thousand feet. Troops had to be clothed, supplied, and equipped for the uneven and ever-changing mountain weather. A wide variety of clothing—body clothing, footwear, gloves and mittens, headgear— and equipment—for packing, sleeping, cooking—now existed in the supply system to meet these needs. Snow was a specific weather threat to survival in the mountains, particularly when hanging overhead in cornices, running in avalanches, or compacted into glaciers, necessitating both training and techniques to minimize risk or conduct a rescue. In addition to clothing, troops operating in snow and extreme cold had to be adequately fed, preferably with hot food and hot drinks as often as possible. Shelter and heat were acute needs in extreme cold, whether tents or improvised timber and snow shelters, and clothing had to be dried in sleeping bags. Crucial to survival in the mountains was the ability to send supplies, particularly rations, up into the mountains and evacuate the injured and wounded back down from the heights.[9]

Mobility in the mountains required proper technique: using a steady rhythmic pace, keeping the feet flat, with knees slightly bent, and a five-foot distance between men over uneven or difficult footing. The time required to cover a distance had to include an hour for each 1,000 feet ascended or 1,500 feet descended, and a battalion in single file could cover almost four miles of trail. Snow would further slow the pace, requiring trail breaking, road marking, and road clearance. In the snow it was understood that most of the men would use snowshoes, for which instructions in the use, care, and maintenance were now laid out. Scouts and reconnaissance units, and a sizable portion of the infantry, if necessary, should use skis in the snow. Skis, bindings, poles, waxes, climbers, and repair kits, and their use, care, and maintenance, were now standardized, and FM 70-15 included a ninety-four-page appendix on ski instruction, towing skiers, and the use of skis in combat, drawing on three winters of military skiing experience on Mt Rainier and at Camp Hale.[10]

The three summers of climbing experience at Homestake Creek and Seneca Rocks provided the basis for a seventy-eight-page chapter in FM 70-10 on military rock climbing. The chapter covered climbing techniques, movement of men and equipment across rock faces, stream crossings, and the tactical employment of climbers, along with directions for establishing a climbing school, training, and tactical exercises. As with skis, the specialized equipment necessary for military rock climbing—ice axe, crampons, rope, snap links, pitons— was now standardized. The manuals also emphasized transport—motor, animal, oversnow—to ensure mobility. Motor transportation was to be used to the fullest extent possible to bring supplies as far forward as possible to reduce the number of personnel required for packing. Given that mountain roads and bridges were often unimproved and narrow, only jeeps and trucks towing artillery pieces were to be taken into combat, with the rest of the vehicles coming forward later. Transport beyond where trucks could go in the mountains relied on pack mules. An infantry battalion in sustained action needed 100 to 150 mules to ensure mobility with weapons, ammunition, and rations, with another 24 mules for the evacuation of the wounded. However, snow depth of more than one foot would restrict pack animal mobility. In winter, therefore, use of oversnow vehicles such as the M29 enabled transport independent of roads and across country, augmented with cargo sleds.[11]

Mountainous terrain caused offensive maneuvers to be piecemeal and divided into isolated efforts characterized by surprise attacks and flanking attempts combined with broad frontal actions. Objectives were the seizure of dominant terrain, and orders emphasized the objectives and routes of advance. Advances took place along ridges and high terrain features, avoiding the more easily defended valleys, but seizing the high ground would often require a frontal attack. Frontal attacks needed to be launched quietly at night, without initial supporting fires. Night attacks in the mountains were generally able to maintain their direction, usually uphill, but difficult to maintain control, requiring slow and methodical movement. A reinforced infantry battalion would be the largest force normally employed in an attack. Given that a battalion advancing along a ridgeline could be a single four-mile-long column, it would take upward of four or five hours to reinforce the advance guard once it made contact. A company serving as advance guard therefore had to be reinforced with heavy weapons and extra ammunition and possibly pack howitzers. As attacking troops in the mountains rapidly became fatigued, pursuit operations required fresh troops. Lacking those, heavily reinforced patrols could follow the enemy closely, preventing a counterattack. In deep snow, the attacker's oversnow mobility had to be fully exploited to allow for cross-country envelopments. Given that winter demanded increased supplies and shelter, enemy lines of communication were the primary objective in winter maneuvers.[12]

Defensive mountain combat took advantage of good observation and firing positions, the difficulties slopes and other terrain imposed on the attacker, impassable zones, and the difficulties of getting tanks or other heavy weapons into action. In winter the defender suffered less from the cold and snow. But the compartmentation created by terrain made it difficult to shift supporting weapons or execute counterattack plans with reserves. The attacker could make surprise attacks at several points, and it took longer to dig in to a position, that duration being increased in the winter by the need to ensure not only cover and concealment but also warmth. Defensive positions had to block all routes of potential enemy penetration, protect friendly lines of communications, protect the flanks, cover all areas to the front, and be organized for all-around defense with positions on successive ridges. In winter these positions were guarded by ski patrols along outer and inner trails. The positions formed a system of mutually supporting tactical groups covering all key terrain. If forward slopes were under enemy observation, a combat outpost on the crest could cover a main line of resistance on the reverse slope. Counterattacks executed downhill had an advantage but could not be pressed too far. Withdrawal in the mountains was even more difficult but could be executed by delaying detachments fighting from key terrain.[13] So, equipped with the experience and knowledge of this doctrine, if not with the actual printed material, the 10th Mountain Division entered into mountain operations in Italy in January 1945.

Mountain Patrols, January–February 1945

On January 8 the 86th Mountain Infantry Regiment entered the Apennine line, joined on its left flank by the 85th Mountain Infantry two weeks later. The 87th Mountain Infantry Regiment relieved the 86th on February 2, with the 85th moving over into what was now the 10th Mountain Division's sector. This sector was a familiar landscape of "steep mountain peaks and snow-filled valleys" quite similar in orientation and relief to Camp Hale, just flipped south to north. The division was in a high mountain basin drained by the Dardagna River flowing north in a deep gorge and dominated by three long ridges with multiple high points. The Monte Grande Ridge lay to the south, at the division's back, and to the west the Spigolino-Campiano Ridge towered. Better known as Riva Ridge, it descended generally south to north for five and a half miles from the high point of Monte Spigolino at 6,400 feet to Monte Campiano at 4,200 feet. Rising 2,000 vertical feet from the basin with an average gradient of 38°, Riva Ridge dominated the approaches to the Belvedere-Torraccia Ridge to the division's north. This massif ran from Monte Belvedere (3,740 feet) west to Monte della Torraccia (3,550 feet) and overlooked Highway 64, one of two major land routes through the North Apennines to Bologna and the Po River Valley.[14]

This landscape meant there would be no impact from altitude. Except for the highest peaks, the Apennines were too low for altitude sickness. The six months in Texas and weeks at sea, however, had sapped much of the mountain stamina from the men, something they would regain as the weeks in the line went on. There was deep snow in spots, up to several feet, and it snowed several more feet in January, but the maritime snowpack and the fact that the division was operating on mainly southern exposures limited risk from avalanches. The snow regularly turned to rain by February, particularly down in the valleys, but the units were able to shelter from the cold and wet in the houses and buildings in the villages and in rural barns and mountain huts. Personal survival in the cold and wet would thus be the main challenge the division faced with their personal kit as the main tool. For this the division had to make do with the M-1943 combat uniform.[15]

This uniform came about because, by late 1942, the quartermaster general had requirements to source specialized clothing and equipment for parachutists, armored forces, units in cold weather, and mountain troops. These requirements proved to be too many to continue production as they competed for limited materials. Thus in 1943 the quartermasters determined to take the best of each specialized uniform, particularly the parachutists' pockets and mountain troops' layers, and produce an all-purpose uniform. Before heading for Italy, the 10th Mountain was issued, and lectured on the use of, windproof and water-repellent field jackets and field trousers made of tightly woven cotton sateen. These were to be layered over the standard wool shirt and trousers, along with the high neck sweater and pile jacket for more insulation. The men received field caps, based on the ski cap, and field boots with integrated leggings. They also drew overcoats and field packs, essentially a waterproofed canvas sack with straps.[16]

With this kit, and four blankets in place of the beloved mountain sleeping bag, the 10th Mountain Division went into the line. As the S-2 (intelligence officer) of the 1st Battalion, 86th Mountain Infantry, put it, it took "superhuman efforts of the regimental and divisional supply officers" to remedy the equipment situation. Drawing on equipment the Fifth Army quartermaster had been stockpiling since the end of 1943, many, though not all, of the infantry troops received field parkas with pile liners and white camouflage, pile caps, field jacket hoods, and shoepacs, waterproof boots with rubber feet and leather uppers. Only at the end of March were some sleeping bags and mountain stoves issued. More equipment slowly trickled in. Each battalion was issued twenty-four and then forty pairs of snowshoes, fifteen and then finally thirty pairs of skis, thirty pairs of mountain boots, and one hundred rucksacks. But no ropes, ice axes, pitons, and crampons were initially available. This lack of equipment hindered mobility. The deep snow in January required snowshoes or skis for patrols to move more than a few hundred feet in a night. February rains turned the snow to slush in valleys but froze the snow on the ridges. Such conditions required creepers (traction devices on the feet) or, even better, ice axes and crampons. Some patrols made creepers for their shoepacs out of knotted ropes, while others chopped steps into the ice with their bayonets, made improvised ropes from their field jackets' drawstrings, and slid down slopes when they slipped, as they had no ice axes for self-arrests.[17]

The training and experience gave the men of the 10th Mountain the ability to survive and be mobile enough to conduct patrols. Mountain patrolling was a familiar experience for the division; a Mountain Training Center outline on the subject from 1943 emphasized the difficulties of patrolling in mountainous terrain. It identified three types of patrols: reconnaissance, combat, and security. Reconnaissance patrols focused on the collection of information but faced difficulties in getting that information back due to the time necessary to cross terrain. The primary role of reconnaissance patrols in the mountains was to determine routes of approach to the enemy and supply lines to support any advance. Combat patrols harassed the enemy, attacking isolated enemy positions, while security patrols were to prevent the enemy from taking friendly forces by surprise. A knowledge of the mountains could aid in patrolling by making use of elevation differences to aid in observation, using terrain for infiltration and movement, and gaining surprise by moving over terrain thought to be inaccessible.[18]

From January 8 to February 17, 1945, the 10th Mountain Division executed nearly three hundred patrols. These lasted an average of nine hours, mostly through the night, and consisted of anywhere from a few men to fifty men often guided by Italian partisans, depending on the mission. The men conducted security patrols, lying in the snow and wet for hours just outside their own lines, listening, straining to hear an enemy patrol. They launched combat patrols, particularly raids on German outposts, often on snowshoes or skis, camouflaged in white. And they carried out reconnaissance patrols. A patrol of five men on skis from the 86th Mountain Infantry Regiment's intelligence and reconnaissance platoon climbed up and around Mt Spigolino and traversed Riva Ridge in just twenty-two hours. The 86th's 1st Battalion was especially interested in finding a way up Riva Ridge. From mid-January it dispatched two to three reconnaissance patrols a day to find routes onto the ridge, locating five up gorges and ravines, across rocky ledges, and over cliffs by the end of the month.[19]

The 10th Mountain Division's patrol actions ultimately showed the division that it could operate in the mountains. The men had some specialized mountain equipment and, more important, the skills and experience to use it or improvise replacements as necessary. This allowed them to survive the climate and move across the terrain. The division did not view the mountains as an obstacle to maneuver, but as a way to maneuver. Had they possessed more of the specialized equipment, they certainly could have done more. Sleeping bags, tents, and stoves would have increased patrol endurance, and ice axes, crampons, and

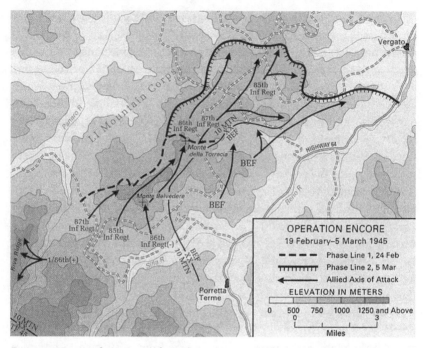

Operation Encore, from Center for Military History Publication 72-34 *North Apennines 1944–1945.*

ropes would have increased their mobility. Ultimately the six weeks of patrolling gave the division valuable experience in a combat zone. The 10th Mountain was still a "green" outfit and would soon have to face its true baptism of fire.[20]

Operation Encore, February 18–March 6, 1945

The US Fifth Army planned Operation Encore as an attack by the 10th Mountain Division with a limited objective to be conducted in two stages. The objective was to clear the Belvedere–della Torraccia–della Spe mountain ridge to set conditions for a general offensive in the spring. For this operation IV Corps reinforced the 10th Mountain Division with a self-propelled 105 mm howitzer battalion, a heavy mortar battalion, two tank destroyer battalions, and a tank battalion to provide extra firepower, where the road network allowed. The Brazilian Expeditionary Force, a division-sized unit, also would attack on the 10th's right flank. Facing the 10th was the German 232nd Infantry Division, with six understrength battalions strung across a ten-mile front and a fusilier battalion and mountain battalion in reserve.[21]

The division issued its orders on February 15, 1945. The plan was for the 85th Mountain Infantry to serve as the divisional and corps spearhead. The regiment's 3rd Battalion would seize Mt Belvedere, supported by a 1st Battalion attack on its left. The 2nd Battalion, 85th Mountain Infantry, was to follow in trace of the 1st and maneuver to attack Mt della Torraccia once Belvedere fell. The 3rd Battalion, 86th Mountain Infantry, advanced on the 85th's right flank while the 87th carried out a series of supporting actions to the left of the 85th. Once Belvedere and della Torraccia fell, the division would conduct Encore's second stage, the attack on Monte della Spe. However, to conduct the first stage of the attack, seizing Belvedere, the division would first have to seize Riva Ridge.[22]

This task fell to the 1st Battalion, 86th Mountain Infantry, which was to occupy, organize, and defend the Riva Ridge's key terrain features from the high ground south of Monte Mancinello to Mt Campiano. From there it would protect the division's left flank and support the 87th Mountain Infantry's advance by fire from four .50-caliber heavy machine guns and a 75 mm pack howitzer hauled to the ridge. Early planning considered climbing Mt Spigolino and attacking down the ridge to the northeast, but there was no route that could supply an entire battalion. The battalion staff considered climbing up the middle of the ridge and fanning out, but the battalion would be vulnerable on just one trail. The staff settled on utilizing multiple routes up the ridge and aiming to seize the summits simultaneously, thereby dispersing the battalion but easing supply. This plan called for five forces on five trails to take five objectives, all summits or high ground. Rifle companies reinforced with machine guns and mortars, including Company F from the 2nd Battalion, made up three of the forces, while a single platoon was the fourth force and a company minus one platoon the fifth. Each force would be preceded by a trail party of three to four men to set ropes at required places. Only trail number one leading to Campiano on the right flank and trail number three to Monte Serrasiccia in the center entailed climbing fixed ropes, held to pitons with carabiners. Trail three would ultimately require six ropes and a hastily built footbridge across the Dardagna to move Company C (reinforced) up onto the ridge.[23]

By the start of February, the 1st Battalion, 86th Mountain Infantry, was off the line and concentrated in the village of Lucca to plan and prepare for the attack. Cold and snow was an initial concern, so early plans had the battalion advancing on skis and snowshoes. On February 12 a reconnaissance by the battalion intelligence section and the lead climbers of each company discovered the snow had melted and hardened and the weather had turned warmer. Skis and heavy packs with extra clothing would not be required. Ropes, pitons, carabiners, and hammers finally found their way forward from the Fifth Army's warehouses, and it was determined that the hammers could be muffled with cloth. Preparation focused on mountain walking, rock climbing with and without ropes, and setting haul lines, utilizing a local quarry. This was a refresher for the roughly 70 percent of the battalion that had gone through the mountaineering course at Camp Hale, but crucial for the 30 percent that had joined in the previous six months. The battalion simply paired up a new men with experienced ones to literally show them the ropes. Hauling the extra weapons to the ridge, along with a supply of ammunition, food, and water and evacuating the wounded would be handled by over one hundred extra men assigned as porters and an Italian pack company with thirty small mules. The mules could only use trail number two up to Monte Cappelbuso. Once the ridge had been seized, Company D, 126th Mountain Engineers, was to build an aerial tramway up to a buttress near Cappelbuso as well.[24]

The attack commenced at 1930 on the night of February 18. All five forces climbed all five trails and seized all five objectives by 0300, February 19. A heavy fog that morning aided the battalion's occupation of defensive positions, and once the fog lifted at 1100 it registered mortar and artillery fire. The climb up onto the ridge took the German company occupying it completely by surprise, and not until 1300 did they launch their first counterattack, which was turned back by Company C. The Germans launched another five counterattacks over the next five days, the last on the morning of February 23. Porters man-packed all four .50-caliber heavy machine guns to the ridge while the battalion's antitank platoon wrestled the pack howitzer up on mules, unfortunately killing one. These weapons played a key role in breaking up the German counterattacks. Also key in holding the ridge was the resupply effort. Porters made up to three roundtrips a day, carrying ammunition up and the dead down. Evacuation of the wounded from Campiano took ten men and thirteen hours, and eight hours from Cappelbuso, though this time was halved once the engineers completed their tramway on February 20. During the five days' fight, men, mules, and trams hauled 10½ tons of ammunition up to the ridge and evacuated thirty-eight wounded and seventeen dead down. After three days food and water were also brought up to the battalion.[25]

With seizure of the ridge on the far-left flank, the main attack of Operation Encore stepped off one hour before midnight on February 19. Following mountain warfare doctrine, it was a frontal attack at night without artillery preparation to gain surprise. The 87th Mountain Infantry attacked on the left with two battalions, which worked their way forward for an hour through minefields and barbed wire, before contacting the Germans. Machine-gun, mortar, and artillery fire slowed the regiment's progress, and the attack devolved into a series of small-unit actions against bunkers and gun emplacements. Familiar with the terrain from patrols and with the support of partisans, the 87th seized the Valpiana Ridge by daybreak on February 20, effectively outflanking Mt

Belvedere on the west, and dug in to repel the German counterattacks. On the 10th Mountain's extreme right flank, the 3rd Battalion, 86th Mountain Infantry, seized the village of San Filomena by 0345, February 20.[26]

The seizure of Mt Belvedere's western and eastern slopes by the 87th and 86th supported the division's main effort, which was the 85th Mountain Infantry's attack in the center against the summit. The 85th attacked with the 3rd Battalion on the left aiming for Belvedere and the 1st Battalion on the right advancing on Monte Gorgolesco, a summit to the northeast. By 0100 on February 19, the 3rd Battalion was within three hundred yards of the top of Belvedere when it came under German fire. The battalion sent Company L to the left (west) and Company K to the right (east) to encircle the summit. Company L fought its way to the summit of Belvedere by 0410, and Company K arrived ten minutes later. The battalion consolidated on the top by 0615 while under heavy artillery fire.[27]

Meanwhile the 1st Battalion was fighting its way over the ridge above San Filomena. By 0300, February 19, the battalion was within three hundred yards of Mt Gorgolesco when German machine-gun fire pinned down Company C. Company B simply swung to its left and took out the German positions, resuming the advance. Two hours later Company B was itself pinned by German fire, but Company C had maneuvered into position to assault the Gorgolesco summit, which the battalion did just after first light at 0610. Daylight allowed the full weight of Allied artillery fire and close air support to come into play, helping to repel German counterattacks and support the continued attack of the 1st Battalion, 85th Mountain Infantry, northeast along the ridge to Mt della Torraccia. The battalion jumped off at 0730 on February 20 with two companies advancing over intermediary ridges and overran a high point on the ridge, Hill 1088, within an hour and a half. Heavy fire from the next high point, Hill 1045, and counterattacks halted the advance for the rest of the day. Not until that evening did Company A secure the lower reaches of Hill 1045.[28]

By then the 2nd Battalion, 85th Mountain Infantry, alerted that afternoon to begin its advance, was passing through the 1st Battalion to seize the Cappella di Ronchidos high point before taking up defensive positions. Throughout the night of February 20 and into the early hours of February 21, the 10th Mountain Division fought off German counterattacks across its entire ridgeline frontage. The 85th's 2nd Battalion attacked at first light to seize Mt della Torraccia, but a German counterattack held up its advance and artillery fire inflicted a large number of casualties. For the rest of the morning, the battalion fought its way forward in unfamiliar terrain. By midday it had to request a resupply of ammunition, food, and water and more supporting fires. The regiment dispatched a pack train of Italian mules and moved up several companies to secure the flanks. By late afternoon the 2nd Battalion resumed the advance, but after twelve more hours of fighting it was still four hundred yards from the della Torraccia summit.[29]

A desultory back-and-forth fight along the southern slopes of della Torraccia occupied most of February 23, and by the end of the day the 2nd Battalion, 85th Mountain Infantry, was down to just four hundred men from over eight hundred. Division ordered it to hold and the 3rd Battalion, 86th Mountain Infantry, to move up from its flanking position, pass through, and take the summit. The 3rd Battalion launched its assault up the slope utilizing artillery and aerial support at 0700. While one company reached the objective at 0855, it took six more hours of fighting to secure the entirety of Mt della Torraccia and most of the night to hold it against German counterattacks. By daylight on the 25th, the first phase of Operation Encore was complete.[30]

For the next few days, the 10th Mountain patrolled, rotated battalions back to rest and recover, and integrated the fourteen officers and 264 enlisted men assigned as replacements for casualties suffered in the attack on Belvedere. The division also shifted right, turning over the Belvedere positions to the Brazilian Expeditionary Force, and massed on della Torraccia in preparation for the second phase of Operation Encore. This phase called for the 10th Mountain to advance northeasterly and seize a line of four peaks—Grande d'Aino, della Spe, della Castellano, and Valbura—four miles away to secure a line of departure for the coming spring offensive. The division expected the four German battalions to conduct "a protracted stand on commanding ground" with four more battalions in reserve to counterattack in increasing strength. This attack would begin with an artillery preparation, after which each regiment would have a field artillery battalion in support, along with an engineer company to clear mines and remove road obstacles, allowing tanks and tank destroyers to move forward in support along with pack trains for resupply. Initially intended to begin on March 1, low clouds, fog, and rain-snow mix delayed the start for two days.[31]

On March 3, after a thirty-minute barrage, the division attacked along the spine of the Apennine divide. The 86th Mountain Infantry was on the left, with the 87th on the right, advancing in columns of battalions and companies to account for the restricted terrain. With support from divisional and corps artillery, "Rover Joe" close air support, and armored vehicles pushing up where the roads allowed, the regiments fought for every crest and village and fought off repeated German counterattacks. In two days the 86th and 87th seized all the intermediate heights, and the 87th took Monte Grande d'Aino on March 4. The next morning General Hays committed the 85th Mountain Infantry, which proceeded to seize della Spe and della Castellano by that afternoon in the face of increasing German fire. The German command directed its major

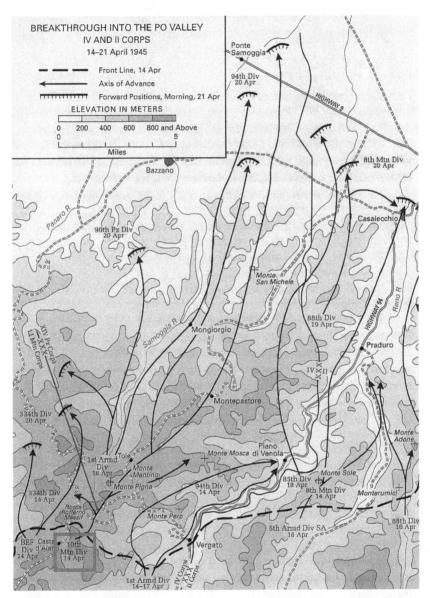

BREAKTHROUGH INTO THE PO VALLEY
IV AND II CORPS
14–21 April 1945

— — — Front Line, 14 Apr
◄──── Axis of Advance
ⅉⅉⅉⅉⅉⅉ Forward Positions, Morning, 21 Apr

ELEVATION IN METERS

0   200   400   600   800 and Above
0   5
      Miles

Ponte Samoggia
94th Div 20 Apr
HIGHWAY 9
8th Mtn Div 20 Apr
Bazzano
Panaro R.
90th Pz Div 20 Apr
Casalecchio
Monte San Michele
Samoggia R.
Mongiorgio
88th Div 19 Apr
HIGHWAY 64
Reno R.
Praduro
XIV Pz Corps
LI Mtn Corps
IV   II
Montepastore
334th Div 20 Apr
Monte Adone
Piano di Venola
Monte Mosca
1st Armd Div 18 Apr
Tole
Monte Mantino
Monte Pigna
94th Div 14 Apr
85th Div 18 Apr
Monte Sole
8th Mtn Div 14 Apr
Monterumici
334th Div 14 Apr
Rocca Rofferno Massif
Monte Pero
6th Armd Div SA 16 Apr
88th Div 16 Apr
BEF Caste Div d'Aiar 14 Apr
10th Mtn Div 14 Apr
Vergato
1st Armd Div 14–17 Apr
IV Corps
II Corps

Detail, Operation Craftsman, from Center for Military History Publication 72-33 *Po Valley 1945.*

reserve, the 29th Panzer Grenadier Division, into the fight, to conduct four counterattacks against the 1st Battalion, 87th Mountain Infantry, on Mt della Spe during the night of March 5. The US Fifth Army commander, Lt Gen Lucian K. Truscott, did not wish to attract any more of the German reserves to the area before the spring offensive, so he called a halt to the attack the next day, ending Operation Encore. It had been, the division narrative recorded, "a most successful limited objective attack."[32]

Encore had also been a successful mountain operation. The division survived the wet and cold conditions of the Apennines. The troops of 1st Battalion, 86th Mountain Infantry, exposed for several days and nights on Riva Ridge, suffered no exposure, frostbite, or trench foot casualties. The division proved its mobility in the mountains. While only two rifle companies, out of twenty-seven, climbed during Encore, the men "had no fear of rugged, precipitous and difficult terrain." The division kept itself in supply, and evacuated casualties, by using jeeps and Weasels where roads were available, a tramway, and ultimately the backs of mules and men. This meant the division was able to maneuver utilizing surprise, secrecy, coordination with close air support and, perhaps most important, advancing along ridges and ridgelines. Units stayed out of draws and ravines where they would have suffered enfilading fire. The maneuver was essentially a series of frontal attacks followed by the defense of a ridge against German counterattacks. Most of the division's losses during Encore came during the first phase, when it took 901 casualties, of which 203 were killed in action. The second phase, with its lavish fire support, cost only 549 casualties with 107 KIA. Ultimately Encore caused the men of the division, who had identified for all those years of training as *ski* troops, to see themselves as *mountain infantry* for whom mountains were not an obstacle, but an avenue of approach.[33]

Operation Craftsman, April 14–20, 1945

The plan for the Allied spring offensive in Italy in 1945 was, as Fifth Army commander General Truscott later recalled, to "debouch into the Po River Valley, and drive north across the Po River to the Brenner Pass." In February, before launching Operation Encore, Truscott concluded that the mountains in the 10th Mountain Division's sector offered the best chance for breaking through the German defenses in the Apennines and into the Po Valley. The 10th Mountain Division would thus attack on the left of IV Corps along the mountain crest between the Reno River in the east and the Samoggia River to the west. By mid-March this plan, designated Operation Craftsman, scheduled its D-Day for April 12, 1945.[34]

The 10th Mountain prepared for this next offensive with the experience of the previous engagement. The staff now clearly understood that they would take casualties and receive replacements for those lost. It would be best if these replacements had at least a modicum of mountain training. Therefore, in late March, the 2662 Mountain Warfare Detachment was reassigned from the Mountain School at Terminillo near Rome to the 10th Mountain Division to train replacements. By May 1945 it had taught over 2,000 replacements, of the more than 6,000 the division would receive, the fundamentals of mountain mobility and mule packing. The latter was important as General Hays, on March 3, requested the division be supported by 2,000 mules and 400 horses, enough to ensure the mobility of one complete mountain infantry regiment. Hays got only half the mules he requested. By the end of March, the 10th Mountain had two Italian pack mule companies with 510 mules. But 558 American mules arrived in Italy by mid-April to outfit two US pack companies in the 10th Mountain Quartermaster Battalion.[35]

By the Fifth Army commander's own admission, the 10th Mountain was to "carry the brunt of the attack to the Po valley—and beyond." The division's plan was simple and straightforward, following the experience of the second phase of Encore. It would attack northeast along a divide from Mt della Spe with the 85th on the left, the 87th on the right, and the 86th moving up in support on the right flank. The division's initial objective was the seizure of the seven-mile Rofferno massif, which ran northeast from Rocca Rofferno to Monte Pigna, then on to Monte Mantino and Monte Mosca. Capture of this terrain would give control of a lateral east–west road over which the 1st Armored Division would move to the 10th Mountain's left flank. Taking the Rofferno massif would also outflank the German defenses between the Samoggia and Reno Rivers. The Germans saw the terrain as their "Achilles heel."[36]

Bad weather postponed D-Day for the 10th Mountain Division's part in Craftsman for forty-eight hours. Finally, on April 14, the operation began at 0945. It was preceded by thirty minutes of attacks from several hundred heavy bombers and over four hundred fighter-bombers and thirty-five minutes of fire from over two thousand artillery pieces. The division faced the challenge of moving off the lower slopes of Mt della Spe and then up onto the Rofferno massif, past a series of five hills running from west to east: Hills 883, 913, 909, 860, and 903. The hills had to be taken first, so the 85th Mountain Infantry advanced on the division's left, in the west, with the 3rd Battalion on the far left and the 2nd Battalion on the right. The 3rd Battalion moved down into a basin at the base of the hills and was quickly pinned down there by German positions along the flanks of the hills above. Meanwhile, the 87th Mountain Infantry advanced on the right flank of the 85th, but it soon found itself also pinned in a ruined village by German artillery and machine-gun fire from Hill 860. But the 2nd Battalion, 85th Mountain Infantry, was able to rapidly cross the valley floor, with most German fire being trained on the 3rd Battalion, and seize Hill 860. From there the 2nd Battalion was able to fire down into the German positions above the 3rd Battalion, allowing the seizure of Hills 913 and 909. With machine-gun fire slacking from Hill 860, the 87th Mountain Infantry resumed its advance, taking Hill 903. This, in turn, allowed the 86th's 2nd Battalion, on the division's eastern or right flank, to advance up and onto the Rocca Rofferno. At nightfall, with all objectives seized, General Hays ordered the division to "button up" in semicircular defense to await German counterattacks and daylight before continuing the advance.[37]

The Germans only launched a minor counterattack during the night, and the division's attack resumed at 0700 on April 15, after a twenty-minute artillery barrage. The 85th Mountain Infantry's hard luck continued as it advanced on the left flank. Heavy and accurate German small arms and artillery fire pinned down the regiment, catching it in a web of minefields. By midday General Hays ordered the 85th to hold and consolidate, while moving up the 10th Mountain Anti-Tank Battalion, fighting as infantry, to secure the division's left flank. The 87th and 86th regiments had a different experience. Attacking down a ridge and able to use the multiple crests to conceal and cover their maneuver, they were continually able to pin German positions from the front and attack them from the flank. In the division's center, the 87th Mountain Infantry took Mt Pigna within an hour of jumping off, the main German force having withdrawn during the night, and proceeded to take Mt Croce. On the right the 86th paced the 87th and took Mt Mantino by the evening. Again, the division held up, linked up, and prepared for a German counterattack that never came. From the afternoon on, the German commander tried to withdraw his troops, but they were continually caught and cut up by the 10th Mountain Division.[38]

April 16 began with another twenty-minute barrage followed by the advance of the 87th Mountain Infantry at 0620. Its 2nd Battalion seized Mt Croce by 1305, with the 3rd Battalion passing through and attacking down the ridgeline, into a stiffening German resistance. Though the 3rd Battalion, 87th Mountain Infantry, reached Mt Mosca by 1415, it took another two hours to clear the hill of German troops, who launched several counterattacks to buy time for the rest of their comrades to escape. The 86th Mountain Infantry, on the 87th's right, took Mt Mantino to the south of Mt Croce by the early afternoon. The division now held the Rofferno massif; as the division's combat narrative noted, the "attack phase had ended . . . and the exploiting had to begin." The 3rd Battalion, 86th Mountain Infantry, did so, stepping off at 1115, advancing northeast over the Croce-Mosca Ridge, supported by direct fire from tanks and tank destroyers. The 85th Mountain Infantry began "a slide-slipping maneuver" behind the division's advance, incorporating replacements to make good its losses over the previous two days. On April 16 the 10th Mountain Division forced a massive German withdrawal to the Po Valley; "the exploitation stage had ended, and the pursuit phase was now in order."[39]

The pursuit began on April 17 down the heights between the Samoggia and Lavino Rivers. There were still many hills to negotiate, but as the division attacked northeastward the terrain became increasingly less rugged, with low rolling hills and good roads. This allowed the 86th and 87th Mountain Infantry Regiments to drive forward, supported closely by tanks and tank destroyers. By the end of the day, the attacking regiments had almost outrun their supporting artillery, but the guns were able to reposition that night. The 86th Mountain Infantry led out the attack on the division's right flank on April 18, followed on the left by the 87th. The Fifth Army sent the 85th Infantry Division to advance on the 10th Mountain's right flank. Additionally, the 1st Armored Division crossed through the 10th's rear areas and was advancing on the division's left flank, down the Samoggia Valley, by the afternoon of the 18th. On April 19 the 85th Mountain Infantry passed through the 86th's position and resumed the division's advance. The next day all three regiments—the 87th on the left, the 86th in the middle, and the 85th on the right—descended out of the Apennines and into the Po Valley, marked by crossing Highway 9. Company A, 86th Mountain Infantry, was the first to cross the highway at 1400. General Hays would later award the company's lead scout, Pfc B. L. Lessmeister, a quart of Scotch from General Truscott. The 10th Mountain Division's mountain operations were over, at least until it reached the Alps, at a cost of another 1,448 wounded and 370 killed.[40]

War's End, April–November 1945

From April 20 to May 2, the 10th Mountain Division continued to pursue the retreating Germans. The mountain infantry became motorized infantry to rush to the Po, then manned assault boats to lunge across the river. Continuing to the foot of the Italian Alps, they executed amphibious attacks on Lake Garda, where they learned that all German forces in Italy surrendered at noon on May 2. The last phase of the war contained much hard fighting, costing another 521 wounded, including the assistant division commander Brigadier General Duff, and 154 killed, including Col William Darby, who replaced Duff. The fighting had been hard on the division. In 114 days of nearly continual combat, the 10th Mountain lost nearly one thousand killed and over three thousand wounded. Over 30 percent of the men in the mountain infantry regiments became casualties.[41]

But with what the division paid in blood, it purchased two mountain operations that broke the Germans' defensive line in the Northern Apennines, their last defensive position in Italy. Captured German generals "showed amazement at the offensive power in the mountains developed by the American divisions, particularly the 10th Mountain Division." Field Marshal Albert Kesselring, the German theater commander, was "surprised" by the 10th Mountain Division's ability to operate in deep snow during Operation Encore. The German corps commander who opposed the 10th Mountain during Craftsman, Gen Frido von Senger und Etterlin, reported that the "10th Mountain Division had been my most dangerous opponent in the past fighting and my corps had been separated from the LI Corps by the breakthrough of the Americans."[42]

On May 20 the 10th Mountain Division moved to Udine in northeastern Italy for occupation duties. There the men of the division continued to do what they did: they went climbing. David Brower and a party made their way to Chamonix, France—the heart of mountaineering country. They skied, using equipment taken from German warehouses; Walter Praeger won a slalom race on Mount Mangart in the Carnic Alps. And they continued to train in the mountains; the 85th and 86th Mountain Infantry Regiments established refresher schools on the Grossglockner glacier, taking advantage of the mountaineering and skiing equipment that was finally making its way out of the warehouses in Naples. But the mountain infantry's Alpine idyll would soon come to an end.[43]

On July 14 the 10th Mountain Division received orders to return to the United States. The men would receive thirty days of leave before reporting back to Camp Carson, Colorado. There the division would replace the few men who qualified for demobilization and then reequip and reorganize into a standard infantry division. Once constituted, it was to head for the Pacific where it would be a follow-on force for the planned invasion of Japan in 1946. The division set sail from Italy the last week of July and arrived back in New York and Virginia on August 9 and 11. While at sea the men learned of the dropping of the atomic bombs on Japan, which surrendered on August 15, 1945. Upon arrival stateside, the mountaineers embarked on leave and reported to Camp Carson on September 15 for demobilization.[44]

Discharge took over a month of paperwork, accounting, and waiting. The regiments were inactivated in the order of their activation. The 87th Mountain Infantry, the first to be activated in 1941, was the first to be inactivated on November 21, 1945. The 86th, activated in 1942, followed on November 27. This left the 85th Mountain Infantry to enjoy a last Thanksgiving together at Camp Carson. Hearing of good early season snow up on Berthoud Pass, men from Company L went skiing, without packs for the first time in a long time. After skiing all day on Saturday, the men spent the night in Idaho Springs before returning to Carson on Sunday. That Friday the 85th Mountain Infantry was inactivated, along with the 10th Mountain Division.[45]

The future of mountain troops occupied Minnie Dole's thoughts in the spring of 1945. After the army canceled the National Ski Patrol's contract in March, Dole wrote to General Marshall asking that if the army wished to continue training for winter and mountain warfare after the war, that the NSP be permanently retained to recruit and screen men for such service. Dole sent the letter on May 10 and a week later received Marshall's reply. Since "the Army was now in a position where it can meet its own requirements for training mountain troops through its own resources," Marshall wrote, "no revision of the decision to terminate the contract can be justified at this time."[46]

The army had evidently determined that Dole's assertion that it was easier to train skiers, or mountaineers, to be soldiers, than to train soldiers to ski, was in fact incorrect. Fundamentally, there were not enough skiers or mountaineers to train as soldiers. The history of the Mountain Training Center written by John Jay in May 1944 noted that mountaineers, both climbers and skiers, were "a surprisingly small proportion of the population" compared to "fun" skiers. The "so-called rugged outdoor types"—teamsters, rangers, miners—often proved unable to master the techniques of modern mountaineering and mountain warfare. The MTC's experience was that "keen, young, physically-fit men without previous experience proved to be the best material from the 'non-mountaineer' group."[47]

As such men were the ideal recruits, the army concluded by the end of 1945 that specialized mountain and winter training was to be conducted only after all other required training was accomplished. Ski training, for example, was something the army now had three seasons of experience with—one on Mt Rainier and two on Cooper Hill. From this the 1944 manual on winter warfare, written by veterans of this experience, insisted that "units engaged in ski training should have completed unit and combined training" before beginning ski training. Adding in basic, this was nearly nine months of training before any specialized training would be conducted.[48] This insight, and the experiences of the 1st Battalion, 87th Mountain Infantry, the Mountain Training Center, the 10th Light Division (Alpine), and the 10th Mountain Division, would guide the army's efforts toward mountain warfare during the coming Cold War.

CHAPTER 7

COLD WAR MOUNTAIN WARFARE, 1946–1970

With the deactivation of the 10th Mountain Division at the end of 1945, several of the division's officers attended the Advanced Officer Course at the Infantry School, Fort Benning, Georgia, during the 1946–47 term. At least three of them wrote papers on their experiences of mountain warfare in Italy in 1945. Capt Edward H. Simpson, S-3 of the 1st Battalion, 85th Mountain Infantry, wrote on the patrol actions; Maj William H. Hard, the adjutant, 85th Mountain Infantry, discussed his regiment's actions on Mt Belvedere; and Capt Erwin G. Nilsson, Company D commander, 1st Battalion, 86th Mountain Infantry, recounted the Riva Ridge assault. All the former 10th Mountain officers argued for the continuation of specialized mountain training and for maintaining a specialized mountain unit.[1]

The strongest case came from Lt Col Robert C. Works, executive officer, 87th Mountain Infantry. Works penned an article while awaiting the deactivation of his regiment, published in the May 1946 issue of *Military Review*, the publication of the Command and General Staff School. Works reviewed the mountain training during World War II, pointed out the value of mountain training for infantry divisions, and the value of specially trained mountain divisions. He recommended that all infantry divisions receive at least one month of mountain training and that the postwar army contain at least one mountain division and several separate mountain infantry battalions. Personnel conscripted for a mountain division were to be selected based on their civilian experiences as skiers and mountaineers and should favor those from northern mountain states. The separate mountain infantry battalions would be attached to standard infantry divisions operating in the mountains to carry out "the highly specialized tasks of Alpine combat." In peacetime these battalions would conduct mountain training for infantry divisions.[2]

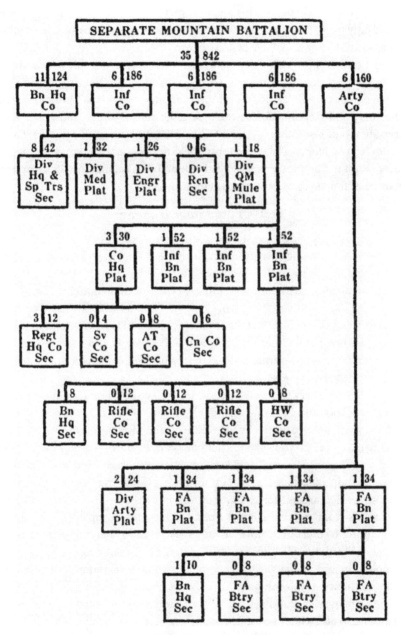

Proposed Separate Mountain Battalion (1946), from Works, "Postwar Mountain Training," 76.

Yet even as Works penned his manuscript, the army was determining that it would only have infantry, armored, and airborne divisions postwar. The influential General Board, US Forces, European Theater concluded after the war that the standard infantry division, with modifications, was able to operate in all types of terrain. Thus, "there is no requirement for divisions specially organized, equipped and trained for ground infantry operations" in mountains. The board did recommend, however, that the armed forces "must spur and keep abreast of research, experimentation and development in equipment and tactics required for special operations," including mountain operations. While there would not be another specialized mountain division in the US Army, the door was left open for postwar mountain training.[3]

Postwar Mountain Training

To carry out this mountain training, the army took two actions in March 1946. First, it announced the transfer of the 38th Regimental Combat Team, part of the 2nd Infantry Division, from Camp Swift, Texas, to Camp Carson, Colorado, to undergo mountain training. Consisting of the 38th Infantry Regiment; 38th Field Artillery Battalion; Company C, 2nd Engineer Battalion; and Company C, 2nd Medical Battalion, the main body of the RCT arrived in late April and incorporated nearly three thousand enlistees and inductees at the end of May. Second, the army decided to create a "permanent mountain training headquarters" at Carson.[4]

This headquarters was activated on June 1 as the Mountain and Winter Warfare School and Training Center (MWWSTC). Given its ungainly title and acronym, it was universally referred to as the Mountain Training Center, or MTC. This MTC received a fourfold mission. First, it was "to preserve and develop the techniques and tactics of mountain and winter warfare." Second, it was to train officers and noncommissioned officers from across the army ground, service, and air forces in mountain and winter warfare, train officers and NCOs from selected combat units "as instructors capable of conducting training of their unit," and "assist in the mountain and winter training of units." Third, the MTC was to "assist boards in conducting tests pertinent to mountain and winter warfare, and to recommend revisions in equipment, clothing, tactics, and techniques." Finally, the center was to "prepare and recommend changes in training literature" and serve as the central repository for all mountain and winter warfare reports from across the army.[5]

Authorized thirty-four officers and 134 enlisted men, the new MTC also had the 611th Field Artillery Battalion (Pack) and 35th Quartermaster Pack Company attached to provide mule packing expertise. Almost all the MTC personnel had experience with the 10th Mountain Division. The division's artillery commander, David Ruffner, in his permanent rank of colonel, served as the MTC's commanding officer, with Col David Fowler, commander of the 87th Mountain Infantry, as his assistant. Lt Col John Hay, who had joined the 1st Battalion, 87th Mountain Infantry, in November 1941 and commanded the 3rd Battalion, 86th, in Italy, was his chief of plans and training (S-3). The S-1, chief of the Tactical and Technical Advisor Section, and the chief medical instructor of the MTC also had both served with the 10th Mountain Division. Of the first eighteen officers and NCOs assigned to the center, thirteen had served with the division. Lieutenant Colonel Hay would eventually hire thirteen civilian instructors, eleven of whom had 10th Mountain experience. This core group of former 10th Mountain Division personnel would heavily influence the army's mountain, winter, cold, and arctic training for the next decade.[6]

The MTC sought to teach the techniques and use of technologies for mountain survival and mobility in both summer and winter, as developed at Camp Hale and the West Virginia Maneuver Area during wartime. The center envisioned approximately eight and a half months of summer and winter training, to run from the end of July to the beginning of April. A crucial lesson learned from the war experience was the need to train a cadre of personnel in each unit and then have them train their units, supervised by the MTC. This would ensure a unit could continue to utilize its mountain skills afterward. Another lesson learned was the need to develop in the army an institutional knowledge of mountain and winter warfare. The MTC thus held a course in 1946 and 1947 for officers and NCOs from all the branches of the army, including Air, Quartermaster, and Transportation Corps. Fifteen officers, including two Marine Corps captains, and thirty-five NCOs received training to qualify them as mountain instructors and to familiarize them with mountain warfare as future commanders and senior enlisted leaders.[7]

Throughout the summer of 1946 along the Front Range near Camp Carson, the MTC conducted training focused on mobility and maneuver. Rock climbing took place in North Cheyenne Cañon, a city of Colorado Springs park just off post. RCT engineers built bleachers in an amphitheater in the canyon to serve as an outdoor classroom. In general, the curriculum and the equipment, a number of instructors recalled, "was familiar to all who had trained at Mount Rainier and Camp Hale." Such was also true of much of the rest of the training: mountain movements and bivouacs, mountain cooking with one-burner stoves, tactics, logistics and supply, patrols, and mountain evacuations. Men learned mule handling and packing, and mule trains made their way along Gold Camp and Old Stage Road to St. Peter's Dome and Gould Creek, where the battalions spent two weeks on tactical problems. The civilian community became the MTC's final training audience. To thank the citizens of Colorado

Springs for the use of North Cheyenne Cañon Park, the MTC held climbing lessons each Saturday in November 1946 at the amphitheater. Any local boy or girl fourteen years and older could participate.[8]

With the coming of winter and snow, the MTC training shifted northwest into the Rocky Mountains, back to the familiar environs of Cooper Hill and Camp Hale. The RCT billeted in winterized, heated tents with electric lights, as most of the barracks had been torn down. The winter phase added more training for survival to that for mobility and maneuver to ensure "the ability of the soldier to move and survive in the mountains under conditions of snow and extreme cold." The training closely resembled that of previous winters at Camp Hale and Cooper Hill. The ski techniques were essentially the same as those used by the 10th Mountain; so too were the skis and boots, while the layers of cold weather clothing were now standard issue.[9]

For eight weeks from late January to the end of March 1947, the cadre trained the entire combat team, again under the supervision of the MTC. The men skied half of one day and devoted the other half to tactics, initially classes on mountain weather, mountain hazards, first aid in snow, and evacuations. As the ski training progressed, the tactics added snowshoeing practice, bivouacs, survival shelters, cooking, and moving cross-country on skis in multiple columns, first as squads, then as platoons, companies, and battalions. Engineers built tramways, medics practiced sled evacuations, artillerymen learned to fire the 75 mm pack howitzer, and signal troops laid wire by ski. All learned to maintain and operate the M29 Cargo Carrier, or Weasel. Ski training finished with two regimental ski movements into bivouac sites below Homestake Peak.[10]

The culmination of the mountain and winter course was to be two weeks of alpine training and maneuvers. Dipping into their experiences of RCT maneuvers and the D-Series, the 10th Mountain veterans of the MTC planned for a series of four exercises: tactical movement, defense, night march, and attack. The 38th RCT received orders, however, to participate in an Army Day parade in Denver, resulting in just a three-day problem along Mitchell Creek north of Tennessee Pass. The final piece of winter mountain training was to be a two-week glacier school on the snowfield between Homestake Peak and Little Homestake Peak. The course of instruction covered movement over glaciers and other snow formations, avalanche rescue, route selection, and building snow shelters above tree line. Unfortunately, after four days, a violent spring storm brought too much snow for the course to continue, so it too was cut short.[11]

Besides training the 38th RCT in 1946 and 1947, the MTC also provided input into the army's education and doctrine. In response to a query from the School of Combined Arms at the Command and General Staff College, the MTC provided a memorandum in November 1946 agreeing that a standard infantry division could be trained to fight in the mountains. This division would require three months of summer and winter training to teach movement, survival, supply, weapons employment, and tactical application in the mountains. This memo provided the basis for a 1948 *Military Review* article, "Infantry in Mountain Operations." Also, in the summer of 1946 the MTC collected and collated material for a revision of FM 70-10 *Mountain Operations*. Published in September 1947, the revised mountain manual thus included twenty more figures illustrating climbing techniques and knots.[12]

The efforts and experiences of the MTC also contributed to the 1949 update to FM 100-5 *Operations*. The mountain operations section of this edition added two substantial paragraphs that clearly drew on the 10th Mountain's Italian experience. In the section's first paragraph, after the well-established statement that mountains were not an obstacle for troops "properly equipped, clothed, supplied, and trained," the manual continued: "such troops by accepting the natural hardships inherent in maneuver through mountain terrain frequently achieve surprise which results in success with relative ease and few casualties." An infantry division was able to operate in most mountains, though it might need to "resort to pack animals and manpower for the movement of equipment and supplies." Troops operating at high altitude in the cold, winds, ice, and snow, however, "must have specialized training and equipment." Significantly, two paragraphs later, the manual stated that it "is essential that all commanders have a thorough understanding of the capabilities of mountain-trained troops." Higher-level staffs had to have mountain experts to ensure equipment was available, and all commanders had to know how the equipment was to be used and maintained.[13]

On April 30, 1947, the army inactivated the Mountain and Winter Warfare School and Training Center, despite the MTC's successful execution of its mission. The move was apparently motivated by the desire to cut a headquarters out of the force structure. The mountain-trained personnel, most of whom were 10th Mountain veterans, were transferred either to the 38th RCT as a mountain training detachment or to the 38th Infantry's intelligence and reconnaissance (I&R) platoon. For the rest of the year and into 1948, the detachment continued the seasonal round of mountain training. Summer training lasted from July to October around Camp Carson, with winter training from October to March at Hale and on Cooper Hill. The winter phase then climaxed in a five-day RCT field exercise, Operation Timberline, in March 1948.[14]

The 38th RCT mountain training detachment conducted six two-week mountain training courses from June to August 1947 for 283 reserve officers. The course was intended to demonstrate to these officers the value of a unit trained to operate in mountain terrain through instruction in the fundamentals of rock climbing. The detachment also dispatched training teams to conduct winter warfare instruction for units from the 2nd Infantry and 82nd Airborne Divisions to carry out exercises in Alaska and Pine Camp, New York, respectively. And the I&R platoon, under 10th Mountain Division veteran 1st Lt Edmund Gulczynski, began public climbing demonstrations in North Cheyenne Cañon Park during the summer of 1947. Tourists selected the exhibition as that year's main attraction in Colorado Springs.[15]

In 1948 the mountain training detachment continued to hold climbing demonstrations for tourists and trained another 320 officers from the Organized Reserve Corps, including Capt David Brower. Brower was not the only 10th Mountain Division associate to take an interest in the mountain training going on at Camp Carson. Minnie Dole met with the new commander of Army Ground Forces, Gen Jacob L. Devers, in late 1946. Dole wrote to Devers throughout the next two years, emphasizing at one point the need for officers with mountain experience to oversee mountain training, something Devers agreed with. In October 1948 Dole tried, once again, to convince the army to allow men to enlist directly for units undergoing mountain training. This Devers refused as "under current regulations individuals *cannot* enlist directly."[16]

The mountain training detachment conducted no cadre training and the regimental combat team planned no mountain training that summer. The reason why became apparent in September when the army announced that forty-one officers and 281 enlisted men from the 38th RCT would depart for Fort Lewis, Washington, to stand up the 38th Infantry as part of the 2nd Infantry Division. The ex-38th personnel remaining in Colorado were transferred to a new 14th RCT at Carson, again with a detachment to conduct mountain training. The 14th's mountain detachment continued rock-climbing instruction and demonstrations in North Cheyenne Cañon during the summer of 1949. The focus of the year's training remained preparing for an upcoming arctic exercise, with 1,200 men of the 1st Battalion Combat Team heading to Camp Hale at the end of November for cold weather training. After six weeks of training, the force departed for Canada at the beginning of January 1950 to participate in the US and Canadian joint exercise Operation Sweetbriar. They returned at the beginning of March. Sweetbriar took place along the Northwest Highway System, between Whitehorse, Yukon Territory, and Northway, Alaska, to "develop procedures, doctrine, and technique for the employment of combined Canadian and United States Armies and Air Forces operating in the Arctic." The mountain training detachment also carried out arctic training for a reserve navy Construction Battalion (Seabees) at Hale from January to March 1950. On May 1, 1950, the 14th RCT began its summer military mountain training program, but it was interrupted when, on June 25, North Korea invaded

South Korea. The Korean War would spur growth in mountain training in the US Army and Marine Corps but would ultimately cause a shift in focus from mountain warfare to cold and arctic operations.[17]

Mountain and Cold Weather Training Command

The Korean War began in June 1950, and fighting continued into the fall and winter. The US and United Nations forces were unprepared for −30°F temperatures and arctic winds found on the Korean Peninsula. More than 5,000 troops suffered from frostbite that first winter, some 1,500 during the Chinese breakthrough of UN lines in early December 1950. The army dispatched quartermaster training teams to Korea. These determined that the weather casualties were the result of ignorance among staff officers of the clothing required for cold weather warfare and the lack of proper supervision by officers in the wearing of cold weather clothing. In fact, units that had trained in cold climate areas suffered few to no cold weather casualties. This demonstrated to the army that cold weather training was required, as living under cold conditions "was an acquired skill you can only get through training."[18]

To conduct and oversee this training, the army reactivated a mountain warfare school at Camp Carson in the summer of 1951, now called the Mountain and Cold Weather Training Command (MCWTC). The new command quickly adopted a new emblem of a mountain sheep ram's head surrounded by a coiled climbing rope, superimposed over crossed skis and an ice axe. As before, a "10th Mountain mafia" dominated the new mountain school. Col Warren S. Shelor, who commanded the 3rd Battalion, 85th Mountain Infantry, in Italy and helped to establish the Mountain and Winter Warfare School and Training Center in 1946, served as the MCWTC's first commander, replaced in 1954 by Lt Col Donald J. Woolley, commander of the 1st Battalion, 85th Mountain Infantry, in Italy. The civilian instructor cadre, all but two of whom were 10th Mountain veterans, was transferred from the 14th RCT to the new command. While training was the primary mission of the MCWTC, it was also tasked with contributing to mountain warfare doctrine and developing the organization for mountain operations.[19]

Both the National Ski Patrol and American Alpine Club sought to aid the new mountain training command. A new director of the NSP, Edward Taylor, visited the Pentagon in November 1951. He found "a lot of thinking" about mountain warfare, but not much interest in assistance from the NSP. He noted the word "ski" had become "taboo" in the Pentagon, as the newspapers had called mountain troops "ski troops" during the last war. Those not associated with the 10th Mountain Division, Taylor wrote to Dole, "have a strictly sour grapes attitude." The AAC proved more successful. It organized a

"Committee on Liaison with the Armed Forces" that provided "recommendations and suggestions" from club members, such as Bob Bates, who contributed
"immeasurably."[20]

The first task of the new mountain training command during the summer
and fall of 1951 was to combine existing mountain and cold weather doctrine
into a single instructor's guide. Totaling twenty-three chapters, the guide
covered instruction in cold weather clothing and equipment, skis and skiing,
winter bivouacking and survival, cooking, hygiene and first aid, oversnow
freighting and evacuations, weather and snow characteristics, and use of the
M29 cargo carrier. This document proved timely as the command dispatched a
party of instructors to Pine Camp, recently renamed Camp Drum, in November 1951 to support Exercise Snow Fall. Following four weeks of training by the
command, focusing especially on the use of cold weather clothing and equipment, the 11th Airborne Division conducted a series of eight parachute drops
in late January 1952, followed by a week of cold weather maneuvers across the
Adirondacks by nearly thirty thousand personnel.[21]

The MCWTC continued unit training in the summer of 1952. The 47th
Infantry Division of the Minnesota National Guard carried out Exercise Pine
Ridge in the West Virginia Maneuver Area from late July to early October.
One hundred men and officers underwent training at Camp Carson in May,
with more trained at Seneca Rocks in July. The cadre and MCWTC instructors
supervised small-unit training in preparation for the regimental combat team
exercises that, as during World War II, completed the training. Individual
mountain training at Camp Carson also went on, with the command conducting six classes of 150 men who had completed their basic training during the
summer of 1952.[22]

This course was to provide mountain-trained infantry replacements for
overseas commands in the Far East and especially in Austria, where now–
Lieutenant General Hays was in command and was carrying on mountain
and ski exercises. For these replacements the command provided three weeks
of basic mountaineering training in North Cheyenne Cañon and three weeks
of field exercises, culminating in a climb of Pikes Peak. Along with replacements, the command continued classes for reserve officers, to fulfill their
summer training commitments. And the MCWTC continued to provide public displays of climbing in the Cañon, every Tuesday and Thursday morning
from June to September.[23]

In September 1952 the mountain command shifted its focus to supporting
the upcoming Exercise Snow Storm, the sequel to Snow Fall, at Camp Drum
from January to March 1953. The MCWTC, including the mules and mule
packers of the 35th Quartermasters, trained a cadre of five hundred men from

the 82nd Airborne Division at Camp Hale for four weeks from mid-November 1952, focusing on survival and mobility in snow and cold. Seventy men, most of the command, then deployed to Camp Drum to supervise six weeks of unit training by the 82nd Airborne Division cadre and oversee a series of RCT exercises in February and March 1953.[24]

The MCWTC also supported other cold weather training efforts. The commanding general, US Army Alaska, organized an Arctic Indoctrination School (AIS) at Big Delta, Alaska, during the winter of 1948–49. The AIS provided mountain and arctic indoctrination for personnel assigned to Alaska and from commands in the lower forty-eight states. After 1951 the MCWTC and AIS regularly conducted exchanges of personnel, providing the AIS with qualified mountaineering instructors. The AIS held winter and summer field exercises, paralleling the training done at Carson and Hale, but with aspects unique to the region, such as using inland waterways in the summer and dealing with severe arctic cold in the winter.[25]

The AIS was part of the army's effort to strengthen its arctic capabilities against the potential Soviet seizure of air bases in the region, as was the recruitment of twenty former Finnish officers to the US Army in 1947. These officers, veterans of the Winter War and the Continuation War against the Soviet Union, observed US exercises, such as Operation Sweetbriar, reviewed cold weather doctrine, and found both wanting. But as their experience was in flat, snow-covered tundra and forests, the Finns were not, by their own admission, mountaineers. They thus sought to separate cold weather operations in general, and arctic operations in particular, from mountain operations. For example, the Finns criticized American skis, boots, and bindings and ski training as too focused on downhill techniques, without comprehending the safety requirements of skiing in steep, mountainous terrain. They were also largely ignorant of the danger avalanches posed to troops maneuvering in the mountains.[26]

Four of the officers, led by Col Alpo K. Marttinen, received the task to review and rewrite doctrine for arctic operations in November 1948; they completed the work, including visits to Camp Hale to take illustrative photos, by March 1951. The result was a series of four field manuals published in 1951 and 1952. FM 31-70 *Basic Arctic Manual* served as the capstone work, a technical guide for individuals, that replaced the previous 1944 manual, which had been classified under mountain operations. FM 31-71 *Northern Operations* was for units below the division level, and FM 31-72 *Administration in the Arctic* was intended for separate battalions and RCTs, focusing on logistic challenges. FM 31-73 *Skiing and Snowshoeing* fulfilled Finnish preferences by the addition of longer, narrower cross-country skis mounted with simpler Balata bindings with toe and ankle straps to the shorter, wider mountain skis with Kandahar bindings.

Marttinen joined the MCWTC as a training officer in November 1953, and his efforts and those of his fellow Finns inadvertently began the process of separating cold weather warfare from mountain warfare.[27]

This emphasis on cold weather brought about by the Korean War and other Cold War concerns is reflected in the decision by the USMC to establish a cold weather training program in November 1950. This effort had indirect connections back to the 10th Mountain Division. The officer initially in charge of field training in the San Jacinto Mountains, Capt William Moore, served with the 38th RCT at Camp Carson in 1947 and 1948 as an exchange officer. Moore, who underwent rock-climbing and skiing instruction in North Cheyenne Cañon and at Camp Hale, proved to be a natural military mountaineer. Designated the Cold Weather Battalion, the Marine Corps training group moved to Pickle Meadows in the Sierra Nevada in 1951. Cold weather training for Korea-bound replacements occupied the battalion until the cease-fire in 1953, after which it began to train Camp Pendleton–based units. This expansion in its mission resulted in the battalion becoming the Cold Weather Training Center in 1956, tasked with carrying out cold weather indoctrination; escape, evasion, and survival training; and mountain leader training.[28]

In January 1953 the army's MCWTC initiated a series of mountain and cold weather instructor courses, divided into seven-week summer and winter sessions. The summer session trained specially selected officers and enlisted men in rock climbing, survival, orientation, cross-country movement, supply, and evacuation techniques. The first four weeks took place in the Camp Carson area, with the last three in glaciated terrain in the Wind River Mountains of Wyoming. The winter training consisted of movement, survival, supply, and evacuation under conditions of snow and cold in the Camp Hale area. For a completely trained mountain warfare expert, attendance at both courses was required. The initial impetus for this training was the need to provide instructors for mountain and cold weather training centers to be established in the Far East and in Austria in 1954. Lt Col Edward Link, an AAC member, organized and commanded the former, while Lt Col John Hay, an Italy veteran and original member of the previous mountain training command, organized the US Forces Austria Center at Saalfelden. Within a few years the MCWTC intended the courses to provide the army with a "substantial cadre of skilled mountain warfare experts."[29]

With this shift in emphasis from providing mountain-trained replacements for overseas commands to creating a mountain warfare cadre in the army, the MCWTC sought to ensure a credible and experienced instructor base. In May 1953 field grade officer tours with the commands were stabilized for three years, while company-grade officer and enlisted man tours were now for a minimum of one year, with intensive instructor training courses. The command did try to recruit qualified draftees working through the AAC and regional clubs to spread the word. At least two instructors were members of the 1956 US Olympic ski team. In 1952 Lieutenant Colonel Link received a letter from Scott Osborn, a 10th Mountain veteran, alerting him that two Pacific Northwest mountaineers, guides on Mt Rainier, had been inducted into the army. Link arranged for Jim Whittaker, who would become the first American to summit Everest and the first president of the outdoor retailer Recreational Equipment Inc. (REI), and his twin brother, Louie, to transfer to the MCWTC in January 1953, where they would serve as mountain warfare instructors (MWIs) until the summer of 1954.[30]

In addition to training MWIs, quickly promoted Cpl Jim Whittaker and the MCWTC also trained members of the army's new 10th Special Forces Group, which deployed to the foothills of the Bavarian Alps at the end of 1953. From January to March 1954 the command, along with the mules and mule packers of the 4th Field Artillery Battalion (Pack) and 35th Quartermaster Pack Company, supported Exercise Ski Jump in the Camp Hale area. An RCT of the 11th Airborne Division provided the exercise force. A four-week cadre training course was followed by five weeks of small-unit training stressing cross-country movement and extended bivouacking and finishing with a five-day exercise. Among the participants was Lt James Earl Jones, the future actor, who "took to the physical challenge, so much that I wanted to stay there testing myself in that awesome environment." As the MCWTC instructors underwent their duties during 1953 and 1954, camera teams shadowed them for an episode of *The Big Picture*, the army's weekly television series. Titled "Mountaineers in Khaki," the episode captured the MCWTC's instructors and students climbing and skiing at locales across the mountains of central Colorado.[31]

In 1954 the command updated its instructor guidance, capturing the experiences of the previous three years and the just-concluded Korean War. The Mountaineering Notebook and Winter Handbook continued to emphasize the basics of survival—especially bivouacking—and mobility—climbing, skiing; there was an increased emphasis on supply, especially "man-packing," the need to be able to carry all supplies forward on the back of a man. Instruction also emphasized individual survival in both winter and summer if separated from a unit and introduced lessons on field fortifications in the mountains, both based on combat experience. The MCWTC found that an infantry battalion, reinforced with artillery, engineers, medical, and logistic support, fighting as a combat team was the best tactical unit for operations in mountains and in extreme cold. It provided a standard operating procedure for such infantry battalion combat teams, some of which would be participating in the large-scale

Airborne Artic Exercise in Alaska in January and February 1955 and the 8th Infantry Division's Camp Hale maneuvers from January to March. In 1956 the army issued Table of Organization and Equipment No. 7-15C for infantry battalions operating under prolonged mountain conditions.[32]

However, though Lt Col Erwin Nilsson of the MCWTC, a veteran of Riva Ridge, reported to the American Alpine Club in 1955 that "mountain training in the U.S. Army is in an excellent state," change was coming. The moving of arctic and cold weather doctrine out from under mountain operations in 1951 had been an early warning, reinforced by the updated TM 10-275 *Principles and Utilization of Cold Weather Clothing and Sleeping Equipment* in April 1956. Gone were the 1945 sections on equipment for packing, cooking, camping, mountain climbing, skiing, and snowshoeing. Only chapters on cold weather clothing and sleeping equipment remained. The army, faced with reduced budgets and now preparing to fight on a "nuclear battlefield," chose to focus on cold weather warfare over mountain warfare.[33]

The axe soon fell in Colorado. In December 1956 the army deactivated the 35th Quartermaster Pack Company and Battery A, 4th Field Artillery Pack Battalion, the two last mule units whose rationale for existence the previous ten years had been the maintenance of mountain warfare capabilities. The MCWTC was next, in 1957, as the army consolidated mountain and cold weather training in Alaska, deactivating the mountain training command and redesignating the Arctic Indoctrination School as the Cold Weather and Mountain School. It now had the mission of developing cold weather and mountain warfare doctrine, tactics, and techniques and training individuals in those subjects.[34]

Cold Warfare

By 1960 the army flipped mountain warfare on its head, emphasizing particular—cold weather and arctic operations—over general capabilities. As the Cold Weather and Mountain School updated field manuals, it made cold weather operations the capstone, with operations in northern latitudes second, and mountain operations a distant third. The new FM 31-70 *Basic Cold Manual* promulgated in February 1959 incorporated the 1952 FMs 31-70 *Basic Arctic Manual* and 31-73 *Skiing and Snowshoeing*. It was "designed to prepare the individual soldier and small unit commander to conduct military operations for extended periods of time under the most severe and varying cold weather climatic conditions." The manual thus included chapters on individual clothing and equipment, small-unit living, skiing and snowshoeing movement, combat techniques, and small-unit leader tips. Clothing consisted of modifications to the M-1943 and M-1951 field uniforms, developments of the World War II mountain jacket and trousers, emphasizing layers of wool and cotton sateen, though now in the army's new olive green color. Gone were the mountain tents because they could not be heated with stoves. The two types of skis and bindings—cross-country and mountain—remained as did the progression of ski techniques from one-step to sidestep to snowplow to sideslip to turns. But movement focused on the generally flat—frozen in winter, wet in summer—landscapes of the far north, as did combat techniques.[35]

FM 31-71 *Northern Operations* (January 1959) provided "doctrinal guidance to commanders and staffs for operation and administration of combat, combat support, and combat service support units in the northern regions of the world." It also provided an outline for a nine-week winter training course. Equipment took up most of week one, living in the field week two, and skiing dominated weeks three, four, and five. Week six started the advanced phase with small-unit training, week seven with unit training and tactics, and weeks eight and nine with battalion problems. However, as with FM 31-70, FM 31-71 focused on the area of northern operations, "the area in the Northern Hemisphere which lies north of the temperate zone where climatic conditions require the application of special techniques and equipment."[36]

The third publication in the cold weather doctrine hierarchy, FM 31-72 *Mountain Operations*, also released in January 1959, superseded the 1949 mountain operations field manual. FM 31-72 was to guide an infantry regiment "commander, his staff, and subordinate leaders in mountain operations. It is designed also as a guide for commanders of supporting units and for staff officers of higher headquarters whose duty it may be to submit recommendations on the employment of units in mountain warfare." Again, the manual presented the army's long-held view that standard infantry and airborne divisions were "suitable for mountain operations," but "in alpine terrain, specialized technical training and the use of special clothing and equipment will be required." The manual had chapters on operations, employment of the arms and services, military mountaineering, snow and glaciers, communications, and training.[37]

For the first time the manual recognized that the avalanche "critical zone lies above 35°," reflecting the advances in avalanche science that understood "most of the dangerous avalanches originate on slopes between 30° and 45°." The manual laid out a five-week program for military mountaineering and glacier work. Mountain marches and bivouacs took up 54 of the 220 hours allotted to the course, assault climbing techniques 50 hours, use of rope installations 16 hours, glaciers 14 hours, and avalanches 2 hours. FM 31-72 laid out a wide variety of factors that had impacts on operations in the mountains, including terrain, climate, weather, and altitude.[38] While the army prioritized operations in the northern latitudes, soldiers and units trained to the standards set in these cold or northern operations manuals would have been at a loss in the mountains, even in the winter.

There was still some mountain training in the army. In the early 1960s the Cold Weather and Mountain School ran a six-week summer mountain course in Black Rapids, Alaska. It generally followed the program from *Mountain Operations* beginning with mountain walking, then climbing, knots, rappelling, rope installations, evacuations, ice climbing, glacier travel, and crevasse rescue. The students used much of the equipment designed two decades prior, including the two-man mountain tent, the larger ice axe, ski-mountain boots, and crampons. Much like their precursors at Hale twenty years earlier, the instructors identified themselves with white tape, worn on their field caps, the descendent of the 10th Mountain's ski caps. There were some changes, understandably. The course utilized helicopters for resupply, given that the comparatively low altitudes of Alaska and the northern latitudes were emphasized; river operations training utilized motorized squad-sized boats. The training included a field exercise, with the students organized into a tactical unit, using boats, mountain walking, and a helicopter lift to cover forty miles in minutes (which some described as "mountaineering at its best") to carry out an assault. A final examination completed the course.[39]

In early 1963, however, the army determined that the training carried out by the Cold Weather and Mountain School would better serve units assigned to Alaska and so redesignated it the Northern Warfare Training Center (NWTC). While the new training center did continue to conduct some individual training in mountain operations, for the first time since the establishment of the 1st Battalion, 87th Infantry Mountain Regiment, in November 1941, there was no specially designated mountain warfare training unit in army. The redesignation was a reflection of the army's priorities. A year before, in February 1962, the army updated its principal operational doctrine, FM 100-5 *Operations*. The manual focused on conventional battle, airborne and airmobile operations, amphibious operations, air defense, unconventional warfare to include guerrilla warfare, and operations against irregulars. It dropped mountain and cold weather operations from the army's main operational set, to which they had been added back in 1939.[40]

The Marine Corps' Cold Weather Training Center followed a similar trajectory. While the center underwent a 45 percent manpower reduction in 1957, leaving eighteen officers and 235 enlisted men, it continued to provide courses in escape, evasion, and survival; winter and summer mountain leader; and unit training. In November 1963, in recognition of the summer mountaineering and survival training, it was redesignated the Mountain Warfare Training Center (MWTC). By this time the center was annually training 760 students in the renamed Survival, Evasion, Resistance, and Escape (SERE) course, 310 students in three winter and seven summer Mountain Operations courses, which had been expanded from three to four weeks to allow for counterguerrilla instruction and exercises, and seven thousand trainees from five infantry battalions and five reserve infantry companies. But with the deployment of the 1st Marine Division to South Vietnam, the Marine Corps closed the MWTC on October 10, 1967.[41]

The reorganization of US Army divisions to include subordinate brigades and battalions starting in 1962 prompted an updating of field manuals by the NWTC to reflect new terminology, including *Northern Operations* in 1963 and *Mountain Operations* in 1964. There were no major changes to either manual, though *Mountain Operations* removed the chapter on communications, added a section on signals to the employment chapter, and added a chapter on the erecting and maintenance of fixed alpine paths "to assist troops in traversing rugged mountain terrain, ascending or descending steep mountain slopes, and to aid in transporting supplies." At the same time the Quartermaster Corps issued an updated TM 10-275, now just titled *Cold Weather Clothing and Sleeping Equipment*. This version reflected the final status of the olive green cold-wet and cold-dry uniforms of layered cotton-wool blend, wool nylon, and cotton nylon sateen with quilted nylon liners and either black or white rubber vapor-barrier boots, developed from the Korean War experience.[42]

Not until 1968 did the base manual, *Basic Cold Weather Manual*, also undergo revision. The general structure of the 1959 manual was left as is, though the appendixes were now lettered, instead of numbered, and rearranged. The 1968 manual did reflect the changes to clothing introduced in the 1964 technical manual as well as the introduction of several new pieces of equipment. These included a nylon rucksack with an aluminum frame, a one-quart vacuum insulated cold climate canteen, and the long-range patrol ration with a dehydrated main component that reconstituted with water. The 1968 manual also demonstrated the army's emphasis on cold warfare over mountain warfare. Gone were mountain skis, bindings, and boots. Instead, the army now just issued all-terrain cross-country skis, 213 cm (7 ft) long, with all-terrain bindings consisting of a toe plate, toe straps, soleplate, heel cup, and quick-release fasteners to be used with the white rubber vapor-barrier boots. However, despite the far less responsive binding and boot, ski technique remained unchanged—still cross-country skills with downhill turns essentially the same since 1943.[43] Troopers skiing on steeper slopes with these skis, bindings, boots, and techniques would have found themselves at a potentially disastrous disadvantage.

While mountain warfare may have been out in the operational cold for the US Army and Marine Corps by the end of the 1960s, mountains were still a subject for the army quartermaster's research efforts, which after 1962 were concentrated in the Natick Laboratories in Massachusetts, under the US Army Material Command, and the US Army Land Warfare Laboratory at the Aberdeen Proving Ground, Maryland. Natick Labs conducted geographic studies of Kashmir, Korea, Tibet, and Colorado and of glaciers in the Northern Hemisphere. The labs supported medical research focused on the effects of high altitudes and engineering research on the physical characteristics of snow at high elevations. The Land Warfare Laboratory took research and development requests from the field for mountain equipment, resulting in such items for testing and possible procurement as the long-range patrol ration (mentioned above), as well as a two-quart arctic canteen, mountaineering rope kits, and crampons, the last two in particular drawing on commercially available models.[44] As these researchers went about studying mountains and mountain equipment, the realization set in around 1969 that the civilian mountaineering and skiing communities possessed far better technologies than did the army. Mountain warfare had to return to its mountaineering roots.

The US Army, and later the Marine Corps, chose to go their own way in pursuit of mountain warfare capabilities after 1945. For a few years the army attempted to train an RCT and then a battalion combat team at Camp Carson and Camp Hale, along with providing summer mountain training to reserve officers. The Korean War reignited mountain warfare efforts at Carson and Hale, though with an understandable emphasis on cold weather, including by the USMC, which established a training center in the California Sierras. At first the new army mountain training command focused on providing mountain-trained replacements for overseas assignments, then on training MWIs for overseas training centers and the larger force. It also provided support via instruction and supervision to larger regimental and divisional winter exercises in upstate New York and in Colorado. These were part of a larger trend in the army to emphasize cold weather and arctic operations ahead of mountain operations. This culminated in the consolidation of all cold weather, arctic, and mountain training in Alaska in 1957. Thus, after 1960 there was less and less interest within the army in mountain warfare. The Marine Corps did rename its cold weather training center a mountain warfare center, albeit a few years before shutting it down. In the army, however, the heirs of the OQMG continued to conduct research into aspects of mountain warfare. By the end of the 1960s, they realized that the military once again needed civilian mountaineering and skiing expertise.

CHAPTER 8

Mountain Warfare Returns,
1970–1990

The return of mountain warfare to the US military began in February 1970 when the army's Land Warfare Lab, Combat Developments Command, and Natick Labs held a two-day "Conference on Mountain Climbing Clothing and Equipment." The goal was to discuss the systems necessary for survival and mobility in the mountains and other environmentally hostile areas. The army labs held the conference because they were finding much of their equipment was increasingly out of date, essentially 1950s technology. Hickory skis were too hard to maintain, stoves were obsolete, tents and clothing were too heavy, cold weather boots were difficult to use with crampons and offered no traction on steep rocks, and the army had no capability to operate at high altitude, those elevations over 10,000 feet.[1]

The conference included over fifty attendees, about half of whom came from the organizing agencies, such as Eldon Metzger of Natick Labs, who had served with the 10th Recon at Camp Hale, 2662 Detachment in Italy, and then as a civilian instructor with the mountain training efforts at Camps Carson and Hale from 1946 to 1957. The rest came from outside agencies, such as the Northern Warfare Training Center in Alaska, the Canadian Forces, and the Arctic Institute. Crucially the attendees included American mountaineers, including Ad Carter and Bob Bates, and two members of the 1953 K2 expedition whom Bates brought with him, Dee Molenaar and Peter Schoening. Also attending were Jim Whittaker, the first American to summit Everest (in 1963) and the president of REI, and William Unsoeld, who also summited Everest. Whittaker further arranged to have John Day from Oregon, a regular mountain guiding client of his and a competitive skier, invited.[2]

Natick Labs organized the conference into discussions on mobility, subsistence, food packaging and cooking, shelters and heaters, clothing, footgear, climbing equipment and sleeping gear, and oxygen equipment. The discussions

OUTSIDE AGENCIES

NAME	ORGANIZATION
LTC D. T. Arcuri	CDC, Fort Belvoir
Dr. William O. Baker	Bell Telephone Lab Inc., Murry Hill, N.J.
Dr. Robert H. Bates	Exeter, New Hampshire
Col. Richard F. Barquist	US Army Alaska
Mr. Adams Carter	Milton, Mass.
Major Benjamin Franklin	Canadian Forces Hqs., Ontario
Mr. Frank J. Civilikas	AMC, Wash., D. C.
CW2 Oliver J. Cooke	CDC Combat Support Group, Fort Belvoir, VA.
Maj. D. C. Davenport	CDC, Fort Bragg, North Carolina
Mr. John Stewart Day	Central Point, Oregon
Col. G. L. Eckert	US Army Alaska
LTC Alfred V. Edwards	CDC, Fort Lee, VA.
Mr. Robert C. Faylor	Arctic Institute of North America, Wash., D. C.
Mr. Benjamin G. Ferris	Weston, Mass.
Maj. Ian Harold Firstbrook	Canadian Forces Hqs., Ontario
Dr. Frank Fisher	NRC, Wash., D. C.
Mr. G. Hattersley-Smith	Canadian Dept of National Defense
Mr. G. Tranter Holmes	Director of Clo & General Engineering Canadian Forces Hqs.
LTC Edward Hunt	US Army Arctic Test Center
Maj. Edwin C. King	CDC, Fort Leavenworth, Kansas
Mr. Ralph A. Lenton	Arctic Institute of No. America, Wash., D. C.
Mr. David Mashburn	Morganton, North Carolina
Prof. Maynard M. Mille.	Dept. of Geology, Mich. State University
Mr. Palle Mogensen	Arctic Institute of No. America
Mr. Dee Molenaar	Fort Orchard, Washington
SGM Virgil Murphy	CDC, Ft. Bragg, No. Carolina
Mr. Charles Morgan (RDLW-MOM)	LWL, Aberdeen Proving Ground, MD.
Col. Edwin M. Rhoads	Arctic Test Center
Maj. Reuben L. Sanders	CONARC, Ft. Lee, VA.
Mr. Martin Savell	CDC, Fort Belvoir, VA.
Mr. Peter Schoening	Seattle, Washington
Dr. William F. Unsoeld	Andover, Mass.
Mr. William Pitt	US Army Alaska

NAME	ORGANIZATION
Maj. David Weir	US Army CDC Infantry Agency, Fort Benning, Georgia
Mr. James W. Whittaker	Redmond, Washington
Maj. J. G. Williamson	US Army CDC, Fort Belvoir, VA.
Mr. Robert L. Woodbury (Chairman)	LWL, Aberdeen Proving Grounds, MD
Mr. Ray Zoberski	US Army Alaska

NLABS

NAME	ORGANIZATION
Dr. S. J. Kennedy	Director, Clothing & Personal Life Support Equipment Laboratory
Dr. Malcolm C. Henry	Deputy Director, Clothing & Personal Life Support Equipment Laboratory
Mr. Theodore L. Bailey	Clothing & Personal Life Support Equipment Laboratory
Dr. Jan H. Vanderbie	Clothing & Personal Life Support Equipment Laboratory
Mr. Eldon C. Metzger	Clothing & Personal Life Support Equipment Laboratory
Dr. Edward A. Anderson	Deputy Scientific Director/DOD Food Program
Dr. Herbert A. Hollender	Associate Director/Food Laboratory
Mrs. Mary V. Klicka	Ration Design Specialist, Food Laboratory
Mr. Herman B. Levitz	General Equipment & Packaging Laboratory
Dr. Rauno A. Lampi	General Equipment & Packaging Laboratory
Mr. Thaddeus S. Bonczyk	General Equipment & Packaging Laboratory
Dr. Edwin R. Dusek	Army Research Institute of Environmental Medicine
Dr. Martin B. Kreider	Army Research Institute of Environmental Medicine
Dr. Paul Dalrymple	Earth Sciences Laboratory

Attendance List for the Mountain Climbing Clothing and Equipment Conference held at the Natick Laboratories on 17–18 February 1970, from Natick Labs, *Proceedings*, v–vi.

around these topics were freewheeling, with the mountaineers providing most of the input, intentionally so as they had the most current experience. As the days went on, it became increasingly clear to the army officers and civilians that they were quite unfamiliar with much of what the mountaineers were talking about. At one point, during a discussion on climbing equipment, Metzger, one of the most experienced army civilians, had to ask for explanations from Unsoeld as he was "using words that I don't pick up."[3]

Postwar Mountaineering

Confusion on the part of so many of the soldiers and civilian employees was quite understandable as rock climbing and high-altitude expeditions drastically changed mountaineering in the decades after World War II. When Brad Washburn returned to Denali in 1951, he pioneered the now-standard West Buttress route from Kahiltna Glacier to Windy Corner to Denali Pass. That July Washburn reached the summit of Denali for a third time. In 1953 Charles Houston, with Bates, Molenaar, Schoening, and three other mountaineers, made another attempt on K2 in the Himalayas. When one member suffered blood clots at 25,300 feet, the whole party attempted to descend roped together. One man slipped, setting off a chain reaction along the rope, broken only by Schoening, who had put the rope around his ice axe that was behind a small boulder. When the rope suddenly tightened, Schoening instinctively put all his weight on the ice axe, halting the fall, something mountaineers still refer to as "The Belay."[4]

Americans finally achieved the grand prize of high-altitude mountaineering, Mount Everest, in 1963. The American Mount Everest Expedition (AMEE) included twenty mountaineers, among them Whittaker, Unsoeld, and Tom Hornbein. The expedition showed the shift in American mountaineering from the amateur ideal of the Eastern gentleman climber to the professional. Thirteen members were from the western United States, nine had worked as professional mountain guides, and many were involved in the growing outdoor industry. But Everest expeditions were still massive undertakings. The AMEE required the support of nine hundred porters and over thirty Sherpa mountaineers. On May 1 Whittaker and Sherpa Nawang Gombu summited Everest, planting an American flag on the summit, having climbed up the now-standard Lhotse Face route. Three weeks later Unsoeld and Hornbein set out to summit Everest via the West Ridge, reaching the top on May 22, a route rarely climbed even today.[5]

These mountaineering expeditions made use of new, lighter technology. No longer were mountaineers swaddled in layers of wool and cotton gabardine. Now they wore "down and nylon," as Whittaker put it when queried about his Everest climb. Down pants and jackets made from nylon served as midlayers, and down pants and parkas with a water-repellent shell made up the outer layer. Outdoor retailer Eddie Bauer manufactured the down parkas worn on K2 by Bates, Molenaar, and Schoening in 1953. The use of down and nylon lightened their entire clothing ensemble to three or four pounds. Mountaineering footwear was now a double boot with an inner felt liner and a leather outer boot, such as the Lowa Eiger boot Whittaker wore on Everest. Mountaineering tents were also constructed of nylon with aluminum poles, and sleeping bags too were made of down and nylon, weighing just eight and five pounds, respectively.[6]

But even as Americans summited Everest in 1963, rock climbing, previously an adjunct to mountaineering, had moved more to its center. After World War II climbers took advantage of all the surplus gear procured for the 10th Mountain Division: snap links, pitons, and especially nylon ropes. Nylon ropes were crucial as they are "dynamic"—designed to stretch under a load—unlike "static" hemp ropes that do not. Dynamic ropes allow the lead climber to fall and recover and climb again, thereby opening up new, riskier, routes. As mountaineering historian Maurice Isserman put it, the lead climber "could be a bolder climber with the knowledge that a skilled and watchful belayer stood below him." Dynamic ropes, combined with cheap pitons and snap links, meant climbers could be self-taught, or lightly mentored, by utilizing the growing number of mountaineering guidebooks and handbooks. These included the AAC's wartime publication *Handbook of American Mountaineering*, joined in 1960 by the now-definitive *Mountaineering: Freedom of the Hills*, which has since been regularly revised and rewritten.[7]

So equipped and informed, rock climbers swarmed over crags and cliffs around the United States in the postwar period, from the Shawagunks in New York to the Front Range of Colorado, to the Tetons in Wyoming, to the North Cascades in Washington. The granite faces of Yosemite National Park continued to serve as the incubator of American climbing. The denizens of the park's Camp 4 in the 1950s and 1960s—Mark Powell, Warren Harding, Yvon Chouinard, Royal Robbins, Layton Kor, Jim Bridwell—made multipitch (a pitch being the length of one rope) multiday climbs the norm. Initially they did so by taking advantage of changes to pitons. John Salathé, a Swiss immigrant blacksmith, made pitons out of alloyed steel in the late 1940s. These pitons were lighter and could be emplaced and removed several times during a climb, meaning climbers could carry more of them, reuse them, and therefore climb even higher than before.[8]

The requirements created by longer and more demanding climbs changed climbing gear. In the mid-1950s climbers still tied into the rope with bowline and butterfly knots, but the ropes used were nylon or the newer Goldline nylon. They attached the rope to the rock with snap links (carabiners), which were now manufactured from lighter aluminum, allowing more to be carried. New shapes, including a safety carabiner with a collar that screwed over the gate to keep it securely closed, joined the previous ovals. Carabiners snapped into pitons, increasingly made of alloys, or onto hangers attached to bolts drilled into the rock where there were no cracks for pitons.[9]

A decade later Perlon climbing ropes were in increasing use as they were even more dynamic. They were of a kernmantle design, with a woven sheath covering a core of woven strand, the forerunners of today's modern dynamic climbing ropes. Soft iron pitons were replaced by chrome-molybdenum steel, allowing a climber to carry thirty-five to forty. Offset-eye pitons were now the most commonly used, and large "bong-bongs," in widths up to six inches, could be used in cracks too wide for regular pitons. For cracks too small, climbers could insert a razor blade–sized, wedge-shaped RURP (Realized Ultimate Reality Piton), invented by Chouinard in 1960. By the early 1970s kernmantle ropes were the most popular, though their ability to protect on long falls led to a change in how climbers tied in to the rope. A lead climber using the previously preferred bowline knot risked suffocating while hanging on the rope after a fall. To alleviate this risk, a "swami belt" could be used—a tubular nylon webbing wrapped around the waist—or a seat harness, which consisted of webbing looped around the waist and upper thighs, tied in to the rope with a figure-eight knot. A "clean climbing" ethic was also taking hold among much of the climbing community; this ethic involved eschewing use of pitons and bolts, which damaged the rock, in favor of "chocks," manufactured hexagonal pieces attached to wires or slings.[10]

The need for all this increasingly complex, expensive, and necessary climbing gear directly contributed to the growth of outdoor companies and retailers. Yvon Chouinard founded what would become the best-known company. He started by making chrome-moly steel pitons from a forge in the trunk of his car, founding Chouinard Equipment in 1965 and redesigning almost every piece of climbing gear in order to make it simpler, lighter, and more functional. By 1970 Chouinard Equipment was the largest supplier of climbing gear in the United States. At about the same time, the company branched out into soft goods, initially selling durable rugby shirts to climbers before ultimately establishing Patagonia in 1981. Jim Whittaker led the best-known retailer, incorporating the Recreational Equipment Co-op of Seattle as REI in 1956. While REI initially had only one retail outlet, plus a mail-order service, its membership blossomed from 50,000 in 1965 to 250,000 in 1972. In 1974 REI opened its first branch store in Berkeley, California, quickly followed by several other locations on the West Coast.[11]

So, when the army's Natick Labs, following up on its 1970 conference, contracted with Artic Institute of North America to test and evaluate mountaineering equipment, it drew almost solely on commercially available items. During July 1972 the institute tested equipment in glacier exploration and alpine climbing in the Saint Elias Mountains of Yukon Territory, Canada. It recommended the best available product that could be purchased off-the-shelf or for which the army could contract with the manufacturer to modify the equipment to military standards. It recommended mountain boots from the Chippewa Shoe Company, gaiters from Eastern Mountain Sports (EMS), and a tent from Bishop's Ultimate Outdoor Equipment. For climbing gear, the institute endorsed mechanical rope ascenders, or "jumars," from Gibbs Products, rescue pulleys from the Dolt Hut of Santa Monica, California, D-shaped carabiners from Chouinard Equipment, Chouinard's Lost Arrow rock pitons, Forrest Mountaineering's hammer with fiberglass handle, and ropes in 7/16-inch diameter and 150-foot lengths from Plymouth Cordage Company. For snow and ice work, the institute recommended the European company Salewa's ice screws, a snow anchor designed by the Ski Hut of Berkeley, California, Simon Grepon ten-point crampons available from REI, and the Mountain Safety Research Thunderbird ice axe with a metal shaft in thirty-inch and thirty-six-inch lengths. The institute suggested the army adopt Dupont's Fiberfill 2 as an insulating fill material for clothing and sleeping bags, along with open-cell foam sleeping pads from EMS.[12]

For most mountaineering equipment the Arctic Institute had several commercial examples to choose from. This was not the case when it came to ski bindings. Most commercially available ski bindings were now specialized for either downhill or cross-country use, but the army required a binding that would be effective for both. An army binding had to fit a comparatively soft combat boot, be loose enough to allow freedom of movement for long distances, but be able to be tightened enough to allow for downhill runs. The institute could find only one binding that could do this, the somewhat obscure Ramy-Securus ski mountaineering binding. Designed back in the 1950s, its toe irons were adjustable to fit any boot with a welt overhang for the cable and a cable clamp for downhill skiing, like the old Kandahar binding. But, unlike the older binding, the toe irons rode on a spring-loaded pin and would release (open) with any excessive twisting force, representing an early version of a safety binding.[13] That the institute could only find one binding that met the army's requirement in 1972 highlighted the fact that skiing had changed even more than mountaineering since World War II.

Postwar Skiing

At first, even before the war ended, there was a thought that postwar skiing would be much like wartime military skiing, both downhill and cross-country.

When interviewed by John Jay in January 1944, General Rolfe, the original ski troop commander, expressed his belief that "military skiing will occupy a much greater place after the war is over." Perhaps in preparation for that wider adoption, David Brower rapidly brought out a second edition of the *Manual of Ski Mountaineering* in early 1946, adding chapters on mountaineering routes, rock climbing, and ice climbing. The Sierra Club published a third edition, with a few changes to account for new waxes and medical practices, in 1961.[14] Yet Rolfe's forecast about postwar skiing could not have been further from what happened.

Buttressed by the "original ski bum" veterans of the 10th Mountain and the 100,000 pairs of army surplus skis, ski poles, boots, and clothing—Brower illustrated the climbing chapter in the second edition of the *Manual of Ski Mountaineering* with figures attired in surplus ski-mountain boots, mountain trousers, ski parkas, and ski caps—skiing became even more of a mass participation sport. While Minnie Dole had exaggerated the number of skiers at 1 to 3 million in 1940, it is quite certain that there were at least 500,000 dedicated skiers in the United States in 1956, 1.5 million in 1962, and 3 million by 1968. But almost none of these skiers were practicing "military skiing." Instead, led in many ways by 10th Mountain veterans who had had enough of going cross-country and uphill with a heavy pack under their own power, these postwar skiers flocked to ski areas with ski lifts.[15]

In 1955 the United States had seventy-eight ski areas with cable (wire rope) lifts, forty-one of which were chairlifts. Over the next ten years the ski industry added 580 areas and 1,392 lifts. Many of these improvements were under the leadership of 10th Mountain veterans, including Friedl Pfeifer in Aspen, Larry Jump at Arapahoe Basin, and Peter Seibert at Vail. Ultimately the old Camp Hale military reservation would be ringed by five areas: Cooper, Breckenridge, Copper, Vail, and Beaver Creek. Tenth alumni fundamentally created the ski industry, not just developing ski areas but managing at least sixty-two ski schools and providing nearly two thousand ski instructors, along with making films, owning shops, and manufacturing equipment. In the 1960s, to draw skiers, ski areas increasingly became ski resorts with lodges, condominiums, and snow-making and -grooming machinery. To accommodate the latter, ski runs were widened and straightened, to follow the fall line. By 1968 ski resorts were expanding their existing terrain and upgrading more than one thousand chairlifts, many of which were now four-seaters.[16]

To ski these new areas and resorts with their lift-served, widened runs, skiers had new styles of skis. Like many ski manufacturers at the time, Howard Head initially skied on hickory skis, but soon he created a metal version. Head assembled aluminum sheets, steel edges, plywood cores, phenolic resin bases, top sheets, and sidewalls—all held together by flexible adhesives. Metal skis resisted twisting, which allowed the skier to better hold a turn. Introduced in 1950 the Standard ski came with a black top sheet and in lengths of 205, 210, and 220 centimeters. By the mid-1950s, it was the best-selling ski in the United States. But by 1962 skiers were winning races with epoxy fiberglass skis in which torsional flex was independent of longitudinal flex. A short ski could thus perform like a longer ski, while allowing the skier to pivot the skis more easily to initiate a turn. By the early 1970s, many skiers were on 180 cm fiberglass skis, a length that is only occasionally exceeded today.[17]

Lightweight aluminum poles, easier to flick forward to plant, added to the shorter skis' ability to turn, as did new boots. In 1963 Robert Lange introduced the buckled, plastic ski boot that was as pliable as leather, with a lower shell riveted to a hinged, overlapping cuff, the now-standard design. Plastic construction allowed manufacturers to steadily increase the height of the cuff well beyond that of a leather boot. Skiers could now pressure the cuff forward to initiate a turn, on the side to edge the ski, and then back to ride the tails, increasing speed. By the 1970s plastic boots allowed for standardized compatible modern heel and toe bindings. Cubco introduced the first modern binding with separate heel pieces and toepieces in 1950, but the style was not popular until the 1960s. By the middle of that decade, heel and toe releasable bindings with ski brakes were increasingly common, and the Kandahar-style cable binding, with its dual cross-country and downhill capability, disappeared from downhill skiing.[18]

Changes to ski technology influenced changes in ski techniques. The immediate postwar years saw continued reliance on the Arlberg method, but a flood of new theories meant, as ski historian Johan Fry noted, the "late 1950s and early 1960s were a bewildering period in ski technique." By the middle of the 1960s, a few "common denominators" came to mark skiing: "feet acting independently, not locked together; keeping the upper body quiet; and anticipating the direction of the oncoming turn." The Professional Ski Instructors of America (PSIA), organized in May 1961, taught this technique at an increasing number of ski schools. As PSIA instructors Charles Roberts and Seth Masia note, the emphasis of 10th Mountain instructors on "a quiet, stable upper body presaged this evolution" in ski technique. By the early 1970s the American Teaching Method "blended the Arlberg's stem-based lower body maneuvers for beginners and intermediates with the Swiss and French-based parallel skiing at the expert level." Adding heel and toe bindings, shorter fiberglass skis, and especially higher plastic boots to the parallel turn led to edged carved turns. In doing this the skier kept the upper body stable as an "anchor to twist the legs and feet" and faced downhill. Subtly unweighting the skis caused them to "twist naturally into the turn." A skier "almost fell into the turn to initiate it, catching the snow with his edges to complete it." Postwar skiing thus came to be dominated by hyperspecialized alpine skiing.[19]

The US Forest Service quickly came to realize that "much of the desirable alpine skiing terrain was on national forest land." To allow for European alpine skiing at Alta, Utah, without a European-level alpine death toll, the Forest Service hired Monty Atwater as the area's snow ranger in 1946. Atwater, a self-described "graduate" of the 10th Mountain with only writing and ski mountaineering as his marketable skills, set about creating American avalanche science, inventing much of the technical language still used today. He established the first avalanche training school in the Western Hemisphere at Alta in 1949, served as its first avalanche instructor, and held classes every other year. Atwater worked with the Wasatch Avalanche Center in Alta, established in 1937, joined in 1950 by one-man avalanche study centers at Berthoud Pass in Colorado and Stevens Pass in Washington. These centers covered all three snowpacks in North America: Maritime, Intermountain, and Continental. Atwater found the Continental snowpack, with its depth hoar and resulting persistent weak layer, the "most difficult riddle."[20]

Ed LaChapelle joined Atwater in Alta in 1952 as the director of the avalanche center, and for the next eight years the two conducted observations and research, utilizing Swiss texts translated by the US Army Corps of Engineers. Together they fundamentally wrote the book on American avalanche science: *Snow Avalanches: A Handbook of Forecasting and Control Measures*, printed by the Department of Agriculture in 1961. The handbook introduced many of the concepts still in use: the snow cycle, avalanche classifications, the slope angle "sweet spot" for avalanches of 35° to 45°, forecasting factors, snow pit profiles, and snow hardness tests using fist, fingers, pencil, or knife blade. Avalanche mitigation, also called "snow stabilization," involved ski cutting, or "protective skiing," and the use of explosive charges, employing artillery pieces as necessary to trigger avalanches at safe distances. Rescue techniques now included recommendations for equipment, forerunners of today's avalanche tools: a collapsible probe, portable shovel, and a fifty-foot brightly colored avalanche cord worn around the waist and trailed behind to allow rescuers to locate a victim. The obvious limitations of the avalanche cord led LaChapelle to work with Cornell Aeronautical Laboratory in Buffalo, New York, to create the first effective avalanche rescue beacon, the "Skadi," in 1968, with the first units sold a few years later. Carried by a skier, the Skadi continuously transmitted a radio signal that could be detected by other nearby beacons switched to receive mode. During a search for an avalanche victim, the Skadi emitted a sound into an earpiece that grew louder as it got closer to the transmitting beacon, increasing the likelihood of a rescue.[21]

While avalanche science, and the Skadi, rapidly spread through steadily professionalizing ski areas, other skiers also took an increasing interest. Turned off by the growing expense of alpine skiing but drawn by the promise of cardiovascular exertion in the quiet of winter, skiers took to cross-country, or Nordic, skiing in the early 1970s. By 1975 over two hundred Nordic touring centers existed where skiers could ski on prepared tracks. The technological revolution quickly came to cross-country skiing with better poles, boots, and skis, the latter increasingly made of fiberglass with metal edges and waxless, fish-scaled bases, for ease of use and better uphill performance. A few Nordic skiers, including Yvon Chouinard, rediscovered the telemark turn, which allowed them to ski steeper slopes, but many cross-country skiers quit the sport during a series of snowless winters in North America in the early 1980s.[22]

But an even smaller number of skiers seized on the parallel and telemark techniques, avalanche science, and cross-country skis for a different purpose. These skiers mounted the obsolete cable bindings or the hybrid Silvretta binding with a heel cable and a hinged toe onto the new cross-country skis, such as the Fischer Europa, a lightweight, narrow ski with sidecut and aluminum edges. This allowed them to go deeper into the mountains touring on flatter terrain to ski steeper lines, often down big mountains. In the Rockies Tom and Jim Carr descended the Cross Couloir on the Mount of the Holy Cross within sight of old Camp Hale in 1977, while Chris Landry skied the East Face of Pyramid Peak outside of Aspen in 1978, the same year that Lou Dawson skied from the summit of nearby Castle Peak, beginning his thirteen-year odyssey skiing all of Colorado's 14,000-foot mountains. While Dawson called what they were doing "ski alpinism," in many ways it was what Bestor Robinson and David Brower called ski mountaineering three decades prior, albeit with far better skis.[23]

New Doctrine and Equipment

While the army, via Natick Labs, did find some new mountaineering and skiing technologies and technologies that could be used by the military, most civilian practice was not that useful. The army was not going to launch multiday, multipitch big wall cliff assaults, nor was it going to just ski downhill. As the army updated its mountain and cold weather doctrine during the 1970s, military mountaineering and skiing remained much simpler than what had developed in civilian communities. Training Circular 21-3 *Soldier's Handbook for Individual Operations and Survival in Cold-Weather Areas* (1974) continued to layer soldiers in cotton/wool, cotton/nylon, and wool/nylon blends, and outfit them in quilted nylon combat boots and overshoes or cold weather boots, increasingly referred to as "Mickey Mouse boots" for their bulbous toes. Sleeping bags consisted of an inner mountain bag and outer arctic bag with a pneumatic mattress. Tents were still large ten-man versions for the high north, with a Yukon stove, hauled in an ahkio sled.[24]

TC 90-6-1 *Military Mountaineering*, promulgated in 1976, was a decade behind the third edition of *Freedom of the Hills*, published two years earlier. Ropes were nylon, but of thrice-twisted strands, not sheathed kernmantle, and were still tied directly around the body with the bowline knot. Pitons were preferred by the army—no "clean climbing" for the military—of just four types: vertical, horizontal, angle, and wafer. *Military Mountaineering* made no mention of bong-bongs, RURPs, or chocks. Military ice axe heads remained straight, not curved, and crampons were without front points. The army did, however, add the commercially procured "nonstandard" ice screw to the standard ice piton. A six-week "Military Mountaineering and Glacier Work" master training program in the training circular totaled 240 hours. Mountain marches and bivouacs took up 54 hours focusing on movement through terrain requiring application of mountaineering techniques. Assault climbing techniques took 50 hours covering mountain walking, route selection, two- and three-party climbing, belay points, rappelling, and use of fixed ropes.[25]

Military skiing was similarly simpler than civilian skiing. Skis remained the wooden all-terrain ski, 208 cm long, with steel ski poles, and mohair climbers attached by five web straps. Bindings were still of the Balata-type with straps across the toe and instep to accommodate ski-mountain boots or cold weather boots. The training circular *Military Skiing* of 1981 did recognize the bifurcation of civilian ski techniques into cross-country/Nordic and downhill/alpine. Military units faced their greatest challenge in developing downhill skiing, as those skills were more difficult to attain. The circular laid out a ski training program of only twenty-six hours divided into three phases. Two hours of basic movement to teach soldiers to walk on skis and perform sidesteps, a controlled fall and recovery, plus herringbone and kick turns made up phase one. Downhill skiing occupied sixteen hours in phase two, progressing from straight running—an archaic term by then—to step turn, to wedge, to wedge turn, then sideslip, basic christie, then stem turns and parallel turns. Eight hours of tactical skiing made up phase three: waxing and diagonal steps, skijoring, use of climbers, pole riding, ski battle drill and firing positions, and a practical exam. Despite the circular's claim that it made use of the most up-to-date instructional techniques, it was in fact at least a decade behind civilian ski schools.[26]

These techniques and technologies fed into a new mountain warfare doctrine. In June 1980 the US Army's Training and Doctrine Command (TRADOC) released FM 90-6 *Mountain Operations*, superseding and renumbering the previous FM 31-72 of May 1964. With FM 90-6's publication, TRADOC returned mountain warfare to the top of the mountain and cold weather doctrinal hierarchy, with plans to publish an FM 90-11 *Winter Operations*, though this never came to fruition. FM 90-6 described how forces were to fight in mountain regions. Rugged compartmentalized steep terrain, with few lines of communication, and a high variability of weather characterized militarily significant mountains. The "focal point" of mountain operations was "the battle to control the heights," and the infantry division remained "the basic maneuver force in the mountains." In the sixteen years since the previous field manual, army aviation had come of age, so the 1980 version noted that helicopter units could "operate in the mountains to support ground maneuver," though pilots required special training in "the combined hazards of variable winds and rugged terrain." While mountains complicated combat support and logistics—there were few roads for heavy vehicles and few firing positions for field artillery and air defense artillery—aviation assets could position guns, conduct resupply, and carry out medical evacuations. Given the "severe environmental conditions," mountain operations required special training and, in some cases, special clothing and equipment.[27]

All soldiers were to be trained in basic military mountaineering including the hazards of movement in mountains, rope care and management, knots, mountain walking, free-climbing, rappelling, the use of mountaineering installations—fixed ropes, roped bridges, haul lines, and traverses—and mountain medical evacuation. Unit mountain training would focus on physical conditioning and acclimatization while stressing land navigation in mountains, cold weather and mountain bivouacs, communications, patrolling, adjustment of supporting fires, and first aid. Selected personnel would undergo more rigorous and detailed mountaineering training conducted by the NWTC at Fort Greely, Alaska, and by the Mountain and Survival Skills Training Committee at Fort Carson, Colorado. To the basic military mountaineering skills, advanced mountaineering added relays and relay positions, use of climbing equipment including the placement of protective devices, roped or party climbing, direct aid climbing, anchors, construction of mountaineering installations, glacier movement, snow and ice climbing, mountain medical evacuation, and mountain and avalanche rescue techniques.[28]

Clothing and equipment for mountain operations were now to be found in the Common Table of Allowances (CTA) 50-900, but FM 90-6 did reflect an increased use of civilian techniques and technologies. Chippewa mountain boots, high-altitude double boots, and down parkas, pants, booties, and mittens were included as possible clothing items. Further, a number of individual mountain equipment items were not in the CTA but were in the military supply system. These included rock and ice piton sets, piton hammers, snap links, mountain ice axes, crampons, rope slings, and climbing ropes. Numerous commercial items were also suggested for use by soldiers and units: goggles, snow pickets, sleeping bags and pads, fuel containers, seat and chest climbing harnesses, snow saws, two-man tents, four-man high-altitude tents, stoves, plastic water bottles and cups, headlamps, and ice screws. In addition, assault climbers were to be trained to use jumars and chocks, in lieu of pitons.[29]

The most successful adoption of civilian mountaineering to military mountain operations in the 1980s was the extended cold weather clothing system (ECWCS). ECWCS resulted from three new technologies and one change to technique. W. L. Gore and Associates announced the first new technology: expanded polytetrafluoroethylene (ePTFE) in 1970. This material was 70 percent air and semipermeable, allowing for water vapor to escape while preventing water droplets from passing through. By 1977 outdoor companies were offering jackets for sale made of a layer of Gore-Tex, as ePTFE was trademarked, between two layers of nylon. The fourth edition of *Mountaineering* (1982) reported that "many [mountaineers] have found raingear made of Gore-Tex to be very satisfactory."[30]

Chouinard's Patagonia developed the other two pieces of technology and the technique to use them. Starting in 1976 Chouinard began to retail jackets made of synthetic pile, in "ugly tan and equally hideous powder blue," that insulated without absorbing moisture. Four years later Patagonia marketed long underwear tops and bottoms made of polypropylene, a synthetic fiber that not only absorbed no moisture but also wicked it away from the skin. Combining pile and polypropylene led Patagonia to alter the technique of layering, explained via essays in their catalogs. Previously layering had been based on wool, cotton, and down, materials that absorbed sweat and kept the mountaineer warm, but damp. Patagonia proposed a new system of layering based on keeping dry and comfortably cool. Polypropylene, or "polypro" as it was often called, worn as the base layer next to the skin, transported perspiration away. A middle layer of pile, increasingly referred to as "fleece," served for insulation, worn or removed as necessary, and an outer shell layer provided wind and water protection, for which Gore-Tex proved ideal.[31]

Natick Labs took this mountaineering technique and technologies and created ECWCS (pronounced "eck-wecks"), issued on a test basis in the early 1980s. The system consisted of twenty-three individual items to be used in combinations of five layers to meet a variety of cold weather conditions. The heart of the system was a base layer of polypro tops and bottoms, a midlayer of pile shirts and pants, and an outer layer of woodland camouflage Gore-Tex jackets and trousers. An additional layer of quilted nylon provided extra warmth when required, with a white layer for snow camouflage. Gloves and trigger finger mittens were still constructed with wool inserts and leather, sateen, and nylon shells. The standard-issue field cap, descendant of the ski cap of 1942, had earflaps and was supplemented by a balaclava hood. The Korean War–era cold weather boots of rubber, latex, and wool fleece were worn as part of ECWCS, the Type I–Black in temperatures down to −20°F and the Type II–White down to −60°F.[32]

By the mid-1980s the military not only had ECWCS for mountain operations; it had several other pieces of modernized equipment. There was a sleeping bag for temperatures down to 10°F and another good down to −50°F. Both used an insulated sleeping pad and were carried in a waterproof bag. The all-purpose lightweight individual carrying equipment (ALICE) external-frame rucksack came in a large size with a top flap for over white camouflage and pack cover, a large inside pocket that could hold a radio, and three upper outside pockets for food to be eaten while on the move. Three large external pockets held the day's rations and spare socks, a cap, and scarf, while skis could be carried in the tunnel behind the outermost two pockets, and the sleeping bag was in the bottom of the main compartment with spare clothes in the upper half. Army snowshoes were now constructed of a white magnesium frame laced with nylon-casted steel cables, forty-eight inches by twelve inches, and weighing just over three pounds. Bindings were of wide nylon webbing with buckles.[33] All this new doctrine and equipment was needed as there were new requirements in both the US Army and the Marine Corps for mountain warfare capabilities by the 1980s.

Marines, Norway, and Skis

In July 1978 the secretary of defense directed the Department of the Navy to plan for "the rapid reinforcement of Norway with an airlifted, brigade-sized force." This directive committed the USMC to the defense of Norway from a Soviet attack along a mountainous littoral in the depth of winter, when off-road mobility was at its best. The marines would thus have to learn of the imperatives of survival, mobility, and maneuver in the mountains in winter. Initial exercises in Norway in the late 1970s showed that the marines were barely able to survive the conditions, never mind fight in them, which caused the normally taciturn Norwegians to publicly question their utility.[34]

The Marine Corps responded to the requirement along two lines. The first was to update their doctrine, expanding the cold weather and mountain operations chapters in a 1978 manual on special operations, which meant nonstandard operations at the time, into the full-fledged Fleet Marine Force Manual (FMFM) 7-29 *Mountain Operations* in January 1980. The second was to alter the training and equipping of units to operate in Norway and other cold weather climates. A 1980 report, accepted by the commandant of the Marine Corps in February

1982, identified two primary requirements: training of a dedicated cold weather force and implementation of a winter infantry mobility program using skis.[35]

To conduct training the Marine Corps did have the Mountain Warfare Training Center, which had been reactivated in 1976 and expanded in 1981, to train four battalions a year in winter mountain operations and five in summer mountain operations, along with over five hundred marines as mountain leaders. Although the Marine Corps did make use of other bases in the northern tier of states, including Minnesota, Michigan, and New York, for cold weather training, the winter Sierra Nevada of the MWTC would be the primary predeployment training venue for the infantry battalions heading for Norway. In 1985, after several years of lackluster marine performance at NATO exercises in Norway, Col Harry W. Jenkins, commanding officer of the 2d Marine Regiment from 1984 to 1986, the ground combat element for the 4th Marine Amphibious Brigade, sent his 1st Battalion, 2nd Marines, to train for five weeks at the MWTC in January and February. Marine Aircraft Group 40, the brigade's air combat element, also deployed Marine Medium Helicopter Squadron 266 (HMM-266) to train at MWTC at the same time. This was followed by another three weeks of cold weather training afterward at Fort Drum with the rest of the brigade, immediately followed by the flight to Norway for Exercise Cold Winter 85.[36]

Colonel Jenkins aimed to train and equip a full battalion and regimental headquarters, over one thousand marines and sailors, on skis. Jenkins, who had served as an instructor at MWTC twenty years earlier, was an experienced mountaineer and cross-country skier. While their initial equipment was the army's wooden all-terrain skis with strap bindings, the Marine Corps looked to civilian backcountry technology and techniques of the time. The Marine Oversnow Mobility System, officially procured in 1991, consisted of skis, climbing skins, bindings, poles, boots, and snowshoes. The skis were European Åsnes Fjellski MT-65 cross-country skis, 200 cm long and 77 mm wide, constructed of composite birch and fiberglass, with steel edges, a tail groove for the included climbing skins, and white top sheets. The bindings were a version of the NATO 120 cable binding, which could also be used with the cold weather boot, and the ski poles had removable handles to allow them to become avalanche probes. The ski-march boots were leather telemark boots with a 75 mm square-tipped toe, worn with vapor barrier socks and gaiters, with an insulated waterproof overboot for extra warmth. For the final phase of an attack, marines removed their skis and put on assault snowshoes, militarized commercial models from Atlas, Tubbs, and Redfeather. And to use this system, marine ski instructors began their lessons with the basic athletic position—knees bent, hands forward—and the telemark position of one ski slightly forward and rear heel lifted. Marine combat skiing focused strongly on cross-country techniques—strides, glides, herringbone—before moving to turns, culminating with the telemark turn.[37]

The marines also had other equipment to ensure survival and mobility in the winter mountains of Norway. In 1981 Norway agreed to procure, store, and maintain a prepositioned equipment set for a Norwegian Air Landed Marine Expeditionary Brigade (NALMEB). This included leased Norwegian Bandvagn (BV) 202 and 206 amphibious, oversnow, tracked, articulated, all-terrain vehicles providing a much better option for ground transport, supply, and evacuation. Colonel Jenkins's 2nd Marines drew a wartime level of BVs for training in 1985. Marines also utilized several components of Natick Labs' cold weather clothing system, what would become ECWCS. In 1984, at Exercise Teamwork 84, some marines wore polypro base layers and Gore-Tex parkas and trousers, to enthusiastic reviews. In Colonel Jenkins's deployment the next year, most of the marines had the Gore-Tex shells, but the rest of the cold weather clothing was still layers of blends of cotton, wool, and nylon with rubber cold weather boots.[38]

Exercise Cold Winter 85 in the last week of March 1985, held 150 miles north of the Arctic Circle, showed that the marines not only had learned to survive and be mobile in the winter mountains, but they also had learned to maneuver. Marine helicopters flew ski-equipped marine infantry at night to landing zones on reverse slopes high in the mountains, concealed from enemy air defenses by the terrain and covered by the darkness. The marines then executed night ski marches, over the heights and down into the rear of the enemy positions, enveloping and encircling. Oversnow vehicles followed up these advances, bringing supplies and support forward, allowing the attacks to continue. Norwegian and Allied officers took notice of the marines' new winter mountain warfare expertise.[39]

The Marine Corps looked to follow up its success in Cold Winter 85 in the next year's Norway exercise, Anchor Express 86. Again, a regimental headquarters and an entire infantry battalion trained on skis at MWTC along with a helicopter squadron, followed by the entire brigade carrying out cold weather training in New York, before flying to Norway and drawing out equipment from the NALMEB supplies. Fully equipped with Gore-Tex and modern cross-country skis, the marines were ready to attack. But at this point, in early March 1986, the Marine Corps learned the critical difference between cold weather warfare and mountain warfare in winter: avalanches. The weather in northern Norway fluctuated between windy, cold, and snowing and warm and raining, which created an unstable snowpack. A resulting avalanche on March 5, 1986, caught a platoon of Norwegian combat engineers, burying them in up to eight feet of snow, ultimately killing sixteen of the thirty-one men. Given this loss of life and the ongoing dangers to the exercise force, Norway canceled Anchor Express 86.[40]

By 1987 the Marine Corps had responded to the requirement for mountain warfare in winter levied on it nearly ten years prior. As proposed by the 1980 study, it had learned how to train and equip forces to survive, be mobile, and maneuver under the winter conditions of coastal Norway. But it had not designated a dedicated cold weather force, as the study had also suggested. Instead the 2nd Marines became the de facto cold weather force. All but one of the nine infantry battalions that participated in Norway exercises between 1983 and 1990 were assigned to that regiment, and the parent 2nd Marine Division assigned any officer or staff noncommissioned officer with mountain, cold weather, or ski experience to the regiment. The round of equipping marines with ECWCS, training them on modern cross-country skis at MWTC, and then deploying for NATO exercises in Norway where they drew NALMEB equipment, particularly the oversnow vehicles, continued for the rest of the decade, with Exercise Cold Winter 89 being a "high water mark."[41]

The MWTC continued to refine Marine Corps mountain warfare capabilities, training several battalions a year in mountain operations and several winter and summer mountain leader and survival courses a year. In 1985 the center purchased mules and sent instructors off to Jackson, Wyoming, to attend a civilian outfitter course, reintroducing animal packing into the syllabus. The MWTC also began offering cliff assault courses for small boat raid companies assigned to the new "Special Operations Capable" Marine Expeditionary Units. This required assault climbers, typically six to eight, to establish lanes with fixed ropes or cable ladders up which a raid force could ascend a cliff and then descend upon withdrawal. Assault climbers were primarily trained and equipped with civilian technologies—hexes, nuts, stoppers, cams—and techniques.[42]

Army Mountain Units Return

As the Marine Corps learned to conduct mountain operations in winter during the 1980s, the army was returning mountain units to its order of battle, organized in the Vermont Army National Guard in September 1982 as part of an army regimental mountain concept plan. Initially consisting of just one company in April 1983, it was expanded to an entire battalion at the end of the year. The 3rd Battalion, 172nd Infantry (Mountain), was the army's only specifically organized, trained, and equipped unit for mountain and cold weather operations. Despite attempts to organize it as a standard infantry battalion in 1989, the "Mountain Battalion" retained several unique additions. The HQ and Headquarters Company had an organic platoon of mountain engineers, an air defense section with Stinger missiles, an enlarged medical platoon to run two aid stations, a support platoon with oversnow vehicles, BV-206s incorporated into the army as small unit support vehicles (SUSVs), and a larger scout/sniper platoon trained as assault climbers. Three mountain infantry rifle companies had one more mortar and three more machine guns than standard units, two SUSVs for oversnow logistic support, and a six-man scout/sniper section to carry out assault climber missions for the company. Further, each soldier in the companies had a full set of cold weather gear—ECWCS, once that system was fielded. They were issued snowshoes, open-purchased Kastinger ski boots, and Dynastar Yvette 180 skis with Silvretta plate alpine touring (AT) bindings.[43]

The battalion had to be proficient in several mountain skill tasks, including crossing vertical obstacles via fixed ropes, conducting cliff assaults, and oversnow mobility by skiing, snowshoeing, ice climbing, and skijoring behind SUSVs, along with survival in an arctic or alpine environment. Thus, in addition to the assault climbers, the leadership billets in the rifle companies required training as military mountaineers. To provide this training the Vermont Army National Guard established a Mountain Warfare School at Jericho, Vermont, on April 5, 1983, the first army mountain school since 1957. In recognition of that fact, the school adopted the ram's head of the old Mountain Warfare and Cold Weather Training Command as its Military Mountaineer badge. TRADOC approved the school's program of instruction, consisting of two-week summer and winter courses, in 1986. And in 1994 the army designated the Mountain Warfare School as the producer of Skill Qualification Identifier-E (SQI-E) "Military Mountaineer," marked by a ram's head. This action finally provided a way for the army to recognize and record qualified individuals, something the Mountain Training Center had asked for back in 1942.[44]

Drawing on several years of experience at the Jericho mountain school, the army vastly updated the 1976 version of TC 90-6-1 *Military Mountaineering* in 1989, quadrupling its size. There were now ten chapters covering terrain, climate, and acclimatization, climbing equipment, mountaineering techniques, building anchors, and roped climbing. Unit movement received a separate chapter, as did evacuations, fixed alpine paths, and glacier and snow operations, including avalanche rescue techniques using transceivers or beacons, probes, and shovels. The training chapter focused on training units in basic mountaineering, but more-advanced training for classes of fifty men was included as an appendix. A major change since 1976 was that the supply system now had Special Operations Forces Mountaineering Equipment kits, which were capable of outfitting twelve men with the latest equipment: ice hammers and ice screws, short (27-inch) ice aces, twelve-point crampons, locking and D-shaped carabiners (no longer called snap links), ascenders and figure-eight descenders, chocks, hexagons, wire stoppers, snow anchors, harnesses, and ropes, both kernmantle (sheath and core) and three-strand nylon. Following best civilian practices, the circular introduced Department of the Army Form 5752-R (May 1989) "Rope Log (Usage and History)." That military mountaineering was more in line with civilian practices was not surprising as the 1989 version of *Military Mountaineering* listed over forty civilian publications as references, likely reflecting those used by the mountain school instructors in Vermont starting back in 1983.[45]

In the same year the Vermont Army National Guard began operating its mountain school, the army began an initiative that would ultimately return the 10th Mountain Division to its rolls, although not as a mountain unit. In October the chief of staff of the army, Gen John Wickham, announced his decision to create new light infantry divisions. For the previous decade the army had focused on developing heavy mechanized and armored forces optimized to fight in Europe. Wickham saw a strategic need for forces that could rapidly deploy to other crisis areas via airlift. Five new light divisions, shorn of heavy equipment, heavy firepower, and large support units, would constitute such a force. Three light divisions would come from the reorganization of the active 7th and 25th Divisions and the National Guard 29th Division. Two more would be new divisions, to be numbered the 6th and the 10th.[46]

Although the announcement of the new 10th in August 1984 stated it would be designated as the 10th Mountain Division, army standardization took over and it was referred to as the 10th Infantry Division (Light). The National Association of the 10th Mountain Division enlisted the support of Senator Bob Dole, a veteran of the division's Italian battles. Senator Dole queried the secretary of the army: "Is there any reason it cannot be known as the '10th Mountain Division'" when reactivated? When the decision passed to General Wickham, he supported the change of designation; after all, the 101st Airborne Division was not a parachute unit. The army therefore redesignated the new division, reactivated on February 13, 1985, at Fort Drum, New York, as the 10th Mountain Division (Light Infantry) replete with the *Mountain* tab "in deference to unit history and soldier pride." However, the new 10th Mountain would have neither "the capability nor mission as a mountain division." In other words, it would be a mountain unit in name only.[47]

Army officers, however, soon questioned this lack of mountain units. One argument was that any rapidly deployable force had to be ready to fight in the terrain to which it might deploy. This readiness would require predeployment training in the most likely environments. Since nearly every contingency area for a potential US Army deployment contained mountain ranges, light divisions needed a training program to operate in mountainous terrain. Of the five light divisions, only the 6th Infantry Division (Light), taking advantage of its basing in Alaska and the presence of the Northern Warfare Training Center, conducted consistent mountain training. Per another line of reasoning, the US Army needed mountain infantry units in its force structure that "will be able to maneuver from an unexpected direction, taking maximum advantage of its firepower while at the same time protecting itself in order to fight and win in the mountains." The organizational, personnel, training, tactical, logistics, and sustainment requirements for mountain operations meant that mountain infantry, modeled on the Mountain Battalion of the Vermont Army National Guard, were needed in the active force.[48]

By 1990 mountain warfare had returned to the US Army and the Marine Corps. The military had been able to make some use of the immense changes to civilian mountaineering and skiing that occurred after 1950. This included the steady adoption of climbing technologies. Marines used the new back-country cross-country skiing, with metal-edged, composite skis and telemark techniques. New layering principles and materials, especially Gore-Tex, came into use with the ECWCS. Training in the use of these, however, took time. The Marine Corps learned to extensively train units for two months or more in the winter mountains, before deploying them to Norway. The army maintained a full-fledged mountain unit, the 3rd Battalion, 172nd Infantry (Mountain), albeit in the National Guard. But more importantly a Mountain Warfare School in Vermont joined the Alaska-based NWTC. The 10th Mountain Division was back, though as a light infantry division, not a mountain division. But the realization was growing that such divisions might have to fight in the mountains. But at this point the Cold War with the Soviet Union ended, and the impetus dropped out of the mountain warfare efforts. They would have to wait another decade for a true mountain warfare renaissance.

CHAPTER 9

MOUNTAIN WARFARE
RENAISSANCE, 1990–2020

While mountain and cold weather warfare was on the back burner for the US military throughout the 1990s, by the end of the decade time overcame inertia as the army realized that its mountain operations manual was nearly two decades old. In November 2000 it published a new *Mountain Operations* field manual, renumbered 3-97.6, describing "the tactics, techniques, and procedures that the United States (US) Army uses to fight in mountainous regions." The key characteristics commanders had to understand about mountainous terrain were "(1) the significant impact of severe environmental conditions on the capabilities of units and their equipment, and (2) the extreme difficulty of ground mobility." The manual characterized mountains into three levels of operational terrain. Level I was the bottoms of valleys and main lines of communications. Level II terrain was the ridges, slopes, and passes that overlooked the valleys, and Level III was the dominant terrain in the summit regions. Following larger doctrinal shifts, FM 3-97.6 included chapters on intelligence, command and control, firepower and protection of the force, maneuver, and logistics and combat service support, with appendixes on mountain illnesses and injuries and forecasting mountain weather. The manual also included historical perspectives on the importance of controlling key terrain from the Gallipoli Campaign in 1915, the use of mountaineering teams from the 10th Mountain Division's seizure of Riva Ridge in February 1945, and the importance of lines of communications from the Soviet campaign in Afghanistan in the 1980s.[1]

The 2000 *Mountain Operations* noted, with some understatement, "Army units do not routinely train for operations in mountainous terrain." It kept the information on preparation and training from the 1980 version, placing it in a section in Chapter 2, "Command and Control." Importantly, taking advantage of the return of mountain warfare schools to the military's education system, the

• Characteristics of the mountain environment (summer and winter). • Mountaineering safety. • Use, care, and packing of individual cold weather clothing and equipment. • Care and use of basic mountaineering equipment. • Mountain bivouac techniques. • Mountain communications. • Mountain travel and walking techniques. • Hazard recognition and route selection. • Mountain navigation. • Basic medical evacuation.	• Rope management and knots. • Natural anchors. • Familiarization with artificial anchors. • Belay and rappel techniques. • Use of fixed ropes (lines). • Rock climbing fundamentals. • Rope bridges and lowering systems. • Individual movement on snow and ice. • Mountain stream crossings (to include water survival techniques). • First aid for mountain illnesses and injuries.

Level 1, basic mountaineering tasks.

• Use specialized mountaineering equipment.
 • Perform multipitch climbing:
   _ Free climbing and aid climbing.
   _ Leading on class 4 and 5 terrain.
 • Conduct multipitch rappelling.
 • Establish and operate hauling systems.
 • Establish fixed ropes with intermediate anchors.
	• Move on moderate angle snow and ice.
	 • Establish evacuation systems and perform high-angle rescue.
	 • Perform avalanche hazard evaluation and rescue techniques.
	 • Be familiar with movement on glaciers.

Level 2, assault climber tasks.

• Recognizing and evaluating peculiar terrain, weather, and hazards. • Preparing route, movement, bivouac, and risk management plans for all conditions and elevation levels. • Using roped movement techniques on steep snow and ice. • Performing multipitch climbing on mixed terrain (rock, snow, and ice).	• Performing glacier travel and crevice rescue. • Establishing and operating technical high-angle, multipitch rescue and evacuation systems. • Using winter shelters and survival techniques. • Leading units over technically difficult, hazardous, or exposed terrain in both winter and summer conditions.

Level 3, mountaineer leader tasks.

Levels of Military Mountaineering, from DA, FM 3-97.61 (2002), appendix A.

2000 manual introduced the concept of three levels of military mountaineers. Level 1 was a basic mountaineer, graduate of a basic mountaineering course, trained in the fundamental travel and climbing skills necessary to move safely and efficiently in the mountains. A Level 2 military mountaineer was an assault climber, responsible for the rigging, use, and operation of rope systems and therefore trained in additional rope management skills, knots, belay, and rappelling techniques. Level 3 was a mountain leader who had all the skills of the other two levels and extensive practical experience in a variety of winter and summer mountain environments and conditions. Mountain leaders advised commanders on all aspects of mountain operations.[2]

Due to this emphasis on trained military mountaineers, many of the specifics on operating in the mountains, particularly the techniques and technologies for survival and mobility, were moved from *Mountain Operations* to a supporting field manual, 3-97.61 *Military Mountaineering,* which updated the 1989 TC and was published in 2002. The manual detailed the techniques soldiers and leaders needed to know to cope with mountainous terrain as a mountaineer tool kit. The tools then had to be applied to a variety of situations to include river crossings, glaciers, snow-covered mountains, ice climbing, rock climbing, and urban vertical environments. The manual also discussed basic and advanced techniques of acclimatization, illness and injury treatment, equipment, anchors, evacuation, movement on glaciers, and training.[3]

The 2002 mountaineering field manual continued to add civilian mountaineer practices to military mountaineering. The additions were quite deliberate as the manual listed only two references: Clyde Soles's 2000 publication, *Rock and Ice Gear: Equipment for the Vertical World,* and the sixth edition of *Freedom of the Hills,* published in 1997. *Military Mountaineering* (2002) included an "Avalanche Hazard Evaluation Checklist" developed by the Alaska Mountain Safety Center, taken from the sixth edition of *Freedom.* The manual called for Levels 2 and 3 mountaineers to use sticky-soled climbing shoes and plastic mountaineering boots with an outer plastic shell and inner insulating liner. Further military mountaineers would need gaiters, climbing helmets, and sunglasses to cover the entire eye socket, none of which were in the supply system. The manual also added spring-loaded camming devices to the protection systems available and emphasized the equalizing of any anchor. Military mountaineers now learned the rewoven or retraced figure-eight knot to secure the rope to the harness and the Münter hitch, a simple reversible hitch clipped into a carabiner to put friction on the line.[4] The adoption of civilian mountaineering techniques and technologies in the 2002 manual demonstrates that the conditions for a mountain warfare renaissance were in place by the start of the new millennium, as there now existed civilian skiing and mountaineering practices that were very adaptable to military requirements.

Light and Fast

During the last decades of the twentieth century, a small if active cohort of mountaineers and skiers adopted techniques and technologies focused on survival and mobility in the mountains. Backcountry skiing, defined by the first handbook to use the term as "skiing away from ski areas, off the beaten track, far from the crowd," arose from a synthesis of equipment and skills by 1980. Of particular importance was the development of alpine touring gear, ultimately referred to as "AT." AT boots were now similar to downhill ski boots but were more flexible and had lug soles. AT bindings were releasable frame bindings with a hinged toepiece for touring and locked down heel piece for skiing, imported from European manufacturers such as Ramer, Emery, Petzl, Salewa, and Silvretta. The Ramer Universal from 1980 was the first to offer a heel-lifter. AT skis were wider and shorter than cross-country or downhill skis. A downhill skier who preferred 205 cm skis would use a 190 cm or even 180 cm AT ski. Climbing skins were now synthetic mohair backed with an adhesive to stick to the ski, thereby doing away with buckles. AT equipment allowed for greater safety, by releasing the boot in a fall, and greater downhill control, since the skier could use short-radius parallel turns in steep and icy terrain.[5]

By the 1990s Nordic and alpine skiing techniques were converging in backcountry skiing. Telemark technologies caught up to AT with plastic double-boots and the return of cable bindings to create a stronger attachment to the ski, with heel-lifters, or "elevators." Skis slowly increased in width, with telemark skis ranging from 54 mm to 70 mm and AT skis from 70 mm to 90 mm. Greater use of ski crampons allowed for more secure climbing on crusty snow. Skiing techniques unified into just ascending and descending. Backcountry descending focused on strong, controlled turns such as the snowplow, stem christie, and a wide-stance parallel, usable by either telemark or alpine skiers.[6]

The trend of backcountry skiing convergence continued, and by the middle of the 2000s, the sport came to include not just ski touring, or moving through the mountains, but also ski mountaineering, ascending a steep mountain to ski down it. Backcountry skiers began to make greater use of mountaineering technologies, including those used by winter alpine climbers. While ski tourers had always preferred thin layers of clothing, they did use the common base-insulation-shell system. From around 2005 many adopted softshell fabrics that were windproof, breathable, and water-repellent, combining the insulation and base layers in drier climates. Skis were now "shaped" with side cuts that gave them a curved, hourglass figure, and the width of backcountry skis, regardless of the binding that was put on them, converged into the 70–90 mm range. Tech bindings, often called Dynafit after the brand that initially sold them in North America in 1993, joined AT frame bindings, now increasingly just one or two rails vice a solid plate. Tech bindings only had a toepiece, with spring-loaded pivot pins that inserted into fittings on the boot toe, and a heel piece with two spring-loaded rods that fit into a metal fitting on the boot heel. These were very strong, very light, and fully releasable bindings. Techniques continued to focus on uphill movement via skins and setting the skin track and on downhill skiing using "survival skiing techniques in the backcountry" with simple wedge and stem turns.[7] Backcountry skiing developed techniques and technologies that were multiuse, fusing Nordic skiing, alpine skiing, and mountaineering to move through the mountains in winter and were thus adaptable for military use.

Also adaptable to the military were backcountry skiing's avalanche risk mitigation practices necessary for survival. These practices required knowledge and gear that were developed in the last decades of twentieth century, often in response to the increased popularity of backcountry skiing. As the first backcountry skiing guidebook put it, "*avalanches are the most unique, the most insidious, and probably the biggest danger facing the adventurous backcountry skier.*" To manage this danger, early backcountry skiers and guidebook authors relied on several resources. The US Forest Service's Rocky Mountain Experiment Station in Fort Collins, Colorado, which took over avalanche research after the closure of the Alta station, published an updated version of the avalanche handbook in 1976. The *Avalanche Handbook* reflected nearly two decades of research into how weather, snowpack, and slope all combined to create potential avalanche conditions that could be forecasted by evaluating snowpack stability, based on standardized snow pit data. Rescue techniques now included search by electronic transceiver and specially trained avalanche dogs.[8]

Two Canadian avalanche researchers, David McClung and Peter Schaerer, wrote the second edition of *The Avalanche Handbook* in 1993, though Ed LaChapelle, the author of the 1961 version, wrote the foreword. McClung and Schaerer capitalized on the maturation of avalanche research and field operations during the 1980s, professionalized under the Canadian Avalanche Association and American Avalanche Association. The handbook expanded sections on snow metamorphism, snow shear strength, avalanche release mechanisms, avalanche motion and effects, and avalanche prediction. Backcountry travelers—skiers, mountaineers, snowmobilers, snowshoers—were intended as potential readers of the handbook. For this reason, a backcountry forecasting analysis was intentionally used as an illustrative example and a major section on terrain was included.[9]

With the improvement in avalanche techniques, there was also an increase in training, but curriculum and quality varied among avalanche education providers. In 1998 three mountain guides working in Crested Butte, Colorado, came together to create the American Institute for Avalanche Research and Education (AIARE). While the American Avalanche Association established guidelines for a recreational avalanche education, there was no recognized curriculum. AIARE thus developed avalanche courses with classroom and field components for backcountry travelers, incorporating "a decision-makers' approach to risk management." These courses emphasized researching the snowpack and weather, with emphasis on snow and meteorological science, before making a travel plan in order to avoid most avalanche hazards, again mainly on 30°–45° slopes. Rescue techniques were taught as was making weather and snowpack observations in the field, the latter by digging a pit. AIARE also created an instructor training program to maintain consistency.[10]

Avalanche rescue techniques and tools were also increasingly understood, available, and usable. In response to the greater number of winter backcountry travelers, The Mountaineers of Seattle reissued LaChapelle's 1961 *ABCs of Avalanche Safety* in 1978. It printed a second edition in 1985 and a third in 2003. The second and third editions introduced practical guidelines for snowpack stability evaluation. These maintained essentially the same steps for survivor rescue: don't panic, mark last seen point, make a quick search, search below last seen point, then make a thorough search before probing for the victim. If a victim was located, they had to be dug out and given care. The third edition, however, added the step "switch transceivers to receive," reflecting the increasing ubiquity of avalanche rescue technology.[11]

Around 1980 rescue equipment included ski poles that could fit together to make a long probe, at least one snow shovel per group, with a Lexan plastic model made by Life-Link being the most recommended, an avalanche cord, and an avalanche radio beacon, or transceiver. By this time the Skadi transceiver had been joined by the Pieps I and Echo models, all of which operated on 2.275 kHz. By the 1990s avalanche cords had fallen out of favor as they often got entangled in the brush when skiing below timberline, which was common in North America. Transceivers operated on the 457 kHz frequency from 1994, extending the search range from twenty meters to seventy meters, but this led to compatibility concerns. Several manufacturers, including Ortovox and Pieps, made beacons that worked simultaneously on both frequencies. In 1998 Backcountry Access of Boulder, Colorado, introduced the Tracker Digital Transceiving System beacon with a three-dimensional antenna and digital display of direction and distance to the victim, easing search efforts. Dedicated collapsible avalanche probes, locked together by a cord running down the length, replaced ski pole probes by the early 2000s. These probes joined aluminum avalanche shovels with sharper blades and removable, increasingly ergonomic, handles in backcountry skiers' packs.[12] This growth of avalanche risk management benefited not only backcountry skiers, but also mountaineers.

From 1980 climbing, which had essentially split off from mountaineering two decades earlier, itself split into sport and traditional. Sport climbing required clipping into preplaced bolts for protection at established locales or crags. It was also practiced at the climbing gyms that began springing up in urban areas from 1987. Traditional, or "trad," climbing required the climber to place their own protection, now almost exclusively removable chocks and cams. Both types of climbers used the sticky-soled climbing shoes that came onto the market in 1983. Yet many of the techniques and technologies of climbing did find their way back into mountaineering, as a small number of climbers began to venture into the high mountains for alpine ascents in the 1980s.[13]

In doing so, these "super-alpine climbers" took advantage of the evolution of the techniques and tools needed to climb snow and ice. Ice climbing long relied on using the ice axe to chop steps into the ice, while climbers ascended wearing crampons, protected by a rope attached to the ice first with ice pitons then, increasingly from the 1960s, with ice screws. By the 1970s American mountaineers were less likely to cut steps instead tended to rely on crampons alone, using the flat-footing technique for moderate slopes and front-pointing on steep to vertical slopes. Front-pointing made increased use of specialized ice tools, short-shafted hammers with a pick on one end. Using two ice tools while front-pointing, a climber could thus maintain three points of contact to the ice. During the 1980s Gore-Tex shells, synthetic fleece, plastic boots, rigid crampons, and curved-shaft ice tools that aided placement of the pick, all contributed to ice climbing progress. Some alpinists adapted ice climbing to climb on rock, snow, ice, frozen mud, and even moss, what was called "mixed climbing" by the end of the 1990s. All this, termed "the ice revolution" by mountaineering writer Andy Selters, allowed mountaineers to move off the rock and onto the ice in the high mountains, a much faster way to go, opening the way to "the most influential transformation in mountaineering history."[14]

This transformation was the development of alpine climbing, perhaps best captured in North America by Mark Twight and James Martin's *Extreme Alpinism: Climbing Light, Fast, & High*, published in 1999. Twight and Martin defined it as climbing in a dangerous alpine environment, "extreme" denoting serious consequences, where "the climber tackles the route, moving as swiftly as possible with the least equipment required" or "climbing the hardest routes with the least gear." In such dangerous environments "speed is safety." The mantra of "keep moving" and the concept of continual mobility permeated alpine climbing. Twight and Martin emphasized maintaining a good attitude, "a psychological state that allows and spurs you to reach a goal," based on both mental and physical training for endurance and strength.[15]

Extreme Alpinism argued for layering clothing on top of an "action layer" of a light hard shell or wind-resistant, breathable, softshell microfibers. But whatever the choice, "keep it light, light, light. Move, move, move." Equipment was discussed in terms of climbing techniques. When "going up "the game is to move quickly and safely, using every trick in the book to get up and off fast," to "take you up the route and back down again," along with "safety, communication, and bivouacs." The latter were best avoided by continuing to move, but if bivouacs had to be done then Twight argued: "Live with the minimum. Do not pursue comfort. Aim for success only." Descending when "exhausted, impatient" was "a time for discipline."[16] Ultimately, "light and fast" alpine climbing, with its emphasis on the bare minimum for survival and the imperative for mobility, was a form of mountaineering far more adaptable to military operations than any had been since World War II. Combining alpine climbing with backcountry skiing practices meant mountain warfare now had a set of civilian techniques and technologies it could call on, as it would beginning with the years following the US invasion of Afghanistan.

The Afghan Crucible

With the start of Operation Enduring Freedom in October 2001, the US military found itself having to conduct operations in mountainous terrain, particularly in the eastern regions of Afghanistan. When army units left the valley floors and moved up the ridges and onto the higher summits (Levels II and III operational terrain in doctrinal terms), as Maj Scott Safer reported, they "fought at a disadvantage because of poor decisions by unit leadership at all echelons of command. Had the unit leadership been trained in mountain warfare, their respective units would have been able to use mountainous terrain to their advantage." Safer found a "lack of understanding in soldier acclimatization, location of units in relation to operational levels of terrain, and the effect of mountainous terrain on operational reach while a unit is in enemy contact." Other analysis concluded that maneuver in Afghanistan required units that were well trained in mountain operations, acclimated to the altitude, and prepared for the cold weather.[17]

Soldiers and marines did have equipment for cold weather, even if they had not received much training or experience with it, but ECWCS, even its second generation, was developed for conventional operations in the low-elevation, wet, and cold climate of northern Europe, not for "go-fast" actions in the high-elevation, dry, cold, and windy conditions of the Hindu Kush. So, in early 2002 retired army ranger Rick Elder at Natick Labs, officially the Natick Soldier Systems Center, received a call from Special Forces Master Sgt Tony Pryor in Afghanistan that he was "freezing his ass off" and that Elder, head of the Special Projects Team, needed to do something about it. Elder assembled a team from across the Special Operations Forces, including SEAL Master Chief Scott Williams, and civilian outdoor communities. The team adopted Mark Twight's layering concepts and experiences. As it was nearly impossible to stay dry under exertion, it was best to dry quickly instead, utilizing body heat to push moisture out of clothing. The resulting system, the protective combat uniform (PCU), thus emphasized many light, synthetic layers on top of each other.[18]

To field the PCU quickly, ultimately in just one year, Elder, Williams, and Twight selected "commercial-off-the-shelf" (COTS) technologies, including Gore-Tex and Polartec's Power Grid technical fleece and synthetic Alpha active insulation. Further, Twight would introduce and explain the PCU in a video, emphasizing that PCU had to be tested to the user's physical needs and configured to their activity. The PCU consisted of fifteen pieces of clothing worn in combinations of seven levels. Level 1, the base layer, consisted of either short or long light, synthetic tops and bottoms. Level 2 comprised a thermal shirt and pants of gridded fleece, with Level 3 being just a long-sleeved fleece jacket for extra warmth. PCU Level 4 was a nylon wind shirt, to be worn inside the system to block wind and retain heat. Twight's greatest contribution was the use of silicon-encapsulated cotton softshell fabric, Nextec's Epic, for the Level 5 jacket and pants; Twight credited Scottish mountaineers with introducing him to softshell fabrics. Gore-Tex rain jacket and pants, with full side zips, made up Level 6, and Level 7 comprised Polartec Alpha high-loft jacket, pants, and vest, worn for maximum warmth.[19]

The levels were to be combined based on climatic conditions, mission requirements, and personal cold weather tolerance. For example, on an active mission in cold weather (30°F to 0°F), soldiers would wear Level 1 and/or Level 2 base layers and the Level 5 softshell. For a static mission in extreme cold (0°F to −50°F), they could use Level 2 base layers, the Level 3 fleece, the Level 5 softshell, and the Level 7 parka and pants. In developing the PCU, Elder, Williams, and Twight deployed to the special operations force a mountaineering clothing system that was more advanced than that used by the general mountaineering community. The *Freedom of the Hills* did not mention softshells until the 2010 edition. The rest of the army adapted the PCU as ECWCS Generation (Gen) III starting in 2008. That same year the Marine Corps began procurement of a PCU-inspired Mountain/Cold Weather Clothing System (M/CWCS) consisting of a Windpro fleece jacket, a lightweight hard-shell rainsuit, and an extreme cold weather jacket, trousers, and booties from the outdoor company Feathered Friends, called the "Happy Suit."[20]

Heavy use of commercial outdoor providers was key to the military's being able to field new mountain and cold weather clothing in a relatively short time. Many companies manufactured various pieces for the various levels of PCU, ECWCS Gen III, and M/CWCS. Some were relatively unknown small firms such as Beyond Clothing, Wild Things Gear, Propper, and Blackhawk. Others were industry heavyweights, including Arc'teryx, Outdoor Research, and Patagonia. These companies maintained distinct clothing lines for military use—Patagonia's Lost Arrow, Arc'teryx's Law Enforcement Armed Forces (LEAF), Outdoor Research Tactical's (now OR Pro)—manufactured in American factories as required by procurement law. This involvement in defense procurement, particularly on Patagonia's part, would ultimately raise the ire of the corporation's more progressive fans, who would question whether such companies really needed to sell to the military. The answer was yes, as LEAF and OR Pro remain whereas Lost Arrow spun off to become Forgeline, a separate company, before Chouinard gifted his shares of Patagonia to a trust in 2022.[21] Ultimately, the crucible of Afghanistan aligned civilian outdoor techniques and technologies along the requirements for military mountain operations to a level not seen since Bestor Robinson identified what the army really needed back in 1941. The stage was set for a renaissance in US mountain warfare.

Renaissance

The renaissance began with a burst of publications on mountain and cold weather warfare in professional journals and monographs. The first was in February 2002 on the need for specialized training and acclimatization at high altitudes, followed by a 2003 thesis on mountain warfare that stated, "Armies that train for mountain combat perform much better than those that do not."[22] The commandant of the US Army's Infantry School, Maj Gen Walter Wojdakowski, who grew up in Gunnison, Colorado (elevation 7,703 feet), dedicated a 2006 issue of *Infantry* to highlighting the demands of operations in the steep grades, rough terrain, thin air, and weather extremes found in the mountains, followed by another issue in 2008. The May–August 2010 *Infantry* also featured articles on historical mountain operations by India in the Himalayas and by the Soviet Union in Afghanistan. The army published translations of Soviet mountain articles on mountain warfare and several other pieces such as *Mountain Warfare and Other Lofty Problems* in 2011.[23] Marines also participated in the intellectual ferment with a 2005 Command and General Staff thesis, a 2006 report, and a 2008 School of Advanced Military Studies monograph.[24]

Doctrinal updates followed upon all this professional discussion. First, in January 2011, prompted by Afghanistan experiences, the army and the USMC jointly issued a *Cold Region Operations* publication, which replaced the 1968 cold weather and 1971 northern operations manuals after nearly four decades. *Cold Region Operations* firmly returned cold weather back under mountain warfare, as it was designed to work with the *Mountain Operations* and *Military Mountaineering* manuals. The *Cold Region* manual, which was an Army Tactics, Techniques, and Procedures (ATTP) publication and a Marine Corps Reference Publication (MCRP), provided a "conceptual framework . . . to conduct cold region operations," to "conduct movement and maneuver," and to "apply sustainment principles unique to cold regions." Such regions required the use of specialized clothing, such as the ECWCS Gen III, equipment, and procedures.[25]

A month later, and again clearly based on experiences in Afghanistan, the army released ATTP 3-21.50 *Infantry Small-Unit Mountain Operations*. ATTP 3-21.50 provided perspective and guidance on "infantry company missions in an operational environment characterized by high altitudes, rapidly changing climatic conditions, and rugged terrain." This required specialized mountaineering and cold weather skills and equipment. For the latter the army acquired three separate but integrated mountaineering kits for issue to replace the old Special Operations Forces Mountaineering kits. The High Angle Mountaineering Kit (HAMK) allowed a "minimally trained" infantry platoon of forty soldiers to move through steep terrain on established rope installations. The HAMK provided each soldier with a harness, two locking carabiners, two nonlocking carabiners, a belay device, accessory cords, and two webbing runners or slings, all commercially procured. Six ascenders or jumars and three 200 m static ropes were also included.[26]

To establish rope installations for soldiers to use the HAMK, the army procured an Assault Climber Team Kit (ACTK). This equipped three assault climbers, Level 2 advanced mountaineers, with a harness, three locking and three nonlocking carabiners, a belay device, and several webbing runners and accessory cords. The kit included four 60 m dynamic ropes and a 200 m static rope, along with six ascenders, a set of seven cams, a set of six chocks, and a set of four tricams, a chock/cam hybrid. Finally, a platoon of forty soldiers trained in operating in steep terrain covered by snow and ice used the Snow and Ice Mobility Kit (SIMK). Each soldier received an avalanche transceiver, crampons, ice axe, and snowshoes from the kit. The SIMK also included twenty avalanche shovels, twenty collapsible avalanche probes, eight snow anchors, three pairs of ice tools, and twenty ice screws. The army fielded the kits, along with a Squad Mountain Leader Kit for Special Operations mountain teams, starting in 2014 with each infantry brigade receiving fifteen HAMKs, eight ACTKs, and one SIMK.[27]

To provide the skills to use all these kits, *Infantry Small-Unit Mountain Operations* directed units to the Army Mountain Warfare School and Northern Warfare Training Center, which could train soldiers to Level 1 basic mountaineer and Level 2 advanced mountaineer (assault climber). However, the status of army Level 3 mountain leader, qualified to advise commanders on all aspects of mountain operations and serve as principal trainers, could only be attained by serving as an instructor at a military training center for mountain warfare or serving as a member of a Special Operations Forces mountain team, neither of which were particularly numerous. Also, to assist in training, the army reissued the 2002 *Military Mountaineering* manual, now labeled a training circular, in 2012. It was only slightly updated, but the reference to *Freedom of the Hills* was changed to the eighth edition, published in 2010. Ultimately TC 3-97.61 *Military Mountaineering* (2012) illustrates the adaptability of alpine-style mountaineering techniques to military uses as it remains current at the time of writing in 2024.[28]

In 2013 and 2014 the Marine Corps, building on *Cold Region Operations* (2011), updated its Cold War–era manuals. Marine Corps Warfighting Publication (MCWP) 3-35.1 *Mountain Warfare Operations* (February 28, 2014) was "a reference for all unit commanders and their staffs (trained or untrained in mountain warfare) and all leaders from the company level through regiment or brigade for use in operations that occur in mountainous terrain, snow, or cold weather." Critically the publication identified the types and numbers of military mountaineers recommended for a unit. Two tactical rope suspension technicians (TRSTs), Level 1 military mountaineers, were recommended per rifle squad. TRSTs were trained in the skills necessary to establish all rope systems used in tactical operations and could serve as a number two climber to a lead climber. *Mountain Warfare Operations* recommended two Level 2 assault climbers, a TRST-qualified marine who received additional training and was certified to lead climbs on vertical to near vertical terrain, per platoon with six TRSTs. The manual also recommended that one rifle platoon per company or one company per battalion be trained as scout skiers, with "the skill to negotiate arduous snow-covered and avalanche-prone terrain on skis and . . . skilled in basic tracking/countertracking, avalanche assessment, and avoidance."[29]

The lynchpin was the Level 3 mountain leader, a lieutenant, captain, or staff noncommissioned officer who had attended both the summer and winter mountain leader courses. The summer-trained mountain leader was a qualified TRST and an assault climber. The winter mountain leader was a scout skier and a certified military skier. The primary role of the mountain leader was to train, advise, and plan company and platoon dispersed operations in complex, compartmentalized terrain. The recommendation was for two mountain leaders per infantry company. The mountain cadre for a marine infantry battalion of around 750 personnel comprised 78 marines—54 TRSTs, 18 assault climbers, and 6 mountain leaders—plus up to 120 scout skiers for oversnow operations. Crucially, mountain leaders could conduct mountain training for their units and the Marine Corps provided a series of reference publications for their use.[30]

MCRP 3-35.1A *Small Unit Leader's Guide to Mountain Warfare Operations* (May 21, 2013) was "a reference for all Marine leaders (team through company) to use when conducting operations in mountainous terrain, snow, cold weather, and/or high altitude." Topics included "the environment, specialized clothing and equipment [including Black Diamond gaiters and Arc'teryx Bora 80 packs], weapons considerations, patrolling considerations, route selection and navigation, basic avalanche hazard assessment and mitigation, crossing streams or ice, snowshoeing, winter camouflage, logistics, fire support, helicopter operations, and casualty evacuation."[31]

MCRP 3-35.1B *Mountain Leader's Guide to Winter Operations* (July 11, 2013) contained "winter operations tactics, techniques, and procedures covering combat ski instruction and skills, crawls, firing positions, avalanche hazard assessment and mitigation, and crossing frozen waterways." It also covered snow tracking and deception, ski patrolling, and oversnow vehicle use. It maintained the Marine Corps' preference for Nordic ski techniques and telemark turns, along with Åsnes skis and cable bindings, but it did note that "Alpine touring (AT) skis are under development (along with an AT binding and mountaineering boot) for use by intelligence, surveillance, and reconnaissance (ISR) assets, mountain leaders, and scout skiers." This placed marine scout skiers about twenty years behind civilian backcountry skiers, but they were up to date in avalanche science as the first chapter covered "operations in avalanche-prone terrain" and included both avalanche decision and data observation checklists.[32]

MCRP 3-35.1C *Mountain Leader's Guide to Mountain Warfare Operations* (February 27, 2014) was "a reference for trained summer mountain leaders to use during operations in complex, compartmentalized, mountainous, high altitude, alpine, and glaciated terrain." It covered "terrain; weather; rope skills; rope systems; climbing; fixed ropes; rappelling; casualty evacuation; planning considerations across all six warfighting functions; chemical, biological, radiological, and nuclear considerations; glacier operations; and processes used to guide units through mountainous/alpine terrain." The publication described a mountaineering kit, the Marine Assault Climber's Kit (MACK), a comprehensive collection of climbing equipment to enable a reinforced rifle company of approximately two hundred marines to negotiate a three-hundred-foot cliff. The kit contained climbing equipment for four two-person climbing teams plus the additional items necessary for the rest of the company. The climbing teams used their equipment to conduct two-party climbs over vertical obstacles while establishing rope installations for the movement of the company. For steep earth and glaciers, the MACK had to be augmented with equipment open-purchased from commercial vendors, including eight ice tools, eight pairs of crampons, and twenty-four snow pickets. For a company to move across a glacier, at least 120 pairs of crampons and ice axes would have to be purchased.[33]

Two years after the Marine Corps, the army published its current mountain warfare and cold weather operations manual, Army Techniques Publication (ATP) 3-90.97, whose purpose was to serve as "the Army's doctrinal publication for operations in mountain warfare and cold weather operations," the current heir to the 1944 manuals developed at Camp Hale and Seneca Rocks. *Mountain Warfare and Cold Weather Operations* combined and superseded two previously separate manuals: *Mountain Operations* (2000) and *Cold Region Operations* (2011). This roughly doubled the size of the publication to ten chapters, covering the severe environmental conditions associated with the mountain and cold regions, the effects of mountains on intelligence operations, mountain operations, movement and maneuver in mountains, engineering, sustainment, military aviation support, indirect fires, and communications in mountainous and cold region environments.[34]

The last chapter covered training and the army's "Mountain Training Strategy." All personnel in a unit operating in the mountains or cold were to be trained to base orientation level with basic mobility skills and basic understanding of fundamentals; this training was to take four to five days and be carried out by a military mountain school or unit military mountaineer. One or two soldiers per platoon would complete a fifteen-day Level 1 Basic Military Mountaineer (SQI-E) course at a military mountain school to learn basic technical skills, as well as how to train soldiers in basic mobility and assist in planning operations. Two soldiers per battalion would attend a Level 2 Advanced Mountaineer (Assault Climber) course, again fifteen days at a mountain school, for advanced technical skills, to qualify to serve as an adviser to the battalion commander and battalion trainer and planner for mountain sustainment and operations. Finally, a brigade operating in the mountains would have one Level 3 master military mountaineer, a mountain leader (certified mountaineering instructor) who had served as a mountain school instructor. An army mountain leader had to possess advanced technical skills and more than two years' experience, in order to serve as the adviser to the brigade commander and be the brigade mountain trainer and planner. This meant that an army infantry battalion would have no more than twenty military mountaineers, about one-fourth what the Marine Corps held to be necessary, and no mountain leaders to conduct unit training. The army's mountain training strategy thus put a premium on military mountain schools.[35]

Military Mountain Schools

The renaissance in mountain warfare extended beyond gear, publications, and doctrine into training. The military's mountain schools grew, expanded, and matured. In 2003 the army redesignated the Vermont Army National Guard Mountain Warfare School as the US Army Mountain Warfare School (AMWS) and made it the executive agent for military mountaineering. To smooth individual mountain training progression, the army approved a single-phase Basic Military Mountaineer Course (BMMC) to earn a Skill Qualification Identifier-E "Military Mountaineer" and the ram's head device in 2008, in lieu of requiring both summer and winter phases. From 2005 the AMWS deployed instructors, who remained national guardsmen, to Afghanistan as trainers and subject matter experts. By 2010 the army also reincorporated the NWTC into its mountain training courses, although the NWTC generally did not accept students from units not assigned to Alaska.[36]

The BMMC (summer) lasted fourteen days at AMWS and fifteen at NWTC, trained soldiers in the skills essential to conduct mountain combat operations during any climatic conditions, focusing on survival and mobility skills. Only AMWS offered the BMMC (winter), again two weeks in length. The basic courses were prerequisites for two-week Advanced Military Mountaineer courses in both summer and winter. The advanced courses trained soldiers to Level 2 assault climber tasks. The NWTC only offered a summer assault climber course. The AMWS also offered a Rough Terrain Evacuation course, a seven-day Mountain Planner course for soldiers qualified as Mountain Leaders to learn the basic skills to plan, support, and execute operations in mountainous terrain, and a Mountain Rifleman course to train snipers and squad-designated marksmen a combination of mountain-specific skills and angle marksmanship fundamentals. The NWTC also provided a four-day Cold Weather Orientation course to familiarize commanders and staffs with planning and conducting cold weather and oversnow operations and a thirteen-day Cold Weather Leader course for squad and platoon leaders.[37]

The numbers that could be trained by these courses were limited. The class sizes were relatively small, no more than forty-eight to sixty students, to ensure a safe student to instructor ratio and owing to the limited facilities in both Vermont and Alaska. The courses were also challenging; from 1999 to

2008 the graduation rate for the Basic Military Mountaineer was 86 percent. In 2008 the AMWS trained 432 basic military mountaineers, though most of these were members of the new National Guard 86th Infantry Brigade Combat Team (Mountain), an expansion of the previous single mountain battalion. The school also only graduated twelve summer and twelve winter assault climbers. By the middle of the decade, by one account, the AMWS could offer only eight basic courses a year, with most of the student slots going to 86th Brigade members, and the NWTC could offer only three. As a result, the military mountain schools provided a maximum of 264 basic military mountaineers for the larger force. By 2020 the AMWS's faculty of fifty-six instructors, who as National Guard members could remain for years if not decades at the school, was offering ten to twelve basic courses a year and eight advanced courses. When combined with the specialty courses, the AMWS was now graduating roughly one thousand military mountaineers. The numbers were set to grow as AMWS began construction of a new 82,668-square-foot facility in 2020 with classrooms, billeting, and dining space for 174 students, and a four-story indoor climbing wall.[38] Yet all this training was for individuals, not units.

The Marine Corps, as it had been doing since the 1960s, offered individual training in military mountaineering at the Mountain Warfare Training Center in Bridgeport, California. Level 1 military mountaineers were trained in a fifteen-day Tactical Rope Suspension Technician course, with another fifteen days required for the Level 2 Assault Climber course. A six-week summer and six-week winter Mountain Leader course certified Level 3 military mountaineers. The MWTC also provided specialist courses. One company per battalion was recommended to undergo the two-week Scout Skier course, while four medical corpsmen per company were to take a twelve-day Mountain Medical Training course or Cold Weather Medical Training course. The center recommended that four marines per platoon attend an eighteen-day Animal Packing course, four per company a fifteen-day Mountain Communicator course, and four marines from the battalion scout sniper platoon a seventeen-day Mountain Scout Sniper course. There were also mountain courses for staff planners, machine gunners, and engineers in both winter and summer.[39]

The MWTC taught many of these courses to prepare entire units for collective training. Starting in 2009, the MWTC exploited training sites in the "greater Bridgeport" area, including Hawthorne Army Depot and Naval Air Station Fallon, Nevada, which were connected via corridors of Bureau of Land Management, Forest Service, and private land, to carry out Marine Air-Ground Task Force (MAGTF) exercises. The "Mountain Exercise" trained to the tasks specified in the *Mountain Warfare Operations Training and Readiness Manual*. This not only referenced USMC doctrine, but also civilian materials including alpine climbing and backcountry skiing guides published by The Mountaineers of Seattle and the AIARE student manuals. "Mountain Collective" training took place in three phases: preenvironmental training, environmental training, and unit exercise. Preenvironmental training lasted three to five days, preferably before a unit deployed to the MWTC, and was focused on individual tasks covering the mountain environment, hazards and mitigation, the use of specialized clothing and equipment, and historical lessons learned. Environmental training took place at the MWTC over seven to eleven days focusing on collective tasks and emphasizing initially survival, mobility, and fighting skills, then environmental considerations. It also included advanced mountain and oversnow mobility training, driver training, medical training, and animal packing. The MAGTF conducted the final unit exercise over four to five days testing the ability of the ground, air, and logistic elements to survive, be mobile, and maneuver "in complex, compartmentalized, mountainous terrain." Ultimately, the MWTC was able to train nearly 14,000 marines annually in both courses and exercises.[40]

Critical to the mountain training at the MWTC was the selection and preparation of mountain warfare instructors, of whom there were rarely more than one hundred. The basic currency of the MWIs was their mastery of civilian skiing and mountaineering skills. The initial entry requirement for an MWI was attendance at either the summer or winter Mountain Leader course and a series of instructor courses, which took eight to ten months. One in five instructors were Level 2 MWIs, who required another year or two to focus on rock climbing, oversnow mobility, and alpine movement. Rock climbing included training on multipitch vertical rock faces, high-tensioned rope systems, and specialized rescue techniques. Snow training involved traveling up to fifty kilometers in subarctic or arctic conditions, fully self-sufficient, and assessing avalanche hazards. Alpine training took instructors to elevations over 14,000 feet, across glaciated terrain, and into dangerous topography. A Level 3 MWI had to qualify as a civilian avalanche instructor, a military ski instructor, and lead a mountaineering expedition into high-consequence terrain away from the MWTC. Given the demands, rarely more than one or two MWIs at any time were Level 3s.[41]

By the end of the 2010s, the MWTC was facing some limitations. Only able to train one reinforced battalion at a time, but with limited live fire, it was not large enough for a true mountain exercise. Marine Sgt Maj Daniel E. Mangrum recommended establishing a mountain training area in Alaska to accommodate a marine expeditionary brigade–level exercise. Marine cold weather clothing was also found to have limitations, especially on the longer winter deployments to Norway that the Corps restarted mid-decade. Fundamentally, marines were unable to layer properly for conditions. The Marine Corps thus sought improvements to base layers and the Level 3 fleece layer and to acquire a softshell layer for better insulation and quick drying. And the skis, boots, and bindings it acquired in 1993 were obsolete.[42]

In 2018 the Marine Corps purchased a new Military Ski System (MSS) designed by Serket and made by Icelantic Skis in Denver, Colorado. The MSS consisted of one of three ski lengths and a binding. Most marines used the Scout, a short (143 cm or 156 cm), wide (105 mm) ski or snow trekker, a cross between skis and snowshoes that was easier to learn to use than skis and required less energy than snowshoes. Scout skiers used the Intrepid 9.7 in 155 cm, 162 cm, or 169 cm lengths, still shorter than civilian skis, and 97 mm underfoot. Mountain leaders and experienced skiers used the Intrepid 10.1 in more standard 171 cm, 178 cm, or 185 cm lengths and 101 mm wide. The bindings were Patrol ski bindings, a plate alpine touring binding, pivoting at the toe for the uphill and locking down at the heel for the downhill, but designed with snowboard binding elements to attach soft military boots, including cold weather mountain boots and vapor barrier boots.[43] In many ways the MSS was the best adaptation of civilian ski technology for military use.

By 2020 the mountain warfare renaissance that began in Afghanistan had matured in the US Army and Marine Corps. Professional intellectual interest in mountain and cold weather operations and training remained, with publications during the 2010s covering the tactical application of military mountaineering; a call for the army to designate active duty units to organize, train, and equip for mountain warfare; overcoming cold and altitude sickness; operating in extreme cold environments; and relations with foreign military mountain schools. The US Army Infantry School, the army's proponent for mountain and cold weather warfare, recently devoted the Winter 2022–23 issue of *Infantry* to mountain operations, past and future.[44] Doctrine was well established with the army's updating of ATTP 3-21.50 *Infantry Small-Unit Mountain and Cold Weather Operations* in 2020 to emphasize "the tactical application of techniques—non-prescriptive ways or methods used to perform missions, functions, or tasks—associated with the offense and defense during Infantry small-unit mountain operations."[45]

The military mountain schools were operating and about to get busier. At the start of 2023, the 10th Mountain Division changed its modified table of organization and equipment coding several hundred additional enlisted positions per brigade for the Special Qualification Identifier-E (Military Mountaineer). It was intended that this would once again, nearly eighty years on, focus the division on mountain and cold weather operations.[46] And the military was still making the best practicable use of civilian mountaineering techniques and technologies, procured from the outdoor industry. In February 2023 the army deployed an interim cold temperature and arctic protection system (CTAPS), as replacement for the ECWCS Gen III, to two brigades of the 11th Airborne Division in Alaska. The CTAPS consisted of five layers—base, insulation, softshell, hardshell, and extreme cold weather—with the base layers and hard shells purchased completely "off-the-shelf" from private-sector vendors, whose models met military specifications.[47] There is an understanding of mountain warfare, there is a doctrine for mountain warfare, there is training available in the techniques of mountain warfare, and there is technology available for mountain warfare, the latter two drawing heavily on civilian backcountry skiing and alpine climbing. What remains to be seen is if this potential mountain warfare capability will be retained by the armed forces in the coming decades.

Epilogue

We began with the 10th Mountain Division in World War II and ended with mountain warfare in the present day. From this journey we can detect a basic pattern to the US military's mountain warfare efforts over the last eight decades. The military generally understands the need to survive and be mobile in the mountains, to be able to maneuver in the mountains. But it does not keep up with the latest techniques and technologies resident in the civilian skiing and mountaineering communities. When the military has the requirement, or suspects it may have the requirement, to operate in the mountains, it must then reach out to civilian experts, adapting current practices and equipment to military needs. From this flows an intellectual engagement with mountain warfare, updated doctrine, and training opportunities. Eventually, however, after a decade or so, the requirement seems to fade, and the military's mountain warfare capabilities decline until the pattern repeats.

This pattern has happened in effect three times over the last eighty years: around 1940, 1970, and 2000. From the last go-round, as noted at the end of the previous chapter, the US military, especially the US Army and the Marine Corps, are decently prepared for mountain warfare. Doctrine is up to date, military mountain schools are in operation, the latest technology is being procured, techniques are current, and units realize the need to train in the mountains. The question before us at the end of this history is what is to be done to ensure this situation holds, that a degradation of mountain warfare does not ensue. For an answer we can turn to one of the most insightful pieces of the intellectual rebirth of US mountain warfare from the last cycle, authored by marine Lt Col Scott W. Pierce, while attending the army's School of Advanced Military Studies in 2008.

Pierce understood "that military operations in high mountains or intense cold require forces with specialized organization, training and equipment." However, he recognized that "the development of a dedicated specialized force is an inefficient and unrealistic goal for the U.S. military." Instead, Pierce recommended a "hedging strategy" to provide "a minimally acceptable 'off-the-shelf' capability." To oversee this Pierce proposed a "Department of Defense executive agent, a high level programs office to direct and coordinate doctrine, training and procurement, and the establishment of modern training centers … [and] organizing, training and equipping specialized units, designed to provide supported general purpose forces with MCW[Mountain Cold Weather]-specific expertise and equipment."[1] I can do little more than to endorse this assessment, as it is an accurate reflection of the reality that has confronted the pursuit of mountain warfare capabilities in the United States since before World War II.

Pierce saw the army, the Marine Corps, or US Special Operations Command as potential candidates for the executive agent for mountain warfare, here understood to include cold weather warfare. Headed by a general officer with a civilian senior executive service deputy and a robust staff for oversight and coordination, a mountain warfare office within the parent service's development command would coordinate and submit mountain warfare doctrine for approval, accredit mountain warfare training, establish certification standards for mountain warfare units, and propose Programs of Record for mountain warfare matériel, facilities, and training. The general officer would coordinate all the activities—funding, procurement, doctrine, training—leading to mountain warfare capabilities and serve as an advocate for mountain warfare to Congress, the Office of the Secretary of Defense, the Joint Staff, the Services, other government agencies, and allies and partners.[2]

From my perspective the lack of a higher-level oversight and coordination office inhibited the development of what became the 10th Mountain Division in World War II and contributed to the decline and fragmentation of mountain warfare capabilities after the war. I would also propose that a mountain warfare executive agent would also coordinate with the outdoor industry and professional organizations. In World War II this consisted of the National Ski Association, National Ski Patrol, and American Alpine Club, among others. Today this would include such organizations as the Outdoor Industry Association, the Professional Ski Instructors of America–American Association of Snowboard Instructors, the American Avalanche Association, and the American Mountain Guides Association (AMGA), along with major outdoor companies and retailers. A connected mountain warfare executive agent would give knowledgeable and interested civilian organizations an established line to the military, not requiring "cold calls" to the chief of staff of the army and the secretary of war as Minnie Dole and the AAC had to do in 1940. And it would give the military regular insight into current best practices and technological changes.

Pierce saw the mountain warfare executive agent as also establishing a system of mountain training centers in the required variety of terrain including high altitudes, glaciated terrain, intense cold, and deep persistent snow cover. Each center would be staffed with observer-controllers, an opposing force, and support and maintenance personnel. Of crucial importance would be each center's ability to issue all necessary mountain warfare equipment to training units. The mountain warfare training centers would have the ability, depending on terrain, to train a battalion or brigade, reinforced with aviation and sustainment units, and might serve as a base for similarly sized units.[3]

I would emphasize the ability to support aviation units, perhaps in partnership with nearby civilian airfields. The Colorado National Guard's High Altitude Army National Guard Training Site (HAATS) is at Eagle County Regional Airport in Gypsum, Colorado, with high elevation (6,547 feet), variable weather, and approaches and departures through mountainous terrain.[4]

While HAATS supports rotary wing aviation, a USAF fighter squadron able to generate a sortie at the airport, especially in winter, would be far better prepared. But a system of mountain training centers across a variety of terrain would answer some of the limitations of mountain warfare training experienced over the decades, as would the emphasis on training entire formed units in the mountains, rather than just training individuals in mountain skills.

Pierce called for personnel and units of "enablers" to be stationed at or nearby the training centers. These would be "specialized personnel and units that provide the requisite added capability to a general purpose organization to enable it to execute" mountain warfare missions. These enablers included "special operations, reconnaissance, engineer, medical, aviation, communications, mule packers, and specialized equipment maintainers." Enablers would not just support units in training, but also augment units in wartime to take them from mountain warfare–familiarized to mountain warfare–capable. Finally, the personnel management of such enablers would be critical, both to allow for the development of the specialized mountain skills and experiences necessary and to contribute back to the force by serving in outside training and operational billets.[5]

To Pierce's enablers I would add another crucial type: military mountain guides. A mountain warfare executive agent should develop a military mountain guide program from the three levels of military mountaineers in current doctrine. To ensure best practices, up-to-date techniques, and knowledge of current technologies, the executive agent should work with the AMGA. The AMGA trains guides in three disciplines—rock, alpine, and ski—at the apprentice, aspirant, and certified guide levels. Certification in all three disciplines totaling eighty-six days of courses and exams is required to become

an AMGA/International Federation of Mountain Guides Association mountain guide.[6]

The AMGA's training programs are adaptable to train military mountain
guides. Military mountain guides assigned to training centers would both
instruct and enable units, attached in numbers that are currently extant in
doctrine. The personnel for military mountain guides should be drawn not just
from the active-duty force, but also from the reserve component to include the
National Guard, Department of Defense civilian employees, and contracted
AMGA-certified guides. The fundamental challenge for mountain warfare
capability was and always will be maintaining knowledge within the military
of civilian-based mountaineering and skiing practices. A military mountain
guide program would help ensure that mountain warfare capability remains
in the military, thereby preventing or easing the next downward trend in the
pattern.

We began by defining mountain warfare as the ways and means military
forces overcome the retarding element mountains introduce into military
operations. To maneuver in the mountains, military forces have to be able to
survive and be mobile in the mountains. The techniques and technologies for
survival and mobility are best found in the civilian mountaineering and skiing
communities as it is they who do it every day. Forces must adapt outside equipment and skills to military use, an unfamiliar and somewhat uncomfortable
practice for militaries, particularly as civilian practices are seemingly ever-
changing. Procurement and individual instruction is not enough to ensure
mountain warfare capability. Entire units must be in the mountains, must
train regularly in the mountains in both winter and summer, which takes time,
perhaps more time than the armed forces want to allocate. Yet procurement,
instruction, and training must all be done for armies to survive, be mobile, and
maneuver in the mountains—and to carry out mountain warfare.

Notes

Abbreviations

AAC	American Alpine Club
AGF	Army Ground Forces
AIARE	American Institute for Avalanche Research and Education
AMGA	American Mountain Guides Association
AMWS	US Army Mountain Warfare School
ASF	Army Service Forces
ATP	Army Techniques Publication
ATTP	Army Tactics, Techniques, and Procedures
CMC	commandant of the Marine Corps
CO	commanding officer
CP	Carter Papers
DA	Department of the Army
Det	detachment
Div	division
DN	Department of the Navy
DP	Dole Papers
FM	field manual
FMFM	Fleet Marine Force Manual
ID	infantry division
Inf	infantry
LD	light division
MCRP	Marine Corps Reference Publication
MCSC	Marine Corps Systems Command
MCTP	Marine Corps Tactical Publication
MCWL	Marine Corps Warfighting Laboratory
MCWP	Marine Corps Warfighting Publication
MCWTC	Mountain and Cold Weather Training Command
MSR	Mountain and Winter Warfare School and Training Center Records
MSU	Metropolitan State University
MTC	Mountain Training Center
Mtn	mountain
MWTC	Mountain Warfare Training Center

MWWSTC   Mountain and Winter Warfare School and Training Center
Natick Labs   US Army Natick Laboratories
NSA   National Ski Association
NSP   National Ski Patrol
OQMG   Office of the Quartermaster General
SSD   Soldier Systems Daily
TC   training circular
T/E   table of equipment
TF   training film
TM   technical manual
TM#   training memorandum no.
TMD   10th Mountain Division Records
T/O   table of organization
USAHEC   US Army Heritage and Education Center
USFS   US Forest Service
WD   War Department

Prologue

1. All the recent histories of the 10th Mountain Division essentially follow this origin story: Whitlock and Bishop, *Soldiers on Skis*; Jenkins, *Last Ridge*; Shelton, *Climb to Conquer*; Isserman, *Winter Army*. Dole recounted his experience in print in Dole, *Adventures in Skiing*, 90–125. See Wilson, *Armies, Corps, Divisions*, 247, for the lineage of the 10th Mountain Division.
2. Clausewitz, *On War*, 417 (quote). The history of mountain warfare is an understudied topic. Schepe, *Mountain Warfare in Europe*; Gregory, *Mountain and Arctic Warfare*; Roulet, Engelberts, and Weck, *La guerre et la montagne*; Grau and Bartles, *Mountain Warfare*; Hinterstoisser, "Soldaten im Hochgebirge"; and Statiev, *At War's Summit*, are the main works in the field.
3. Lechner, Küpper, and Tannheimer, "Challenges of Military Health."

Chapter 1

1. Falls, "Mountain Troops of Europe," 27, 29, 30, 31, 34, 36, 37; Bates, *Love of Mountains*, 161–62 (quote p. 162).
2. Balck, *Development of Tactics*, 122–28 (quotes p. 123). See Schifferle, *America's School for War*, for the education of American officers between 1918 and 1939.
3. Vollmer, "Attack in Mountain Warfare"; Command and General Staff School, Mountain Warfare Map Exercise 46, 7 February 1936, and Map Exercise 48, 11 February 1936—both in US Army Heritage and Education Center (USAHEC); Pasdermadjian, "Mountain Warfare," 428.
4. War Department (WD), Field Manual (FM) 100-5 (1939): 222–27 (quote p. 222). Roll, *George Marshall*, is a recent biography.
5. Army Ground Forces (AGF), *Mountain and Winter Warfare*, 1–2. At this time in 1940 the General Staff consisted of the G-1 (Personnel), G-2 (Intelligence), G-3 (Operations and Training), G-4 (Supply), and War Plans Divisions. See Millett, "War Department," and Watson, *Chief of Staff*.
6. Nenye, Munter, and Wirtanen, *Finland at War*; Van Dyke, *Soviet Invasion of Finland*; Edwards, *Winter War*.

7. Dole, *Adventures in Skiing*, 90 (quote); Allen, *Culture and Sport of Skiing*, 216–30; Allen, *From Skisport to Skiing*, 89–173.

8. Dole, *Adventures in Skiing*, 57–76; Besser, *National Ski Patrol*, 25–40; Dole, *National Ski Patrol System Manual*.

9. Isserman, *Winter Army*, 2–4, 250; Conn and Fairchild, *Framework of Hemisphere Defense*, 5–7; Leonard, "War in the Snow?"; "Six Ways to Invade," *Life*, March 2, 1942, 16–20.

10. Shelton, *Climb to Conquer*, 12–13; Charles M. Dole to President Franklin D. Roosevelt, July 18, 1940, Dole Papers (DP), Box 9; Dole, *Adventures in Skiing*, 90–98; Burton, *Ski Troops*, 63–74. See Dole's correspondence from this period in DP, Boxes 7–9. He would recount the experience in a speech to the first postwar reunion: "Birth Pains of the 10th Mountain Division," DP, Box 8, reprinted in Baumgardner, *10th Mountain Division*, 2:49–53.

11. Dole, *Adventures in Skiing*, 99–102; Isserman, *Winter Army*, 11–13; Memorandum for Assistant Chief of Staff, G-3, September 12, 1940, in Bland, *Papers of George Marshall*, 2:303–4 (quotes); General George C. Marshall to Charles Minot Dole, November 9, 1940, DP, Box 7; Dole, *National Ski Patrol System Manual*, 75–81. Also see Simonson, *Creating the 10th Mountain Division*.

12. Grotelueschen, "Joint Planning for Global Warfare"; "Joint Army and Navy Basic War Plan—Rainbow No. 4," in Ross, *U.S. War Plans*, 34–54. For the crisis of 1940 see Conn and Fairchild, *Framework of Hemisphere Defense*, 30–67; and Neiberg, *When France Fell*.

13. AGF, *Mountain Training Center*, 1–6; AGF, *Mountain and Winter Warfare*, 2.

14. Shelton, *Climb to Conquer*, 20–22; AGF, *Mountain and Winter Warfare*, 3.

15. Bates, *Love of Mountains*, 164–67 (quote p. 165); "National Defence"; American Alpine Club (AAC), *Proceedings* (1938–41): 166–67; Jenkins, *Last Ridge*, 27–28.

16. Isserman, *Continental Divide*, 161–67.

17. Isserman, *Continental Divide*, 201–13; Taylor, *Pilgrims of the Vertical*, 1–90; Underhill, "Rope in Rock Work"; Maduschka, "Modern Rock Technique."

18. Roberts, *Last of His Kind*, 33–84; Isserman, *Continental Divide*, 235–51.

19. Bates, *Love of Mountains*, 167 (Bates discussed the equipment used on K2 on 102–4); AGF, *Mountain and Winter Warfare*, 3; Memorandum of a meeting called in New York to consider the letter of Colonel Harry L. Twaddle, Acting Assistant Chief of Staff, U.S. Army, dated 20 December 1940, 10th Mountain Division Records (TMD), Box 1.

20. McNeil, "Skiing and National Defense," 12, 14.

21. AGF, *Mountain Training Center*, 7; McNeil, "Skiing and National Defense," 14. For a description of military skiing at the time, see Firsoff, *Ski Track on the Battlefield*.

22. Robinson, "Camping on Snow"; Robinson, "Winter Warfare Leadership"; AGF, *Mountain Training Center*, 7–8; Brower, *Manual of Ski Mountaineering*, viii (quote)—unless otherwise noted, all citations are from the 1st ed.; Taylor, *Pilgrims of the Vertical*, 54–55.

23. McNeil, "Skiing and National Defense," 15–17; Shelton, *Climb to Conquer*, 21, 24; Brower, *Manual of Ski Mountaineering*, viii–ix.

24. Carter, "Mountain Intelligence." (Much of Carter's intelligence work can be found in Carter Papers (CP), Boxes 1 and 2.)

25. Bates, *Love of Mountains*, 167–81 (quote p. 167); Memo, AAC, 20 December 1940, TMD, Box 1. See the Wood Yukon Expedition Report, TMD, Box 1.

26. Bates, *Love of Mountains*, 183–89 (quote p. 189); House, "Mountain Equipment."

27. AGF, *Mountain and Winter Warfare*, 4.

28. Burton, *Ski Troops*, 68. For the importance of the division to the US Army, see Wilson, *Maneuver and Firepower*.

29. WD, FM 100-5 (1941): 213–33 (1st quote p. 213, emphasis in original); WD, FM 31-5 (1941): 1 (2nd quote).

30. AGF, *Mountain Training Center*, 9–10.

31. AGF, *Mountain Training Center*, 10–11 (quotes); Hays, *10th Mountain Division, 1942–1945*, vol. 5/I: 1–4; Sayen, *US Army Infantry Divisions*, 5–8.

32. Simonson, *Creating the 10th Mountain Division*, 13; AGF, *Mountain Training Center*, 10–11.

33. AGF, *Mountain Training Center*, 11.

34. Grotelueschen, "Joint Planning for Global Warfare," 16–19; "Joint Army and Navy Basic War Plan—Rainbow No. 5," in Ross, *U.S. War Plans*, 135–58.

35. Kirkpatrick, *Unknown Future*, 91–102.

36. "Ultimate Requirements Study Estimate of Army Ground Forces," September 1941, in Kirkpatrick, *Unknown Future*, 126–38.

37. Buchner, *Narvik*; McGilvray, *Narvik and the Allies*; WD, *German Campaign in Norway*, v (quote).

38. Cervi, *Hollow Legions*; Battistelli, *Balkans1940–41*; AGF, *Mountain Training Center*, 11 (quotes).

39. Dole, "Birth Pains of the 10th Mountain Division"; Dole to Marshall, July 30, 1941—both in DP, Box 7; National Ski Association (NSA), Resolution of the National Volunteer Defense Committee, October 8, 1941, DP, Box 7; Dole to Marshall, October 8, 1941, DP, Box 8; Simonson, *Creating the 10th Mountain Division*, 14–15; Whitlock and Bishop, *Soldiers on Skis*, 2–3.

40. AGF, *Mountain Training Center*, 12.

Chapter 2

1. Dole, *Adventures in Skiing*, 108 (quote); AAC, *Proceedings* (1938–41): 157–58; An application and letters are reproduced in Chabalko, *Forging the 10th Mountain Division*.

2. Simonson, *Creating the 10th Mountain Division*, 18–19; McLane, "Of Mules and Skis"; AGF, *Mountain Training Center*, 12.

3. AGF, *Mountain and Winter Warfare*; Hays, *10th Mountain Division*, 5/II: 23, 25.

4. Hays, *10th Mountain Division*, 5/II: 31–32, 37–38.

5. McLane, "Of Mules and Skis," 23–24; AGF, *Mountain Training Center*, 13; WD, FM 21-5 (1941), 68–70; WD, FM 22-5 (1941), 2; Rock Climbing Section and Ski Mountaineering Section of the Sierra Club Lessons, TMD, Box 3.

6. Outline of Proposed Course of Instruction for Mountain Troops at Fort Lewis, CP, Box 3; AGF, *Mountain Training Center*, 12 (quotes), 23.

7. WD, FM 100-5 (1941), 213–33 (quote p. 214); WD, FM 31-15 (1941), ii, 23–27, 51–53.

8. AGF, *Mountain Training Center*, 16; McLane, "Of Mules and Skis," 25–27; Woodward, quoted in Sanders, *Boys of Winter*, 62.

9. Lang, *Downhill Skiing*, 5 (quote); "Days of Innocence"; WD, Training Film (TF) 11-168 (1941); WD, FM 21-7 (1943), 99.

10. AGF, *Mountain Training Center*, 16, 21; McLane, "Of Mules and Skis," 27–28 (quote p. 28); Brower, *Manual of Ski Mountaineering*, 127–29; Military Ski Qualification Memo, 17 April 1942, TMD, Box 1; Skoog, *Written in the Snows*, 163–66.

11. AGF, *Mountain Training Center*, 21–22 (quote); Roberts and Masia, "10th Mountain Division Ski Technique"; Allen, *Culture and Sport of Skiing*, 261–62.

12. Chapter 5: "Military Ski Technique," *Experimental Ski Manual* (Mountain and Winter Warfare Board, Fort Lewis, WA), TMD, Box 1.

13. McLane, "Of Mules and Skis," 28, 31; AGF, *Mountain Training Center*, 21.

14. McLane, "Of Mules and Skis," 32; AGF, *Mountain Training Center*, 21–22.

15. AGF, *Mountain Training Center*, 26.

16. AGF, *Mountain Training Center*, 26 (quote); Eyerman, "Mountain Troops"; Henderson, *American Alpine Club's Handbook*; 87th Mountain (Mtn) Infantry (Inf) Mountaineering School Training Schedule, TMD, Box 1; Mountaineering School Examination Grades, TMD, Box 1; Jenkins, *Last Ridge*, 41–42.

17. AGF, *Mountain Training Center*, 23 (quote); McLane, "Of Mules and Skis," 33–34 (quote p. 33).

18. Essin, *Shavetails and Bell Sharps*, 156–57; WD, FM 25-5 (1939); Dole, *Adventures in Skiing*, 113.

19. AGF, *Mountain Training Center*, 26, 97; McLane, "Of Mules and Skis," 32–33; Eyerman, "Mountain Troops," 62–63; Hays, *10th Mountain Division*, 5/II: 1; Burton, *Ski Troops*, 121–22; Shelton, *Climb to Conquer*, 35.

20. AGF, *Mountain Training Center*, 96; McLane, "Of Mules and Skis," 24–25; Burton, *Ski Troops*, 93; Office of the Quartermaster General (OQMG), *Equipment for Special Forces*, 78–79.

21. OQMG, *Equipment for Special Forces*, 83–88, 114.

22. OQMG, *Equipment for Special Forces*, 90–95, 102–4, 106, 109–10; Pvt John L. Wigdahl to Company Commander, Report covering my use of U.S. Speed Wax and U.S. Wet and Corn Wax, 23 April 1942, TMD, Box 8; Myers, "Rucksack History."

23. WD, TF 7-677 (1942) WD, TF 7-678 (1942); WD, TF 7-679 (1942); WD, FM 21-7 (1943), 91.

24. WD, TF 7-680 (1942); WD, TF 7-681 (1942); WD, TF 7-682 (1942); WD, FM 21-7 (1943), 91.

25. OQMG, *Equipment for Special Forces*, 95–100, 116–17; Mount Rainier Test Expedition, 1942, TMD, Box 1; Shelton, *Climb to Conquer*, 39–42.

26. Bates, "Mt. McKinley 1942"; Bates, *Love of Mountains*, 189–205; Roberts, *Last of His Kind*, 205–11 (quote p. 206); OQMG, *Equipment for Special Forces*, 116–17. Also see Alaskan Test Expedition, 1942, TMD, Boxes 1 and 2.

27. OQMG, *Equipment for Special Forces*, 118–19.

28. AGF, *Mountain and Winter Warfare*, 3; AGF, *Mountain Training Center*, 27; Witte, *Camp Hale*, 34.

29. AGF, *Mountain Training Center*, 9; Henderson, *American Alpine Club's Handbook*, 150–51.

30. AGF, *Mountain Training Center*, 9–10, 27; Witte, *Camp Hale*, 34–42.

31. AGF, *Mountain and Winter Warfare*, 4n22; Burton, *Ski Troops*, 89–90; Report of Investigation by Board of Officers, Eight Corps Area, of Proposed Camp Site in

Pando, Colorado, Area, June 23, 1941, Metropolitan State University (MSU) Denver Camp Hale, 3 (quote).

32. AGF, *Mountain Training Center*, 27–29; Hays, *10th Mountain Division*, 5/I: i.

33. Witte, *Camp Hale*, 43–92; Camp Hale Colorado Completion Report (Job Number Pando T 1, 1942), MSU Denver Camp Hale.

34. Hays, *10th Mountain Division*, 5/I: i; AGF, *Mountain Training Center*, 29–31.

35. AGF, *Mountain Training Center*, 31.

36. AGF, *Mountain Training Center*, 34–35; National Ski Patrol (NSP), Bulletin #12, DP, Box 9.

37. AAC, *Proceedings* (1938–41): 174; AAC, *Proceedings* (1942–46): 2–4, 27–29; Stimson to Case, August 15, 1942; The Adjutant General to AAC, July 7, 1942; List of Men Recently Enlisted under Plan for Junior Officers for Mountain Units—all in AAC Library, courtesy of Christian Beckwith.

38. Matloff and Snell, *Strategic Planning*, 266–93; AGF, *Mobilization of the Ground Army*, 7–8; AGF, *Mountain Training Center*, 35–36.

39. AGF, *Mountain Training Center*, 35–38.

40. AGF, *Mountain Training Center*, 38, 53–54; Simonson, *Creating the 10th Mountain Division*, 19–20.

Chapter 3

1. Palmer, Wiley, and Keast, *Procurement and Training*, 433–55. For a recent study of this process that makes comparisons with British and German practices, see Lauer, *Forging the Anvil*.

2. Analysis of NSP System Recruiting for Mountain Troops, December 1941–July 1945, DP, Box 7; AGF, *Mountain Training Center*, 53–58; Chabalko, *Forging the 10th Mountain Division*, 36–27, 126.

3. AGF, *Mountain Training Center*, 53 (quotes), 58; Recruiting: correspondence sent/received, 1943, DP, Box 9.

4. Henderson, *American Alpine Club's Handbook*, 113–42; Brower, *Manual of Ski Mountaineering*, 9–24.

5. WD, Table of Equipment (T/E) 21 (1943), 8, 25–26; Army Service Forces (ASF), *Quartermaster Supply Catalog Section 1*, 5, 9–11, 21, 23; WD, TF 7-677. For illustrations and descriptions of the equipment, see Rottman, *US 10th Mountain Division*, esp. 25–30, 43–47. Sumner and Vauvillier, *French Army, 1939–45 (1)*, 20, notes that the French introduced a similar mountain uniform concept, based on layered shirts and sweaters worn under a hooded anorak, just before the start of World War II.

6. WD, T/E 21 (1943), 25–26; ASF, *Quartermaster Supply Catalog Section 1*, 14, 18–19; OQMG, *Equipment for Special Forces*, 87; WD, TF 7-677.

7. WD, T/E 21 (1943), 25–26, 28; ASF, *Quartermaster Supply Catalog Section 1*, 2–3; House, "Mountain Equipment," 56–58; Clothing and Equipment Arrangement, 87th Mt Inf Regt, Camp Hale, Colo, TMD, Box 8. Bramani founded the Vibram footwear company; see https://www.vibram.com/us/brand/br_history.html.

8. WD, T/E 21 (1943), 25, 27; ASF, *Quartermaster Supply Catalog Section 1*, 27; WD, TF 7-677.

9. WD, T/E 21 (1943), 26; ASF, *Quartermaster Supply Catalog Section 1*, 31–32; OQMG, *Equipment for Special Forces*, 103–5; WD, TF 7-677.

10. WD, T/E 21 (1943), 27; ASF, *Quartermaster Supply Catalog Section 1*, 30, 35; OQMG, *Equipment for Special Forces*, 105–9; House, "Mountain Equipment," 59–60.

11. OQMG, *Equipment for Special Forces*, 119–32.

12. AGF, *Mountain Training Center*, 41; Henderson, *American Alpine Club's Handbook*, 150–51; Burton, *Ski Troops*, 122–24.

13. AGF, *Mountain Training Center*, 46–48; Shelton, *Climb to Conquer*, 59–64.

14. AGF, *Mountain Training Center*, 46–49; OQMG, *Equipment for Special Forces*, 128–29; Burton, *Ski Troops*, 127–30.

15. AGF, *Mountain Training Center*, 47–48; Jenkins, *Last Ridge*, 60–61; Isserman, *Winter Army*, 60–63.

16. Dole to Col Ridgley Gaither, Observations Made at Camp Hale, Colorado, February 4–19, 1943, DP, Box 8 (quote); AGF, *Mountain Training Center*, 48; Shelton, *Climb to Conquer*, 64.

17. AGF, *Mountain Training Center*, 42–46, 50–51 (quotes p. 42); AGF, *Mountain and Winter Warfare*.

18. AGF, *Mountain Training Center*, 41, 63–64.

19. *Camp Hale Ski-Zette*, April 21 and 28, 1943; Isserman, *Winter Army*, 55–56; William W. Boddington Oral History, 10th Mountain Division Resource Center, Denver Public Library, OH203-2018-1421.

20. AGF, *Mountain Training Center*, 58–59 (quote p. 59); Ringholz, *On Belay!*, 154–55. For a study of early mountain guiding in the United States, see Coleman, "House of Leisure."

21. AGF, *Mountain Training Center*, 51, 79, 114–15 (quote p. 115); Black and Hampton, *10th Recon/MTG*.

22. AGF, *Mountain Training Center*, 112–15; Witte, *Camp Hale*, 160–63.

23. AGF, *Mountain Training Center*, 61–62 (quotes p. 61). For technician ratings in World War II, see Hogan, Wright, and Fisch, *Noncommissioned Officer Corps*, 38–39, 295–96.

24. Burton, *Ski Troops*, 135–36. The original 1942 mountain division table of organization called for 139 second lieutenants and 259 first lieutenants; see Hays, *10th Mountain Division*, 5/I: 3.

25. *Camp Hale Ski-Zette*, May 12 and 19, 1943; Burton, *Ski Troops*, 136–37.

26. Chapter 5: "Military Ski Technique," *Experimental Ski Manual* (Mountain and Winter Warfare Board, Fort Lewis, WA), TMD, Box 1; Chapter 11: "Military Skiing," *Proposed Manual for Mountain Troops* (Mountain Training Center, Camp Hale, CO, 1942), TMD, Box 2; WD, TF 11-168.

27. Harper, *Military Ski Manual*, 183–253; Holden, "Let's Get Together."

28. Woodward Interview; HQ Mountain Training Center (MTC), Ski School Schedule, TMD, Box 3; Roberts and Masia, "10th Mountain Division Ski Technique," 15 (quote).

29. HQ MTC, Ski School Schedule, TMD, Box 3; AGF, *Mountain Training Center*, 63; WD, TF 7-680.

30. HQ MTC, Ski School Schedule, TMD, Box 3; AGF, *Mountain Training Center*, 63; Roberts and Masia, "10th Mountain Division Ski Technique,"14.

31. WD, T/E 21 (1943), 27; ASF, *Quartermaster Supply Catalog Section 1*, 28–29; OQMG, *Equipment for Special Forces*, 90–94; WD, TF 11-168; WD, TF 7-677; WD, TF 7-680. My thanks to David J. Little of the Tenth Mountain Division Foundation for providing the ski widths.

32. WD, T/E 21 (1943), 27; *Quartermaster Supply Catalog Section 1*, 28, 30; OQMG, *Equipment for Special Forces*, 94–95; WD, TF 7-680; WD, TF 7-681; WD, TF 7-682.

33. AGF, *Mountain Training Center*, 35; *Camp Hale What's My Name?*, December 18, 1942; *Camp Hale Ski-Zette*, December 25, 1942; Isserman, *Winter Army*, 70–73.

34. AGF, *Mountain Training Center*, 42, 63; WD, T/E 21 (1943), 27; ASF, *Quartermaster Supply Catalog Section 1*, 29; OQMG, *Equipment for Special Forces*, 95; Snowshoe and Toboggan Technique, TMD, Box 3.

35. Young, *Mountain Craft*, 280 (quote); AGF, *Mountain Training Center*, 64.

36. Henderson, *American Alpine Club's Handbook*, 120; OQMG, *Equipment for Special Forces*, 96–97; House, "Mountain Equipment," 55–56.

37. Henderson, *American Alpine Club's Handbook*, 124–25; OQMG, *Equipment for Special Forces*, 100; House, "Mountain Equipment," 59; ASF, *Quartermaster Supply Catalog Section 1*, 2.

38. AGF, *Mountain Training Center*, 64, 70; Hays, *10th Mountain Division*, 5/II: 35–36; ASF, *Quartermaster Supply Catalog Section 1*, 30.

39. 87th Mountain Infantry Mountaineering School, TMD, Box 1; Henderson, *American Alpine Club's Handbook*, 40–54, 79–85; ASF, *Quartermaster Supply Catalog Section 1*, 30.

40. Manual (cold weather clothing), TMD, Box 2; Brower, *Manual of Ski Mountaineering*, 3–7; Ringholz, *On Belay!*, 156.

41. AGF, *Mountain Training Center*, 64, 108; WD, FM 20-15 (1944), 6–9; House, "Mountain Equipment," 59–60 (quote p. 59); WD, TF 8-1297.

42. AGF, *Mountain Training Center*, 64, 108; WD, FM 31-15 (1941), 35–37; Brower, *Manual of Ski Mountaineering*, 68–74; Henderson, *American Alpine Club's Handbook*, 94–99; Manual (cold weather clothing), TMD, Box 2; WD, TF 7-678; WD, TF 7-679.

43. AGF, *Mountain Training Center*, 42, 64, 73, 89; OQMG, *Equipment for Special Forces*, 112–14; Snowshoe and Toboggan Technique, TMD, Box 3; Doyle, *M29 Weasel*, 1–3.

44. Thompson, *White War*, 204; Chapter 10: "Snow Avalanches," *Proposed Manual for Mountain Troops* (Mountain Training Center, Camp Hale, CO, 1942), TMD, Box 2; Seligman, *Snow Structures and Ski Fields*; Brower, *Manual of Ski Mountaineering*, 79–98; Brower, *For Earth's Sake*, 88 (quote).

45. Chapter 10: "Snow Avalanches."

46. Chapter 10: "Snow Avalanches"; OQMG, *Equipment for Special Forces*, 115.

47. Chapter 10: "Snow Avalanches."

48. Chapter 10: "Snow Avalanches"; OQMG, *Equipment for Special Forces*, 115.

49. AGF, *Mountain Training Center*, 64; HQ MTC, Ski School Schedule, TMD, Box 3; Shelton, *Climb to Conquer*, 100–101, discusses avalanche encounters; Bruce Tremper's *Avalanche Essentials* is a recent work on avalanche danger and risk management.

50. AGF, *Mountain Training Center*, 53; Jenkins, *Last Ridge*, 82–97, 122 (quote); Medical Department, *Cold Injury, Ground Type*, 99.

Chapter 4

1. Hays, *10th Mountain Division*, 5/I: 2–4; AGF, Mountain Training Center, 31–32; AGF, Tenth Light Division (Alpine), 2.

2. Greenfield, Palmer, and Wiley, *Organization of Ground Combat Troops*, 339–47.

3. HQ 10th Light Division (LD), Camp Hale, CO, General Order No. 1, 15 July 1943, TMD, Box 5; HQ, 10th Infantry Division (ID), Camp Hale, CO, Training Memorandum No. (TM#) 17, 9 October 1943, TMD, Box 5; AGF, *Tenth Light Division (Alpine)*, 2; AGF, *Mountain Training Center*, 50; Isserman, *Winter Army*, 64.

4. Hays, *10th Mountain Division*, 5/I, 1–7; Wilson, *Maneuver and Firepower*, 188.

5. AGF, *Tenth Light Division (Alpine)*, 1; *Camp Hale Ski-Zette*, July 16, 1943; Putnam, *Green Cognac*, 66–67.

6. AGF, *Tenth Light Division (Alpine)*, 3–4.

7. AGF, *Tenth Light Division (Alpine)*, 3–4; AGF, *Mountain Training Center*, 115–19; Isserman, *Winter Army*, 82.

8. HQ 10th LD, Camp Hale, CO, TM#3, 26 July 1943, TMD, Box 5.

9. AGF, *Tenth Light Division (Alpine)*, 5–6; AGF, *Mountain and Winter Warfare*, 10fn47; Greenfield, Palmer, and Wiley, *Organization of Ground Combat Troops*, 347.

10. AGF, *Mountain Training Center*, 70; Mountain Combat Rock Climbing, TMD, Box 3; HQ 10th LD, TM#2, 21 July 1943, TMD, Box 5.

11. HQ 10th LD, TM#7, 28 August 1943, TMD, Box 5; AGF, *Tenth Light Division (Alpine)*, 6; House, "Mountain Equipment," 58 (quote).

12. OQMG, *Equipment for Special Forces*, 95–98 (quote p. 96); House, "Mountain Equipment," 58–59 (quote p. 59).

13. OQMG, *Equipment for Special Forces*, 98–100.

14. ASF, *Quartermaster Supply Catalog Section 1*, 30, 3; Henderson, *American Alpine Club's Handbook*, 11, 122–24.

15. AGF, *Mountain Training Center*, 58, 89; *Camp Hale Ski-Zette*, July 16, 1943; Brower, *For Earth's Sake*, 95; Shelton, *Climb to Conquer*, 85; Taylor, *Pilgrims of the Vertical*, 99.

16. HQ 10th LD, TM#7, 28 August 1943, TMD, Box 5; HQ MTC, Orientation Lecture, 26 August 1943, TMD, Box 3 (quotes).

17. HQ MTC, Check-list for Basic Climbing Schedule, 21 July 1943, TMD, Box 2; Mountain Combat Rock Climbing, TMD, Box 3; HQ MTC, Knots, 24 August 1943, TMD, Box 3.

18. Mountain Combat Rock Climbing, TMD, Box 3.

19. HQ MTC, Check-list for Basic Climbing Schedule, 21 July 1943, TMD, Box 2; Mountain Combat Rock Climbing, TMD, Box 3.

20. Mountain Combat Rock Climbing, TMD, Box 3.

21. HQ 10th LD, TM#7, 28 August 1943, TMD, Box 5; HQ MTC, Check-list for Basic Climbing Schedule, 21 July 1943, TMD, Box 2; Mountain Combat Rock Climbing, TMD, Box 3.

22. Mountain Walking, TMD, Box 3.

23. Mountain Walking, TMD, Box 3; Group Mountain Walking, TMD, Box 3; HQ MTC, Orientation Lecture, 26 August 1943, TMD, Box 3.

24. HQ MTC, Orientation Lecture, 26 August 1943, TMD, Box 3; HQ MTC, March Formation (Squad or more men), 26 August 1943, TMD, Box 3; WD, FM 7-10 (1942).

25. HQ MTC, March Formation (Squad or more men), 26 August 1943, TMD, Box 3; HQ MTC, Scouting and Patrolling, 26 August 1943, TMD, Box 3.

26. HQ 10th LD, TM#7, 28 August 1943, TMD, Box 5; Black and Hampton, *10th Recon/ MTG*, 18, 25; AGF, *Tenth Light Division (Alpine)*, 6; HQ MTC, Orientation Lecture, 26 August 1943, TMD, Box 3.

27. HQ MTC, Orientation Lecture, 26 August 1943, TMD, Box 3; Henderson, *American Alpine Club's Handbook*, 100–101, 131–33; OQMG, *Equipment for Special Forces*, 109–12; Maintenance Instruction Cooking Stove M-1942, TMD, Box 2; Hays, *10th Mountain Division*, 5/II, 35–36; Brower, *Manual of Ski Mountaineering*, 36.

28. Henderson, *American Alpine Club's Handbook*, 107–11; Brower, *Manual of Ski Mountaineering*, 35–36.

29. OQMG, *Development of Special Rations*, 64–73.

30. AGF, *Mountain Training Center*, 64; HQ MTC, Orientation Lecture, 26 August 1943, TMD, Box 3; Chapter 5: "Mountain Ration," *Proposed Manual for Mountain Troops* (Mountain Training Center, Camp Hale, CO, 1943), TMD, Box 3.

31. Chapter 5: "Mountain Ration."

32. HQ 10th LD, TM#7, 28 August 1943, TMD, Box 5; WD, TF 7-677.

33. HQ 10th LD, TM#7, 28 August 1943, TMD, Box 5; Black and Hampton, *10th Recon/ MTG*, 29–31; Shelton, *Climb to Conquer*, 83–86.

34. The unit sections—"The 90th in Action," "At Ease with the 86th," "With the 85th"—of the *Camp Hale Ski-Zette* during this time provide snapshots of the variety of unit training. Also see Isserman, *Winter Army*, 76–77, for descriptions of the battle courses and WD, FM 7-10 (1942), Appendix II, "Directives for Tactical Training of Rifle Company," for examples of tactical exercises and field maneuvers.

35. HQ 10th LD, TM#3, 26 July 1943, TMD, Box 5; Witte, *Camp Hale*, 130, 209; Holly, "Military Aerial Tramways."

36. HQ 10th LD, TM#5, 14 August 1943, TMD, Box 5; HQ MTC, Scouting and Patrolling, 26 August 1943, TMD, Box 3; HQ 10th LD, TM#9, 11 September 1943, TMD, Box 5; AGF, *Tenth Light Division (Alpine)*, 6.

37. HQ 10th LD, TM#12, 22 September 1943, TMD, Box 5 (quote); HQ 10th LD, TM#16, 6 October 1943, TMD, Box 5; AGF, *Tenth Light Division (Alpine)*, 7 (quote).

38. HQ 10th ID, TM#13, 11 October 1943, TMD, Box 5; HQ 10th ID, TM#13, 3 December 1943, TMD, Box 5.

39. *Camp Hale Ski-Zette*, December 24, 1943; McGrath, *Brigade*, 54–56; HQ 10th ID, TM#13, 11 October 1943, TMD, Box 5.

40. HQ 10th ID, TM#19, 11 October 1943, TMD, Box 5.

41. HQ 10th ID, TM#20, 20 October 1943, TMD, Box 5; AGF, *Tenth Light Division (Alpine)*, 7.

42. HQ 10th ID, TM#18, 11 October 1943, TMD, Box 5; WD, FM 7-10 (1942), Appendix II, para. 7a (quotes), para. 158.

43. HQ 10th ID, TM#23, 18 November 1943, TMD, Box 5; HQ 10th ID, TM#36, 22 December 1943, TMD, Box 5.

44. Jackman, "Tenth Mountain Division"; AGF, *Mountain Training Center*, 80; OQMG, *Equipment for Special Forces*, 129–32.

45. AGF, *Mountain Training Center*, 112; HQ MTG, Detachment (Det) Pine Camp, NY, Instructors Notes, 23 November 1943, TMD, Box 4.

46. AGF, *Mountain and Winter Warfare*, 9; AGF, *Mountain Training Center*, 80; Marzoli, "Best Substitute," 9.

47. AGF, *Mountain and Winter Warfare*, 9; Marzoli, "Best Substitute," 9–12.

48. AGF, *Mountain and Winter Warfare*, 9; Marzoli, "Best Substitute," 12–15.

49. Brower, *For Earth's Sake*, 95; Handbook for Assault Climbers, TMD, Box 2; Marzoli, "Best Substitute," 16–17.

50. Marzoli, "Best Substitute," 18–20 (1st quote p. 20); Brower, *For Earth's Sake*, 95 (2nd quote).

51. Marzoli, "Best Substitute," 20–21; History of the 2662 Mountain Warfare Det, TMD, Box 4.

52. History of the 2662 Mountain Warfare Det, TMD, Box 4; Granger, "British Army Cold Weather," 84; Bates, "Pay-Off in Winter Training."

53. AGF, *Tenth Light Division (Alpine)*, 7.

Chapter 5

1. 10th Reconnaissance Troop to Commanding Officer (CO), 15th HQ Det, Special Troops, Second Army, Report of Three-Day Mountaineering Trip of 10th Reconnaissance Troop and Mountain Training Group, 28–30 December 1943, 6 January 1944, TMD, Box 9; *Camp Hale Ski-Zette*, January 7, 1944.

2. 10th Reconnaissance Troop to CO; *Camp Hale Ski-Zette*, January 7, 1944.

3. 10th Reconnaissance Troop to CO; *Camp Hale Ski-Zette*, January 7, 1944.

4. 10th Reconnaissance Troop to CO; *Camp Hale Ski-Zette*, January 7, 1944.

5. Black and Hampton, *10th Recon/MTG*, 69–79; *Camp Hale Ski-Zette*, January 21, 1944.

6. Patrol reports, January 1944, TMD, Box 9.

7. HQ 10th ID, TM#22, 10 November 1943, TMD, Box 5; AGF, *Mountain Training Center*, 94.

8. HQ 10th ID, TM#22, 10 November 1943; HQ 10th LD, Training Memoranda, 1944, TMD, Box 5; AGF, *Role of Army Ground Forces*, 79–83.

9. HQ 10th ID, TM#22, 10 November 1943; HQ 10th ID, TM#23, 18 November 1943; HQ 10th ID, TM#34, 17 December 1943—all in TMD, Box 5; HQ 15th Det, Sp Tps, 2d Army, Instructors Guide: Individual Instruction: 1st Week, 21 December 1943; HQ 10th ID, Instructors Guide: Individual Instruction: 2nd Week, 12 November 1943—both in TMD, Box 3.

10. HQ 10th ID, Instructors Guide: Individual Instruction: 3rd Week, 13 November 1943; HQ 10th ID, Instructors Guide: Individual Instruction: 4th Week, 15 November 1943—both in TMD, Box 3.

11. *Camp Hale Ski-Zette*, January 7, January 21, and January 28, 1944; Elkins, "GI Skiing."

12. *Camp Hale Ski-Zette*, March 3, 1944; Black and Hampton, *10th Recon/MTG*, 48–58; Rocker, "Trooper Traverse—1944."

13. *Camp Hale Ski-Zette*, March 3, 1944; Black and Hampton, *10th Recon/MTG*, 48–58; Rocker, "Trooper Traverse—1944."

14. *Camp Hale Ski-Zette*, March 3, 1944; Black and Hampton, *10th Recon/MTG*, 48–58; Rocker, "Trooper Traverse—1944." See Lou Dawson, "Trooper Traverse Colorado," for more route descriptions and materials.

15. *Camp Hale Ski-Zette*, March 17, 1944.

16. Palmer, Wiley, and Keast, *Procurement and Training*, 447 (quote); AGF, *10th Light Division (Alpine)*, 7–8; HQ 10th LD, Training Memoranda, 1944, TMD, Box 5.

17. AGF, *10th Light Division (Alpine)*, 4–5; AGF, *Mountain Training Center*, 115; Hays, *10th Mountain Division*, 5/I: 3, 7.

18. HQ 10th LD, Training Memoranda, 1944, TMD, Box 5; AGF, *10th Light Division (Alpine)*, 7; *Camp Hale Ski-Zette*, February 25, 1944; WD, FM 7-20 (1943); WD, FM 7-40 (1942).

19. HQ 10th LD, TM#1, 19 July 1943, TMD, Box 5; WD, FM 7-20 (1943), 190–218 (quote 193).

20. HQ 10th LD, TM#1, 19 July 1943, TMD, Box 5; WD, FM 7-20 (1943), 96–116 (quote 101); Palmer, Wiley, and Keast, *Procurement and Training*, 451; Gibson, "O.K. Fellows."

21. HQ 10th LD, TM#1, 19 July 1943, TMD, Box 5; Witte, *Camp Hale*, 17; *Camp Hale Ski-Zette*, February 25, 1944.

22. *Camp Hale Ski-Zette*, March 24, 1944; HQ 10th LD, Training Memoranda, 1944, TMD, Box 5; Chapter 10: "Snow Avalanches," *Proposed Manual for Mountain Troops* (Mountain Training Center, Camp Hale, CO, 1942), TMD, Box 2; Supplement to Troop History, 10th Reconnaissance Troop (Mech), 22 March 1944, TMD, Box 9; Check List for Small Unit Leaders, 23 March 1944, TMD, Box 4.

23. Check List for Small Unit Leaders, 23 March 1944, TMD, Box 4; Radio Broadcast on WSYR, DP, Box 9; Dusenbery, *Ski the High Trail*, 21.

24. Proposed Manual for Firing on Skis, Camp Hale, CO, 3 February 1944, TMD, Box 3; Check List for Small Unit Leaders, 23 March 1944, TMD, Box 4; Chapter 5: "Mountain Ration," *Proposed Manual for Mountain Troops* (Mountain Training Center, Camp Hale, CO, 1943), TMD, Box 3; Dusenbery, *Ski the High Trail*, 91; Jenkins, *Last Ridge*, 111.

25. *Camp Hale Ski-Zette*, January 21 and January 28, 1944; Jenkins, *Last Ridge*, 105–6; HQ 10th ID, Camp Hale, CO, Memorandum #19, 2 March 1944, courtesy Tenth Mountain Division Living History Display Group, Inc.

26. Some Points Concerning Winter Warfare and Mountain Tactics (Maneuver Director Headquarters, XVI Corps, Camp Hale, 6 April 1944), TMD, Box 3.

27. Some Points Concerning Winter Warfare.

28. Some Points Concerning Winter Warfare (emphasis in original).

29. AGF, *10th Light Division (Alpine)*, 7; *Camp Hale Ski-Zette*, March 24 (quotes) and March 31, 1944. Casualties during "D" Series, in DP, Box 7, lists "Strength at the beginning of Exercises" as 9,296. Of these, 623 were "In hospital and quarters." The 10th Division's "Effective Strength" for the D-Series was thus 8,673.

30. WD, FM 100-5 (1941), 69–96 (quote p. 69), 217–19, 228; *Camp Hale Ski-Zette*, April 7, 1944 (quote).

31. *Camp Hale Ski-Zette*, April 7, 1944; WD, FM 100-5 (1941), 137–64, 222–25, 231–32; Dusenbery, *Ski the High Trail*, 14.

32. *Camp Hale Ski-Zette*, April 21, 1944; WD, FM 100-5 (1941), 97, 219–20 (quote p. 219); Dusenbery, *Ski the High Trail*, 15–81; Map of Vail Pass during D Series, TMD, Box 7.

33. *Camp Hale Ski-Zette*, April 21, 1944; Dusenbery, *Ski the High Trail*, 91–154.

34. *Camp Hale Ski-Zette*, April 21, 1944; AGF, *Mountain and Winter Warfare*, 11; Dusenbery, *Ski the High Trail*, 155.

35. *Camp Hale Ski-Zette*, April 21, 1944; WD, FM 100-5 (1941), 165 (quote); Putnam, *Green Cognac*, 70–71.

36. Casualties during "D" Series, DP, Box 7; Dusenbery, *Ski the High Trail*, 83–90. The brutal conditions of the D-series feature in all the studies of the 10th Mountain Division; see Burton, *Ski Troops*, 137–38; Whitlock and Bishop, *Soldiers on Skis*, 42–43; Jenkins, *Last Ridge*, 116–20; Shelton, *Climb to Conquer*, 104–6; Isserman, *Winter Army*, 109–15; Witte, *Camp Hale*, 175–80.

37. Isserman, *Winter Army*, 109–11 (quote p. 109); Witte, *Camp Hale*, 181; Mansoor, *GI Offensive in* Europe, 28–29, 60, 68; *Camp Hale Ski-Zette*, May 12, 1944 (quotes). Culin took command of the 87th Infantry Division in May 1944.

38. AGF, *10th Light Division (Alpine)*, 1 (quote), 7; *Camp Hale Ski-Zette*, May 19, 1944.

39. Greenfield, Palmer, and Wiley, *Organization of Ground Combat Troops*, 347–48; Wilson, *Maneuver and Firepower*, 188–90; AGF, *10th Light Division (Alpine)*, 8–10.

40. AGF, *10th Light Division (Alpine)*, 9–10 (quote p. 9). For radios see Thompson, et al., *Signal Corps*, 58–78.

41. AGF, *10th Light Division (Alpine)*, 9–10.

42. AGF, *Mountain and Winter Warfare*, 11–12.

43. HQ 10th LD, Training Memoranda, 1944, TMD, Box 5; *Camp Hale Ski-Zette*, April 28, June 9, June 2, 1944.

44. HQ 10th LD, Training Memoranda, 1944, TMD, Box 5; HQ 10th ID, TM#29, Advanced Skiing, 29 April 1944, TMD, Box 3; Gibson, "On Cooper Hill."

45. HQ 10th LD, Training Memoranda, 1944, TMD, Box 5; *Camp Hale Ski-Zette*, May 26, June 9, June 23, 1944; Witte, *Camp Hale*, 181; Letter to Dole from 87th Trooper, May 17, 1944, DP, Box 9.

46. Dole, "The President and Aide Go Travelling—II;" Dole to Marshall, April 11, 1944; Maj Max Besler to Dole, April 15, 1944—both in DP, Box 8; Dole, *Adventures in Skiing*, 146–47; Jenkins, *Last Ridge*, 121.

47. Dole to Marshall (draft), c. April 1945, DP, Box 8; Dole, *Adventures in Skiing*, 147–48; Jenkins, *Last Ridge*, 122.

48. Burton, *Ski Troops*, 147; Whitlock and Bishop, *Soldiers on Skis*, 54; Clark, *Calculated Risk*, 236–37, 417 (quote). For the Fifth Army's mountain fighting see Blumenson, *Salerno to Cassino*; and Fisher, *Cassino to the Alps*. For the FSSF see David, *The Force*; and for the French see Gaujac, *Le Corps Expeditionnaire Français*.

49. AGF, *Mountain and Winter Warfare*, 12; Palmer, Wiley, and Keast, *Procurement and Training*, 470–71; Ringholz, *On Belay!*, 157–58; *Camp Swift Baron*, July 5, 1944; HQ 10th LD, Training Memoranda, 1944, TMD, Box 5.

50. AGF, *Mountain and Winter Warfare*, 12; Hays, *10th Mountain Division*, 5/II: 3, 24.

51. AGF, *Mountain and Winter Warfare*, 12; Hays, *10th Mountain Division*, 5/I: 7, 9–11, 26–27, 32, 53, 89–92; 5/II: 33–34, 44, 51, 90.

52. Rottman, *US 10th Mountain Division*, 21–24; Hays, *10th Mountain Division*, 5/I: 9–11; AGF, *Mountain and Winter Warfare*, 12.

53. HQ 10th LD, Training Memoranda, 1944, TMD, Box 5; HQ 3rd Bn, 85th Inf, Animal Management Instruction, 28 October 1944, TMD, Box 6; WD, FM 25-7 (1944).

54. HQ 10th LD, General Order 37, 6 November 1944, TMD, Box 5; Rottman, *US 10th Mountain Division*, 21, 46.

55. AGF, *Mountain and Winter Warfare*, 12; HQ 10th LD, General Order 37, 6 November 1944, TMD, Box 5; 10th Mtn Division (Div), *Combat History*, 1. Duff joined the division as ADC at the end of May 1944. See *Camp Hale Ski-Zette*, May 26, 1944.

56. 10th Mtn Div, *Combat History*, 1; Dole, *Adventures in Skiing*, 126, 149–50 (quotes); Richard Thruelsen, "The 10th Caught It All at Once," *Saturday Evening Post*, December 8, 1945; Burton, *Ski Troops*, 139–40; Jenkins, *Last Ridge*, 126–27.

57. 10th Mtn Div, *Combat History*, 1–4.

58. Letter to Dole, December 6, 1944, DP, Box 8.
59. Dole to Marshall, December 8, 1944, DP, Box 8; Burton, *Ski Troops*, 141 (quotes).

Chapter 6

1. 10th Mtn Div, *Combat History*, 3–5.
2. AGF, *Mountain Training Center*, 91–93. Some of the *Proposed Manual for Mountain Troops* chapters can be found in TMD, Boxes 2 and 3.
3. AGF, *Mountain Training Center*, 93.
4. AGF, *Mountain Training Center*, 94.
5. Carter, "Mountain Intelligence," 71–72; German Training Regulations for Mountain Troops, *The Mountain Officer's Manual*, Mountain Warfare, CP, Box 2; WD, *German Ski Training and Tactics*; WD, *German Mountain Warfare*; and WD, *German Mountain Troops*.
6. WD, FM 100-5 (1944), 252, 254, 256, 258, 273.
7. WD, FM 100-5 (1941), 219–20; WD, FM 100-5 (1944), 260–61.
8. Brower, *For Earth's Sake*, 98–99. Brower notes that the "printed books reached the mountain troops just before they pushed off for the Po Valley"—i.e., in mid-April 1945.
9. WD, FM 70-10 (1944), 56–62, 144–90, 199–223; WD, FM 70-15 (1944), 5–40, 68–75; WD, Technical Manual (TM) 10-275 (1944), 1–55.
10. WD, FM 70-10 (1944), 5–9; WD, FM 70-15 (1944), 41–46, 104–20, 160–253; WD, TM 10-275 (1944), 64–78.
11. WD, FM 70-10 (1944), 63–140, 191–99; WD, FM 70-15 (1944), 47–67; WD, TM 10-275 (1944), 58–64.
12. WD, FM 70-10 (1944), 13–20; WD, FM 70-15 (1944), 120–23.
13. WD, FM 70-10 (1944), 20–24; WD, FM 70-15 (1944), 123–27.
14. Wellborn, *86th Mountain Infantry*, 3; Woodruff, *85th Mountain Infantry*, 2; Earle, *87th Mountain Infantry*, 2; 10th Mtn Div, *Combat History*, 5 (quote); Scott, "Power of Place and Landscape"; Ware, "Italy."
15. Simpson, *Operations of the 1st Battalion*, 21; Ware, "Italy," 38; 10th Mtn Div, *Combat History*, 7; Rottman, *US 10th Mountain Division*, 34.
16. Risch and Pitkin, *Clothing the Soldier*, 47–60; Clothing: The New Uniform, TMD, Box 2; WD, TM 10-275 (1944), 5–8, 16–17, 35–38. For the development of the M-1943 combat uniform, see Gross, "Layering for a Cold War"; and Stanton, *U.S. Army Uniforms*, 81–87, 110–27.
17. Ware, "Italy," 40 (quote); Simpson, *Operations of the 1st Battalion*, 15–16, 26; Richardson and Allen, *Quartermaster Supply*, 104; WD, TM 10-275 (1944), 14, 25–26, 31, 34; Lund, "Combat Ski Patrols."
18. HQ MTC, Camp Hale, CO, Scouting and Patrolling, 26 August 1943, TMD, Box 3.
19. Teuscher, "Life on the Line"; 10th Mtn Div, *Combat History*, 5–12; Wellborn, *86th Mountain Infantry*, 3–21; Woodruff, *85th Mountain Infantry*, 2–5; Earle, *87th Mountain Infantry*, 4–9; Ware, "Italy," 41–43.
20. Simpson, *Operations of the 1st Battalion*, 36–38.
21. Fisher, *Cassino to the Alps*, 425–28; Truscott, *Command Missions*, 466; Norton, et al., *Battle Analysis: Operation Encore*, 2–3, 34–35.
22. 10th Mtn Div, *Combat History*, 12–15.

23. HQ 86th Mtn Inf, Report on the Mancinello-Campiano Ridge Operation of the 1st Battalion, 86th Mountain Infantry, 12 June 1945, TMD, Box 7, edited and reproduced in Dusenberry, *North Apennines and Beyond*, 177–200; Ware, "Italy," 41–42.

24. HQ 86th Mtn Inf, Report on the Mancinello-Campiano Ridge Operation, TMD, Box 7; Neidner, *Operations of Company A*, 8; Nilsson, *Operations of the First Battalion*, 8–9; Ware, "Italy," 44–45.

25. HQ 86th Mtn Inf, Report on the Mancinello-Campiano Ridge Operation, TMD, Box 7; 1st Battalion, 86th Mountain Infantry, Journal, 18–22 February 1945, TMD, Box 7; Ware, "Italy," 45–46.

26. 10th Mtn Div, *Combat History*, 17–18; Earle, *87th Mountain Infantry*, 12–14; Wellborn, *86th Mountain Infantry*, 12; Herrington, *Operations*, 10.

27. 10th Mtn Div, *Combat History*, 18; Woodruff, *85th Mountain Infantry*, 7–8; Hard, *Operations*, 14–15.

28. 10th Mtn Div, *Combat History*, 19; Woodruff, *85th Mountain Infantry*, 9.

29. 10th Mtn Div, *Combat History*, 20–23; Woodruff, *85th Mountain Infantry*, 9–13; Hard, *Operations*, 18–19.

30. 10th Mtn Div, *Combat History*, 23–24; Wellborn, *86th Mountain Infantry*, 15–17; Hard, *Operations*, 20–21.

31. 10th Mtn Div, *Combat History*, 26–29 (quote p. 29); Fisher, *Cassino to the Alps*, 432–33.

32. 10th Mtn Div, *Combat History*, 30–35 (quote p. 35); Wellborn, *86th Mountain Infantry*, 20–28; Earle, *87th Mountain Infantry*, 27–40; Woodruff, *85th Mountain Infantry*, 17–23; Fisher, *Cassino to the Alps*, 433–34; Truscott, *Command Missions*, 468.

33. Nilsson, *Operations of the First Battalion*, 32; Hard, *Operations*, 21, 24 (quote); Herrington, *Operations*, 22; 10th Mtn Div, *Combat History*, 26, 35; Wellborn, *86th Mountain Infantry*, 18.

34. Truscott, *Command Missions*, 475–83 (quote p. 480); Fisher, *Cassino to the Alps*, 455–57.

35. History of the 2662 Mountain Warfare Det, TMD, Box 4; Rottman, *US 10th Mountain Division*, 41; Richardson and Allan, *Quartermaster Supply*, 75, 147.

36. Truscott, *Command Missions*, 487 (quote); 10th Mtn Div, *Combat History*, 47; Fisher, *Cassino to the Alps*, 471.

37. Fisher, *Cassino to the Alps*, 470–74; 10th Mtn Div, *Combat History*, 47–49; Scott, "Power of Place and Landscape," 232–36.

38. 10th Mtn Div, *Combat History*, 49–51; Fisher, *Cassino to the Alps*, 474.

39. Fisher, *Cassino to the Alps*, 474–75; 10th Mtn Div, *Combat History*, 51–52 (quotes).

40. th Mtn Div, *Combat History*, 52–58; Fisher, *Cassino to the Alps*, 475–82; Truscott, *Command Missions*, 489–90.

41. Rottman, *US 10th Mountain Division*, 37–41.

42. Clark, *Calculated Risk*, 441 (1st quote); Kesselring, *Memoirs of Field-Marshal Kesselring*, 221 (2nd quote); Senger und Etterlin, *War Diary*, 9 (3rd quote).

43. Shelton, *Climb to Conquer*, 220–23.

44. Rottman, *US 10th Mountain Division*, 40–41. Given Japanese plans to retreat from around Tokyo to bastions in the mountains and to defend the mountainous northern island of Hokkaido, the division's mountain skills may have come into play once again. See Giangreco, *Hell to Pay*.

45. Rottman, *US 10th Mountain Division*, 41; Putnam, *Green Cognac*, 204–5; Wilson, *Armies, Corps, Divisions*, 247.

46. Jenkins, *Last Ridge*, 250; Dole to Marshall (draft), c. April 1945; Marshall to Dole, May 17, 1945 (quote)—both in DP, Box 8.

47. AGF, *Mountain Training Center*, i, 122–23 (quotes).

48. WD, FM 70-15 (1944), 45.

Chapter 7

1. Simpson, *Operations of the 1st Battalion*, 37–38; Hard, *Operations*, 25; Nilsson, *Operations of the First Battalion*, 33.

2. Works, "Postwar Mountain Training," 76; Brower reprinted Works's article in the *Sierra Club Bulletin* (December 1946): 46–56.

3. Wilson, *Maneuver and Firepower*, 222–24; General Board, *Types of Divisions*, 26, 31.

4. *Camp Carson Mountaineer*, March 28, 1946; May 2, 1946; May 30, 1946.

5. *Camp Carson Mountaineer*, June 20, 1946. The MWWSTC will be referred to in this chapter as the MTC.

6. *Camp Carson Mountaineer*, May 16, 1946; May 30, 1946; June 6, 1946; June 13, 1946; June 20, 1946; July 4, 1946; August 15, 1946; Stu Dodge, Leon Wilmot, Sidney Peterman, and Edwin Gibson, "The Mountain and Winter Warfare School and Training Center: 1 March 1946–1 April 1947" (12 August 1992), Mountain and Winter Warfare School and Training Center Records (MSR), Box 1.

7. *Camp Carson Mountaineer*, June 13, 1946; July 11, 1946; September 5, 1946; Mountain and Winter Warfare School and Training Center (MWWSTC) Training Schedules 1946, Mountain School Records; HQ MWWSTC, Final Report of the Summer Mountain Training Regimental Cadre Training Course (22 July–30 August 1946), 1 November 1946, MSR, Box 1.

8. MWWSTC Training Schedules 1946; HQ MWWSTC, Final Report of the Summer Mountain Training Regimental Cadre Training Course (22 July–30 August 1946), 1 November 1946; MWWSTC, Rock Climbing Notebook (10 August 1946); Dodge, et al., "Mountain and Winter Warfare School" (quote)—all in MSR, Box 1; *Camp Carson Mountaineer*, July 11, 1946; September 5, 1946; September 12, 1946; September 19, 1946; October 24, 1946; October 31, 1946.

9. *Camp Carson Mountaineer*, October 3, 1946; Dodge, et al., "Mountain and Winter Warfare School"; HQ MWWSTC, Final Report of Winter Training (quote p. 7); MWWSTC, Instructors Handbook of Winter Training—all in MSR, Box 1; MWWSTC, Ski School Notebook, TMD, Box 2.

10. *Camp Carson Mountaineer*, January 30, 1947; February 27, 1947; March 13, 1947; March 20, 1947; MWWSTC Training Schedules, 1946; HQ MWWSTC, Final Report of Oversnow Engineering School, 10 February to 21 March 1947; MWWSTC, Oversnow Vehicle School; HQ MWWSTC, Final Report of Oversnow Artillery School (3–7 March 1947), 14 April 1947—all in MSR, Box 1.

11. HQ MWWSTC, Final Report of Winter Training; HQ MWWSTC, Final Report of Glacier Training (2–10 April 1947), 30 April 1947; MWWSTC, Glacier School Notebook—all in MSR, Box 1; *Camp Carson Mountaineer*, March 13, 1947; March 27, 1947; April 17, 1947.

12. HQ MWWSTC, Request for Information, 15 November 1946, MSR, Box 1; Chapla, "Infantry in Mountain Operations"; Dodge, et al., "Mountain and Winter Warfare School," MSR, Box 1; WD, FM 70-10 (1947), 63–158.

13. Department of the Army (DA), FM 100-5 (1949), 202–3.

14. *Camp Carson Mountaineer*, May 1, 1947; May 22, 1947; July 17, 1947; September 18, 1947; November 13, 1947; January 8, 1948; March 11, 1948.

15. *Camp Carson Mountaineer*, August 28, 1947; July 24, 1947; August 14, 1947.

16. *Camp Carson Mountaineer*, September 9, 1948; Capt David Brower, Mountain Training Critique, 1 July 1948, MSR, Box 1; Dole to John EP Morgan, February 13, 1947, DP, Box 4; Gen Jacob L Devers to Dole, July 21, 1947; Devers to Dole, November 12, 1948 (quote, emphasis in original)—both in DP, Box 8.

17. *Camp Carson Mountaineer*, December 16, 1948; February 3, 1949; May 19, 1949; September 1, 1949; November 24, 1949; January 5, 1950; March 2, 1950; May 1, 1950; "Exercise 'Sweetbriar' Lessons Learned," in Lackenbauer and Kikkert, *Lessons in Arctic Operations*, 51–82 (quote p. 52); Baker, "Arctic Training at Camp Hale."

18. Cutter, "Extreme Weather Conditions"; Westover, *Combat Support in Korea*, 141–75 (quote p. 175).

19. Nilsson, "Post War Mountain Training."

20. Taylor, National Director, NSP to Dole, November 9, 1951, DP, Box 9; Nilsson, "Post War Mountain Training."

21. Untitled instructors guide (winter operations training), TMD, Box 2; *Camp Carson Mountaineer*, November 2, 1951; OQMG, A Soldier's Guide for Keeping Warm in Cold Climates with Special Reference to Exercise Snowfall (December 1951), 10th Mountain Division Field and Technical Manuals Collection, Box 5; *New York Times*, January 26, 1953; February 6, 1952.

22. *Camp Carson Mountaineer*, April 4, 1952; May 30, 1952.

23. *Camp Carson Mountaineer*, June 6, 1952; Nilsson, "Post War Mountain Training"; Hays, "U.S. Forces in Austria."

24. *Camp Carson Mountaineer*, September 12, 1942; October 24, 1952; November 14, 1952; March 13, 1953.

25. Nilsson, "Post War Mountain Training"; Army Arctic Indoctrination School, Field Exercise Summer 1951 Program of Instruction; Army Arctic Indoctrination School, Field Exercise Winter 1954–55 Program of Instruction—both in MSR, Box 1.

26. Tuunainen, "Training the US Army."

27. Tuunainen, "Training the US Army," 123–27, 136–37; DA, FM 31-73 (1952), 17–21.

28. Steele and Moffett, *Mountain Warfare Training Center*, 19–60.

29. Nilsson, "Post War Mountain Training" (quote); *Camp Carson Mountaineer*, March 13, 1953; May 8, 1953. The Saalfelden center would be featured in a short segment of *The Big Picture*, available at https://www.youtube.com/watch?v=GTtHJx8D_Ic.

30. *Camp Carson Mountaineer*, May 8, 1953; March 13, 1953; Whittaker, *Life on the Edge*, 56–61; Annie Addison, "Camp Hale's 'Second Generation,'" *Aspen Times*, March 21, 2007.

31. Whittaker, *Life on the Edge*, 58; Nilsson, "Post War Mountain Training"; Jones and Niven, *Voices and Silences*, 83 (quote); DA, "Mountaineers in Khaki."

32. Mountain and Cold Weather Training Command (MCWTC), Mountaineering Notebook (Camp Carson, CO, 1954); MCWTC, Winter Handbook (Camp Hale, CO, c. 1954); MCWTC, Standing Operating Procedure for an Infantry Battalion Combat Team Operating in Mountains and Extreme Cold (Fort Carson, CO, 10 November 1954)—all in MSR, Box 1; Nilsson, "Post War Mountain Training"; Ney, *Evolution of the US Army*, 138–41.

33. Nilsson, "Post War Mountain Training" (quote); DA, TM 10-275 (1956). Also see Bacevich, *The Pentomic Era*.

34. Essin, *Shavetails and Bell Sharps*, 1; US Army, "NWTC History."

35. DA, FM 31-70 (1959), 3 (quote); Stanton, *U.S. Army Uniforms*, 148–53, 225–35.

36. DA, FM 31-71 (1959), 3, 5.

37. DA, FM 31-72 (1959), 3.

38. DA, FM 31-72 (1959), 151; LaChapelle, *ABCs of Avalanche Safety*, 24.

39. DA, "U.S. Army Cold Weather" (quote at 22:00).

40. US Army, "NWTC History"; DA, FM 100-5 (1962).

41. Steele and Moffett, *Mountain Warfare Training Center*, 61–89.

42. DA, FM 31-71 (1963); DA, FM 31-72 (1964), 118 (quote); DA, TM 10-275 (1964). For the reorganization of army divisions, see Mahon and Danysh, *Army Lineage Series*, 100–111.

43. DA, FM 31-70 (1968), 17, 19, 37, 63–91.

44. Hastings, "Mountain Research" (Hastings, a physical geographer with US Army Natick Laboratories [Natick Labs], was a 10th Mountain Division veteran who had served as a ski instructor and with Company E, 85th Mountain Infantry, in Italy); Mortland, *U.S. Army Land Warfare Laboratory*, vol. 2, Appendix B, B-251, B-288, B-295, B-312.

Chapter 8

1. Natick Labs, *Proceedings*, 35, 61, 65, 83, 106.

2. Natick Labs, *Proceedings*, v–vi; Bates, *Love of Mountains*, 257–89; Whittaker, *Life on the Edge*, 70–119.

3. Natick Labs, *Proceedings*, 130.

4. Isserman, *Continental Divide*, 284–96.

5. Isserman, *Continental Divide*, 329–36.

6. Natick Labs, *Proceedings*, 65–66, 85 (quote), 105–6; Isserman, *Continental Divide*, 272.

7. Isserman, *Continental Divide*, 267–73 (quote pp. 267–68); Manning, *Mountaineering*; Stevenson, "Higher Calling."

8. Isserman, *Continental Divide*, 303–29; Taylor, *Pilgrims of the Vertical*, 125–27; Jones, *Climbing in North America*, 222–33, 267–81.

9. Manning, *Mountaineering*, 116–20, 150–58.

10. Manning, *Mountaineering*, 2nd ed., 129–32, 171–72; Ferber, *Mountaineering*, 3rd ed., 114, 116–18, 163–68, 219–25; Isserman, *Continental Divide*, 324–25, 340–41.

11. Isserman, *Continental Divide*, 310, 336; Taylor, *Pilgrims of the Vertical*, 238, 245; Chouinard, *Let My People Go Surfing*, 10, 20–23, 26–27; Whittaker, *Life on the Edge*, 63–69, 204.

12. Labelle, *Mountaineering Equipment Evaluation*.

13. Labelle, *Mountaineering Equipment Evaluation*, 2–5; Dawson, "Ramy-Securus."

14. AGF, *Mountain Training Center*, 22; Brower, *Manual of Ski Mountaineering*, 2nd ed.; Brower, *Manual of Ski Mountaineering*, 3rd ed.

15. Isserman, *Winter Army*, 240; Fry, *Modern Skiing*, 51.

16. Fry, *Modern Skiing*, 44–59; Shelton, *Climb to Conquer*, 225–35. For the role played by 10th veterans in two locales, see Leach, "Impact," 62–94.

17. Fry, *Modern Skiing*, 74–80.

18. Fry, *Modern Skiing*, 81–89; Masia, "Release!"; Oliver, "Bindings."

19. Fry, *Modern Skiing*, 92–106, 114–15 (quotes pp. 100, 103, 104); Roberts and Masia, "10th Mountain Division Ski Technique," 14.

20. US Forest Service (USFS), *Snow Avalanches*, 7; Atwater, *Avalanche Hunters*, 4, 42–43, 111, 124; Barronian, "Meet the First Guy."

21. USFS, *Snow Avalanches*; LaChapelle, *ABCs of Avalanche Safety*; Dawson, "Skadi." The Skadi, called a "hot dog" for its length and red case, was about 7 3/4 inches long, weighed 14.5 ounces (412 grams), with a rechargeable battery that lasted for a month in receive mode, a week in transmit.

22. Fry, *Modern Skiing*, 190–204.

23. Dawson, *Wild Snow*, 16–17, 187–90; Dawson, "Silvretta Saas Fee Cable Binding."

24. DA, Training Circular (TC) 21-3 (1974).

25. DA, TC 90-6-1 (1976).

26. DA, TC 21-3 (1974), 2-10–2-11; DA, TC 90-11-1 (1981).

27. DA, FM 90-6 (1980), i–ii.

28. DA, FM 90-6 (1980), C-1–C-2.

29. DA, FM 90-6 (1980), B-1–B-7, C-4.

30. Gross, "Bob Gore's Cozy Revolution"; Peters, *Mountaineering*, 4th ed., 21 (quote).

31. Chouinard, *Let My People Go Surfing*, 42–46.

32. Natick Labs, *Use and Care*.

33. DA, TC 21-3 (1986), 2-5–2-9; Lillquist, "Mountain Snowshoes."

34. Durrant, *In Every Clime and Place*, 2 (quote); Donlon, "Different Ballgame"; John Vincour, "U.S. Marine Units Struggle to Cope with Norway's Arctic," *New York Times*, March 26, 1979.

35. Department of the Navy (DN), Fleet Marine Force Manual (FMFM) 8-1 (1974), 61–168; DN, FMFM 7-29 (1980); Commandant of the Marine Corps (CMC), Impact of Cold Weather; Hyndman, "U.S. Marine Corps Cold Weather," 4–5.

36. Steele and Moffett, *Mountain Warfare Training Center*, 95–112; Donlon, "Different Ballgame," 15–30, 36.

37. Jenkins, *Challenges*, 42–64, 182–93; Marine Corps Order 3470.2 w/Ch1; Hickey, Hanlon, and Oblak, *Mobility and Human Factors*; DN, Fleet Marine Force Reference Publication 7-25 (1991).

38. Donlon, "Different Ballgame," 23–27; Steele and Moffett, *Mountain Warfare Training Center*, 113–18.

39. Durrant, *In Every Clime and Place*, 13–15; Donlon, "Different Ballgame," 30–31.

40. Donlon, "Different Ballgame," 38; Lied, "Avalanche Accident at Vassdalen"; "NATO Maneuvers Cancelled."

41. Crookston, *Marine Corps Roles*, 29–36; Steele and Moffett, *Mountain Warfare Training Center*, 120–25.

42. Steele and Moffett, *Mountain Warfare Training Center*, 119; Marine Corps Warfighting Laboratory (MCWL) and Mountain Warfare Training Center (MWTC),

X-File 3-35.23 (2000); Hobbs, *Marine Amphibious Unit*, 33–44; MCWL and MWTC, X-File 3-35.21 (2000). While I was a US Marine infantry officer assigned to a small boat raid company, I attended a winter survival course in January and a cliff assault package in July 1990 at MWTC.

43. US Army Center of Military History, Lineage and Honors Information, 172d Infantry Regiment (The Mountain Battalion), 2 June 2014; US Army Mountain Warfare School (AMWS), "History"; Commander Forces Command to Vice Chief of Staff of the Army, Subj: 3-172 Inf Bn (Mountain) Organization, 17 March 1989, USAHEC; Campbell, "Mountain Infantry Company Winter Raid"; Greer, *Mountain Infantry*, 64–70, 92.

44. Campbell, "Mountain Infantry Company," 41–42; AMWS, "History"; AMWS, "Ram's Head Device."

45. DA, TC 90-6-1 (1989).

46. Wray, *Army's Light Infantry Divisions*; Chief of Staff, US Army, White Paper 1984: Light Infantry Divisions (16 April 1984), Combined Arms Research Library Digital Library, https://cgsc.contentdm.oclc.org/digital/collection/p4013coll11/id/1446.

47. National Association of the 10th Mountain Division, Inc to Senator Bob Dole, 7 January 1985; Senator Dole to Secretary of the Army, January 11, 1985 (1st quote); Chief of Staff, Army, Redesignation of the 10th Infantry Division (Light)—Action Memo, 18 January 1985 (3rd quote); Secretary of the Army to Senator Dole, 22 January 1985; Redesignation of 10th Infantry Division (Light), 24 January 1985 (2nd quote)—all courtesy of the 10th Mountain Division and Fort Drum Museum.

48. Richmond, *Combat Operations*; Greer, *Mountain Infantry*, 95 (quote).

Chapter 9

1. DA, FM 3-97.6 (2000), v–vi (quotes).

2. DA, FM 3-97.6 (2000), v–vi (quote); 2-19–2-22.

3. DA, FM 3-97.61 (2002).

4. DA, FM 3-97.61(2002); Soles, *Rock and Ice Gear*; Graydon and Hanson, *Mountaineering*, 6th ed.

5. Tejada-Flores, *Backcountry Skiing*, 1 (quote), 3, 16, 114–71; Dawson, "Ramer Universal 1980."

6. Vives, *Backcountry Skier*, vi, 20–21, 27–29, 32, 38, 70–117.

7. Tejada-Flores, *Backcountry Skiing*, 193–200; Vives, *Ski Randonée*, 5–12, 33; Volken, Schell, and Wheeler, *Backcountry Skiing*, 11–17, 22–27, 37, 140–77, 236–45 (quote p. 238); Dawson, "Dynafit Low Tech Tourlite."

8. Tejada-Flores, *Backcountry Skiing*, 237 (quote, emphasis in original); USFS, *Avalanche Handbook*.

9. McClung and Schaerer, *Avalanche Handbook*, 2nd ed.

10. American Institute for Avalanche Research and Education (AIARE), "About"; AIARE *Field Book* (2007).

11. LaChapelle, *ABCs of Avalanche Safety*, 27–29; LaChapelle, *ABCs of Avalanche Safety*, 2nd ed., 62–64; Ferguson and LaChapelle, *ABCs of Avalanche Safety*, 3rd ed., 84–87.

12. Tejada-Flores, *Backcountry Skiing*, 205, 242–43; LaChapelle, *ABCs of Avalanche Safety*, 2nd ed., 84, 87; Vives, *Backcountry Skier*, 194–96; Edgerly and Hereford,

"Digital Transceiving Systems"; Volken, Schell, and Wheeler, *Backcountry Skiing*, 66–75.

13. Taylor, *Pilgrims of the Vertical*, 226–32; Selters, *Ways to the Sky*, 190, 226, 280–81.

14. Selters, *Ways to the Sky*, 191, 193 (quotes). For the evolution of ice climbing during this time see Ferber, *Mountaineering*, 3rd ed., 289–300; Peters, *Mountaineering*, 4th ed., 330–66; Graydon, *Mountaineering*, 5th ed., 338–71; and Cox and Fulsaas, *Mountaineering*, 7th ed., 390–440.

15. Twight and Martin, *Extreme Alpinism*, 15–16, 27.

16. Twight and Martin, *Extreme Alpinism*, 91, 197, 205.

17. Safer, *Alpini Effect*, 46–47 (quotes); Grau and Billingsley, *Operation Anaconda*, 351–55; Combs, "Combat Operations."

18. ITS Crew, "PCU Protective Combat Uniform"; Howe, "Stone Cold Campers"; Siler, "Special Forces Can Teach Us."

19. Howe, "Stone Cold Campers"; ITS Crew, "PCU Protective Combat Uniform"; ADS, Inc., "Protective Combat Uniform"; *Protective Combat Uniform*; Polartec, "Power Grid Technical Fleece"; Polartec, "Alpha Direct"; Nextec Military Technology, https://nextec.com/military/.

20. Howe, "Stone Cold Campers"; ITS Crew, "PCU Protective Combat Uniform"; Protective Combat Uniform; Eng, *Mountaineering*, 8th ed., 24; DA, TM 10-8415-236-10 (2008); Marine Corps Systems Command (MCSC), "USMC Mountain/Cold Weather Clothing," 10–11 May 2007.

21. ITS Crew, "PCU Protective Combat Uniform"; Soldier Systems Daily (SSD), "Lost Arrow Project by Patagonia"; Verde Brand Communications, "Outdoor Research"; Reeder, "Arc'teryx LEAF"; Reiss, "Outdoors Companies"; SSD, "Forgeline Solutions."

22. Grau and Vázquez, "Ground Combat"; Malik, "Mountain Warfare" (2003); Malik, "Mountain Warfare" (2004), 94.

23. Wojdakowski, "Mountain Operations"; Moss, "General's Success"; Wojdakowski, "Adaptability"; Eno, "Mountain Operations"; Thomas, "Ambush in Gumbad Valley"; Mulherin, "Planning for Support Operations"; O'Brien, "Constructing a Platoon FOB"; Fry, "Battle in the Death Zone"; Grau, "Mountain Operations"; Grau and Bartles, *Mountain Warfare*.

24. Carpenter, "USMC Capability"; Stephan, "Mountain and Cold Weather Training"; Pierce, *Mountain and Cold Weather Warfighting*.

25. DA, Army Tactics, Techniques, and Procedures (ATTP) 3-97.11/DN, Marine Corps Reference Publication (MCRP) 3-35.1D (2011), iv–v.

26. DA, ATTP 3-21.50 (2011), iv, 5–10.

27. DA, ATTP 3-21.50 (2011), 5-10–5-12; Doug Graham, "Army Introduces Four New Mountaineering, Climbing Kits," *ARNEWS*. February 26, 2014.

28. DA, ATTP 3-21.50 (2011), 6-28–6-30; DA, TC 3-97.61 (2012).

29. DN, Marine Corps Warfighting Publication (MCWP) 3-35.1 (2014) [changed to Marine Corps Tactical Publication (MCTP) 12-10A (2016)], i, 10-5.

30. DN, MCWP 3-35.1 (2014) [changed to MCTP 12-10A (2016)], 10-6.

31. DN, MCRP 3-35.1A (2013) [changed to MCRP 12-10A.1 (2016)], i, A-2.

32. DN, MCRP 3-35.1B (2013) [changed to MCRP 12-10A.2 (2016)], i, 4–1.

33. DN, MCRP 3-35.1C (2014) [changed to MCRP 12-10A.3 (2016)], i, 13-18–13-21.

34. DA, Army Techniques Publication (ATP) 3-90.97 (2016), v, vii–viii.

35. DA, ATP 3-90.97 (2016), 10-1–10-2.
36. AMWS, "History"; AMWS, "Ram's Head Device"; DA, ATTP 3-21.50 (2011), 6–30.
37. DA, ATP 3-90.97 (2016), 10-4–10-9; AMWS, "Basic Military Mountaineer Courses"; Pennell, "Northern Warfare Training Center."
38. Rosenburgh, "Higher Calling"; Safer, *Alpini Effect*, 51; Benitz, "Close-up"; Hughes, "Legacies of Excellence"; Vermont National Guard, "Construction."
39. DN, MCTP 12-10A (2016), 10-5–10-9; MWTC, *Formal Schools Course Catalog*.
40. Steele and Moffett, *Mountain Warfare Training Center*, 140–41; DN, Navy Marine Corps 3500.70B (2016); Cosley and Houston, *Alpine Climbing*; Volken, Schell, and Wheeler, *Backcountry Skiing*; DN, MCTP 12-10A (2016), 10-4–10-5.
41. Jenkins, "Winter to the Corps"; Kinser, "Mountain Warfare Instructor."
42. Mangrum, "Marine Corps Needs"; "Marines' Cold Weather Gear"; MCSC, "USMC Mountain/Cold Weather Clothing" and "Military Ski System."
43. SSD, "Marine Corps Has Awarded Provengo"; Serket, "Skis"; Serket, "Bindings."
44. Mitscherling, Elledge, and O'Rear, "Tactical Application of Military Mountaineering"; Safer, *Alpini Effect*; Henry, "Meeting Our Enemies"; Wade, "Winter Is Coming"; Fry, "Mountain Troops Rope Up"; Burris, "Commandant's Note."
45. DA, ATP 3-21.50 (2020), vii.
46. Darack, "Sky Becomes the Enemy"; Kidney, "Army Mountain Warfare School"; Kumes, "Making It Mountain."
47. SSD, "PEO Soldier."

Epilogue

1. Pierce, Mountain and Cold Weather Warfighting, iv.
2. Pierce, *Mountain and Cold Weather Warfighting*, 60–61.
3. Pierce, *Mountain and Cold Weather Warfighting*, 62–63.
4. Colorado National Guard, "High-altitude ARNG Aviation Training Site."
5. Pierce, *Mountain and Cold Weather Warfighting*, 62–63.
6. American Mountain Guides Association (AMGA), "Mountain Guide Programs."

Bibliography

Archival Collections

Denver Public Library. Denver, Colorado.

10th Mountain Division Resource Center. 10th Mountain Division Collection.
    Carter, H. Adams. Papers.
    Field and Technical Manuals Collection, 1926–1976.
    10th Mountain Division Records.
Western History Collection.
    Dole, Charles Minot. Papers.
    Mountain and Winter Warfare School and Training Center.

Metropolitan State University of Denver. Denver, Colorado.

Camp Hale Colorado Completion Report (Job Number Pando T 1, 1942).
Report of Investigation by Board of Officers, Eight Corps Area, of Proposed Camp
    Site in Pando, Colorado, Area. June 23, 1941.

10th Mountain Division and Fort Drum Museum. Fort Drum, New York.

U.S. Army Heritage and Education Center. Carlisle, Pennsylvania.

Command and General Staff School. Mountain Warfare Map Exercise 46. 7 Febru-
    ary 1946.
Command and General Staff School. Mountain Warfare Map Exercise 48. 11
    February 1946.

Government Documents

Army Ground Forces. *History of the Mountain Training Center.* AGF Historical Sec-
    tion, 1948.
———. *History of the Tenth Light Division (Alpine).* AGF Historical Section, 1946.
———. *The Mobilization of the Ground Army.* AGF Historical Section, 1946.
———. *The Role of Army Ground Forces in the Development of Equipment.* AGF His-
    torical Section. 1946.
———. *Training for Mountain and Winter Warfare.* AGF Historical Section, 1946.

Army Service Forces. *Quartermaster Supply Catalog Section 1: Enlisted Men's Clothing and Equipment.* August 1943.

Chief of Staff, US Army. White Paper 1984: Light Infantry Divisions (16 April 1984), Combined Arms Research Library Digital Library. https://cgsc.contentdm.oclc.org/digital/collection/p4013coll11/id/1446.

Commandant of the Marine Corps. Impact of Cold Weather on MAGTF Amphibious Assaults Study. 12 February 1982.

Department of the Army. Army Tactics, Techniques, and Procedures 3-21.50. *Infantry Small-Unit Mountain Operations.* February 28, 2011.

———. Army Tactics, Techniques, and Procedures 3-97.11. *Cold Region Operations.* January 28, 2011.

———. Army Techniques Publication 3-21.50. *Infantry Small-Unit Mountain and Cold Weather Operations.* August 27, 2020.

———. Army Techniques Publication 3-90.97. *Mountain Warfare and Cold Weather Operations.* April 29, 2016.

———. Field Manual 3-97.6 *Mountain Operations.* November 28, 2000.

———. Field Manual 3-97.61 *Military Mountaineering.* August 26, 2002.

———. Field Manual 31-70 *Basic Cold Weather Manual.* February 1959.

———. Field Manual 31-70 *Basic Cold Weather Manual.* April 1968, Change No. 1 December 1968.

———. Field Manual 31-71 *Northern Operations.* January 1959.

———. Field Manual 31-71 *Northern Operations.* January 1963.

———. Field Manual 31-72 *Mountain Operations.* January 1959.

———. Field Manual 31-72 *Mountain Operations.* May 1964.

———. Field Manual 31-73 *Skiing and Snowshoeing.* May 1952.

———. Field Manual 90-6 *Mountain Operations.* June 30, 1980.

———. Field Manual 100-5 *Operations.* August 1949.

———. Field Manual 100-5 *Operations.* February 1962.

———. "Mountaineers in Khaki." *The Big Picture.* Episode 339.

———. Technical Manual 10-275 *Principles and Utilization of Cold Weather Clothing and Sleeping Equipment.* April 1956.

———. Technical Manual 10-275 *Cold Weather Clothing and Equipment.* October 1964.

———. Technical Manual 10-8415-236-10 *Operator's Manual for Extended Cold Weather Clothing System Generation III (ECWCS GEN III).* June 30, 2008.

———. Training Circular 3-97.61 *Military Mountaineering.* July 26, 2012.

———. Training Circular 21-3 *Soldier's Handbook for Individual Operations and Survival in Cold-Weather Areas.* September 30, 1974.

———. Training Circular 21-3 *Soldier's Handbook for Individual Operations and Survival in Cold-Weather Areas.* March 17, 1986.

———. Training Circular 90-6-1 *Military Mountaineering.* September 30, 1976.

———. Training Circular 90-6-1 *Military Mountaineering.* April 26, 1989.

———. Training Circular 90-11-1 *Military Skiing.* December 30, 1981.

———. "U.S. Army Cold Weather and Mountain School." *The Big Picture.* Episode 525.

Department of the Navy. Fleet Marine Force Manual 7-29. *Mountain Operations.* January 1980.

———. Fleet Marine Force Manual 8-1 *Special Operations.* August 13, 1974.

———. Fleet Marine Force Reference Publication 7-25 *Instructor's Guide to Combat Skiing.* November 1991.

———. Marine Corps Reference Publication 3-35.1A *Small Unit Leader's Guide to Mountain Warfare Operations.* May 21, 2013. (Changed to Marine Corps Reference Publication 12-10A. May 2, 2016.)

———. Marine Corps Reference Publication 3-35.1B *Mountain Leader's Guide to Winter Operations.* July 11, 2013. (Changed to Marine Corps Reference Publication 12-10A.2. May 2, 2016.)

———. Marine Corps Reference Publication 3-35.1C *Mountain Leader's Guide to Mountain Warfare Operations.* February 27, 2014. (Changed to Marine Corps Reference Publication 12-10A.3. May 2, 2016.)

———. Marine Corps Reference Publication 3-35.1D *Cold Region Operations.* January 28, 2011.

———. Marine Corps Warfighting Publication 3-35.1 *Mountain Warfare Operations.* February 28, 2014. (Changed to Marine Corps Tactical Publication 12-10A. May 2, 2016.)

———. NAVMC 3500.70B *Mountain Warfare Operations Training and Readiness Manual.* November 4, 2016.

General Board. *Types of Divisions—Postwar Army.* United States Forces, European Theater, 1945.

Marine Corps Order 3470.2 w/Ch1. Material Fielding Plan (MFP) for the Marine Oversnow Mobility System (MOMS) Components. 26 July 1991.

Marine Corps Systems Command. "Military Ski System." April 2018.

———. "Program Manager Infantry Combat Equipment." 6 November 2019.

———. "USMC Mountain/Cold Weather Clothing Initiative." 10–11 May 2007.

Marine Corps Warfighting Laboratory and Mountain Warfare Training Center. X-File 3-35.21. *Cliff Assault.* August 2000.

———. X-File 3-35.23. *Animal Packers Manual.* August 2000.

Office of the Quartermaster General. *The Development of Special Rations for the Army.* September 1944.

———. *Quartermaster Equipment for Special Forces.* February 1944.

Medical Department. *Cold Injury, Ground Type.* Washington, DC: Department of the Army, 1958.

Mortland, J. E. *U.S. Army Land Warfare Laboratory,* vol. 2. Appendix B, Task Sheets. June 1974.

Senger und Etterlin, F. von. *War Diary of the Italian Campaign: Formal Surrender of Army Group G at Florence.* Headquarters US Army Europe, History Division, 1953.

10th Mountain Division. *Combat History of the 10th Mountain Division, 1944–1945.* Headquarters, 10th Mountain Division, APO#345, U.S. Army, 1945.

US Army. "NWTC [Northern Warfare Training Center] History" (June 24, 2016). https://www.army.mil/article/170431/nwtc_history.

US Army Center of Military History. Lineage and Honors Information. 172d Infantry Regiment (The Mountain Battalion). 2 June 2014.

US Army Mountain Warfare School. "071-SQIE Basic Military Mountaineer Courses (BMMC)." https://www.moore.army.mil/Infantry/AMWS/Courses.html.

———. "The History of the Army Mountain Warfare School" (17 November 2011). https://www.moore.army.mil/Infantry/AMWS/content/pdf/The%20History%20of%20the%20AMWS.pdf.

———. "The History of the Ram's Head Device." 5 September 2013. https://www.moore
.army.mil/Infantry/AMWS/content/pdf/The%20History%20of%20the%20Rams
%20Head%20Device.pdf.

US Army Natick Laboratories. *Proceedings of the Conference on Mountain Climbing
Clothing and Equipment, 17–18 February 1970.* Natick, MA: Natick Laboratories,
1970.

———. *Use and Care of the Extended Cold Weather Clothing System (ECWCS).* Natick,
MA: US Army Natick R,D&E Center, 1986.

US Forest Service. *Avalanche Handbook.* Agriculture Handbook 489. Department of
Agriculture, July 1976. Slightly revised, November 1978.

———. *Snow Avalanches: A Handbook of Forecasting and Control Measures.* Agriculture Handbook 194. Department of Agriculture, January 1961.

US Marine Corps Mountain Warfare Training Center. *Formal Schools Course Catalog.*
2016.

War Department. Field Manual 7-10 *Rifle Company, Rifle Regiment.* June 2, 1942.

———. Field Manual 7-20 *Infantry Battalion.* March 27, 1943.

———. Field Manual 7-40 *Rifle Regiment.* February 9, 1942.

———. Field Manual 20-15 *Tents and Pitching.* August 5, 1944.

———. Field Manual 21-5 *Military Training.* July 16, 1941.

———. Field Manual 21-7 *List of Training Films, Film Strips, and Film Bulletins.* January 1, 1943.

———. Field Manual 22-5 *Infantry Drill Regulations.* August 4, 1941.

———. Field Manual 25-5 *Animal Transport.* June 15, 1939.

———. Field Manual 25-7 *Pack Transportation.* August 25, 1944.

———. Field Manual 31-15 *Operations in Snow and Extreme Cold.* September 18, 1941.

———. Field Manual 70-10 *Mountain Operations.* December 30, 1944.

———. Field Manual 70-10 *Mountain Operations.* September 16, 1947.

———. Field Manual 70-15 *Operations in Snow and Extreme Cold.* November 4, 1944.

———. Field Manual 100-5 *Tentative Field Service Regulations, Operations.* October 1,
1939.

———. Field Manual 100-5 *Operations.* May 22, 1941.

———. Field Manual 100-5 *Operations.* June 15, 1944.

———. *The German Campaign in Norway.* Military Intelligence Service. September 30,
1942.

———. *German Mountain Troops.* Military Intelligence Division. December 1944.

———. *German Mountain Warfare.* Military Intelligence Division. February 29, 1944.

———. *German Ski Training and Tactics.* Military Intelligence Division. January 31,
1944.

———. Table of Equipment 21 *Clothing and Individual Equipment.* December 15, 1943.

———. Technical Manual 10-275 *Principles of Cold Weather Clothing and Equipment.*
October 26, 1944.

———. Training Film 7-677 *Ski Equipment.* 1942.

———. Training Film 7-678 *Snow Camping above Timberline.* 1942.

———. Training Film 7-679 *Snow Camping in Timber.* 1942.

———. Training Film 7-680 *Ski Safety.* 1942.

———. Training Film 7-681 *Ski Safety—First Aid and Emergency Repair of Equipment.*
1942.

——. Training Film 7-682 *Ski Sled*. 1942.

——. Training Film 7-683 *Ski Mountaineering*. 1942.

——. Training Film 8-1297 *Personal Health in Snow and Extreme Cold*. 1943.

——. Training Film 11-168 *The Basic Principles of Skiing*. 1941.

Books, Articles, and Unpublished Works

ADS, Inc. "Protective Combat Uniform (PCU)." https://www.youtube.com/playlist?list=PL514CB3C956B82B2E.

Allen, E. John B. *The Culture and Sport of Skiing: From Antiquity to World War II*. Amherst: University of Massachusetts Press, 2007.

——. *From Skisport to Skiing: One Hundred Years of an American Sport, 1840–1940*. Amherst: University of Massachusetts Press, 1993.

American Alpine Club. *Proceedings*. 1938–41.

——. *Proceedings*. 1942–46.

AIARE (American Institute for Avalanche Research and Education). "About." https://avtraining.org/about-aiare/.

——. *Field Book*. 2007.

American Mountain Guides Association. "AMGA Mountain Guide Programs." https://amga.com/programs/mountain-guide-programs.

Atwater, Montgomery M. *The Avalanche Hunters*. Philadelphia: Macrae Smith, 1968.

Bacevich, A. J. *The Pentomic Era: The U.S. Army between Korea and Vietnam*. Washington, DC: National Defense University Press, 1986.

Baker, George H. "Arctic Training at Camp Hale." *Military Engineer* (May–June 1950): 204–5.

Balck, William. *Development of Tactics—World War*. Trans. Harry Bell. Fort Leavenworth, KS: General Service Schools Press, 1922.

Barronian, Abbie. "Meet the First Guy to Chuck a Bomb at an Avalanche Hazard." *Adventure Journal* (July 29, 2021). https://www.adventure-journal.com/2021/07/meet-first-guy-chuck-bomb-avalanche-hazard/ (accessed July 30, 2021).

Bates, Robert H. *The Love of Mountains Is Best: Climbs and Travels from K2 to Kathmandu*. Portsmouth, NH: Peter E. Randall, 1994.

——. "Mt. McKinley 1942." *American Alpine Journal* (1943).

——. The Pay-Off in Winter Training." *American Alpine Journal* (1946): 78–81.

Battistelli, Pier Paolo. *The Balkans 1940–41 (1): Mussolini's Fatal Blunder in the Greco-Italian War*. New York: Osprey, 2021.

Baumgardner, Randy W., ed. *10th Mountain Division*. 2 vols. Paducah, KY: Turner, 1998.

Benitz, Jennifer. "Close-up on Army Mountain Warfare School, Vermont." *Army* (May 2020): 67.

Besser, Gretchen R. *The National Ski Patrol: Samaritans of the Snow*. Woodstock, VT: Countryman Press, 1983.

Black, Andy, and Charles M. Hampton. *The 10th Recon/MTG*. N.p., 1996.

Bland, Larry I., et al., eds. *The Papers of George Catlett Marshall*, vol. 2: *"We Cannot Delay," July 1, 1939–December 6, 1941*. Baltimore: Johns Hopkins University Press, 1986.

Blumenson, Martin. *United States Army in World War II: Mediterranean Theater of Operations; Salerno to Cassino*. Washington, DC: United States Army Center of Military History, 1993.

Brower, David R. *For Earth's Sake: The Lafe and Times of David Brower.* Salt Lake City, UT: Peregrine Smith, 1990.

——, ed. *Manual of Ski Mountaineering.* Berkley: University of California Press, 1942.

——, ed. *Manual of Ski Mountaineering.* 2nd ed. San Francisco: Sierra Club, 1946.

——, ed. *Manual of Ski Mountaineering.* 3rd ed. San Francisco: Sierra Club, 1961.

Buchner, Alex. *Narvik: The Struggle of Battle Group Dietl in the Spring of 1940.* Trans. Janice W. Ancker. 1958. Reprint, Philadelphia: Casemate, 2020.

Burris, Larry. "Commandant's Note." *Infantry* (Winter 2022–23): 1.

Burton, Hal. *The Ski Troops.* New York: Simon and Schuster, 1971.

Campbell, James. "Mountain Infantry Company Winter Raid." *Infantry* (September–December 1998): 39–44.

Carpenter, Clifton B. "USMC Capability: Mountain/Cold Weather Operations." Master of Military Studies thesis, USMC Command and General Staff College, Quantico, VA, 2005.

Carter, H. Adams. "Mountain Intelligence." *American Alpine Journal* (1946): 70–73.

Cervi, Mario. *The Hollow Legions: Mussolini's Blunder in Greece, 1940–1941.* Trans. Eric Mosbacher. New York: Doubleday, 1971.

Chabalko, Justin J. *Forging the 10th Mountain Division for War, 1940–1945: How Innovation Created a Highly Adaptive Formation.* Fort Leavenworth, KS: US Army Command and General Staff College, 2017.

Chapla, B. C. "Infantry in Mountain Operations." *Military Review* (March 1948): 14–20.

Chouinard, Yvon. *Let My People Go Surfing: The Education of a Reluctant Businessman.* 2nd ed. New York: Penguin Books, 2016.

Clark, Mark W. *Calculated Risk.* New York: Harper and Brothers, 1950.

Clausewitz, Carl von. *On War.* Ed. and trans. Michael Howard and Peter Paret. Princeton, NJ: Princeton University Press, 1976.

Coleman, Annie Gilbert. "The Rise of the House of Leisure: Outdoor Guides, Practical Knowledge, and Industrialization." *Western Historical Quarterly* 42 (2011): 437–57.

Colorado National Guard. "High-altitude ARNG Aviation Training Site." https://co.ng.mil/About/Schoolhouse-HAATS/.

Combs, David. "Combat Operations in a Mountainous Cold Weather Environment." United States Army Sergeants Major Academy. 14 July 2009.

Conn, Stetson, and Byron Fairchild. *The Framework of Hemisphere Defense.* Washington, DC: United States Army Center of Military History, 1960.

Contiguglia, Georgianna. "Searching for the Perfect Ski Gear: Equipment Development for the Tenth Mountain Division." *Colorado Heritage* (1992): 2–16.

Cosley, Kathy, and Mark Houston. *Alpine Climbing: Techniques to Take You Higher.* Seattle: The Mountaineers, 2004.

Cox, Steven M., and Kris Fulsaas, eds. *Mountaineering: The Freedom of the Hills.* 7th ed. Seattle: The Mountaineers, 2003.

Crookston, Joseph A. *Marine Corps Roles and Missions: A Case for Specialization.* Quantico, VA: Marine Corps Command and Staff College, 1987.

Cutter, Lara. "Extreme Weather Conditions: Military Medicine Responds to a Korean War Winter." *Military Medicine* (2015): 1017.

Darack, Ed. "When the Sky Becomes the Enemy: The Marine Corps Mountain Warfare Training Center." *Weatherwise* (January–February 2019): 14–22.

David, Saul. *The Force.* New York: Hachette Books, 2019.

Dawson, Lou. "Dynafit Low Tech Tourlite 1993." *Wild Snow.* https://wildsnow.com /backcountry-skiing-history/binding-museum-backcountry-skiing/dynafit -tourlite-tech-1993/.

———. "Ramer Universal 1980." *Wild Snow.* https://wildsnow.com/backcountry-skiing -history/binding-museum-backcountry-skiing/ramer-universal-ski-binding-1980/.

———. "Ramy-Securus." *Wild Snow.* https://wildsnow.com/backcountry-skiing-history /binding-museum-backcountry-skiing/ramy-securus-ski-binding-history/.

———. "Silvretta Saas Fee Cable Binding for Ski Touring—1960s." *Wild Snow.* https:// wildsnow.com/14164/ski-binding-silvretta-saas-fee/.

———. "Skadi—First Avalanche Rescue Transceiver 'Beacon.'" *Wild Snow.* https:// wildsnow.com/10527/skadi-history-avalanche-rescue-beacon-transceiver/.

———. "Trooper Traverse Colorado Ski Route Introduction & Index." https://www .loudawson.com/ski-mountaineering-history/trooper-traverse-intro-index/.

———. *Wild Snow: 54 Classic Ski and Snowboard Descents of North America.* Golden, CO: AAC Press, 1997.

"Days of Innocence: A Training Film for a Non-existent Outfit." *Skiing Heritage* (Fall 1995): 4–5.

Dole, Charles Minot. *Adventures in Skiing.* New York: J. Lowell Pratt, 1965.

———, ed. *The National Ski Patrol System Manual.* New York: National Ski Patrol System, 1941.

———. "The President and Aide Go Travelling—II." *American Ski Annual* (1945): 73–81.

Donlon, Brian. "A Different Ballgame: The Marine Corps and NATO Cold Weather Exercises in Norway, 1976–1986." Texas A&M Research Paper. February 11, 2022.

Doyle, David. *M29 Weasel: Tracked Cargo Carrier and Variants.* Philadelphia: Pen & Sword, 2019.

Durrant, Jerry L. *In Every Clime and Place: USMC Cold Weather Doctrine.* Fort Leavenworth, KS: US Army Command and General Staff College, 1992.

Dusenbery, Harris. *The North Apennines and Beyond with the 10th Mountain Division.* Portland, OR: Binford & Mort, 1998.

———. *Ski the High Trail: World War II Ski Troopers in the High Colorado Rockies.* Illustrated by Wilson P. Ware. Portland, OR: Binford & Mort, 1991.

Earle, George F. *History of the 87th Mountain Infantry in Italy, 3 January 1945—14 August 1945.* 1945. Reprint, edited by Barbara Imbrie, 2004.

Edgerly, Bruce, and John Hereford. "Digital Transceiving Systems: The Next Generation of Avalanche Beacons." *International Snow Science Workshops (ISSW) Proceedings of Professional Papers* (1998): 120–27.

Edwards, Robert. *The Winter War: Russia's Invasion of Finland, 1939–1940.* New York: Pegasus Books, 2008.

Elkins, Frank. "GI Skiing." *American Ski Annual* (1945): 49–51.

Eng, Ronald C. *Mountaineering: The Freedom of the Hills.* 8th ed. Seattle: The Mountaineers, 2010.

Eno, Russell A. "Mountain Operations: A Historical Perspective." *Infantry* (January–February 2008): 23–25.

Essin, Emmett M. *Shavetails and Bell Sharps: The History of the U.S. Army Mule.* Lincoln: University of Nebraska Press, 1997.

Eyerman, J. R. "Mountain Troops: They Fight from Craggy Peaks amid Snow, Ice and Rocks." *Life* (November 9, 1942): 58–63.

Falls, De Witt C. "The Mountain Troops of Europe." *Journal of the Military Service Institution* 44 (1909): 27–37.

Ferber, Peggy, ed. *Mountaineering: The Freedom of the Hills*. 3rd ed. Seattle: The Mountaineers, 1974.

Ferguson, Sue A., and Ed LaChapelle. *The ABCs of Avalanche Safety*. 3rd ed. Seattle: The Mountaineers, 2003.

Firsoff, V. A. *Ski Track on the Battlefield*. New York: A. S. Barnes, 1943.

Fisher, Ernest F., Jr. *United States Army in World War II: Mediterranean Theater of Operations; Cassino to the Alps*. Washington, DC: United States Army Center of Military History, 1993.

Fry, John. *The Story of Modern Skiing*. Lebanon, NH: University Press of New England, 2006.

Fry, Nathan. "Battle in the Death Zone: High-Altitude Mountain Warfare in Operation Chumik." *Infantry* (May–August 2010): 30–34.

———. "Mountain Troops Rope Up and Strengthen Bonds during the Partnership for Peace Program in Switzerland." *Alpinist* (April 2, 2020). www.alpinist.com/doc /web20s/wfeature-swiss-alps-partnership-for-peace. Accessed August 5, 2021.

Gaujac, Paul. *Le Corps Expeditionnaire Français en Italie: 1943–1944*. Paris: Histoire et Collections, 2003.

Giangreco, D. M. *Hell to Pay: Operation DOWNFALL and the Invasion of Japan, 1945–1947*. Revised and updated. Annapolis, MD: Naval Institute Press, 2017.

Gibson, Edwin. "O.K. Fellows." *American Ski Annual* (1944): 21–22.

———. "On Cooper Hill." *American Ski Annual* (1945): 60–61.

Granger, Rob. "British Army Cold Weather and Mountain Warfare Training in the Second World War." *British Journal for Military History* 8 (2022): 69–86.

Grau, Lester W. "Mountain Operations: Lessons from the Soviet-Afghan War." *Infantry* (May-August 2010): 35–42.

Grau, Lester W., and Charles K. Bartles. *Mountain Warfare and Other Lofty Problems: Foreign Perspectives on High Altitude Combat*. Fort Leavenworth, KS: Foreign Military Studies Office, 2011.

Grau, Lester W., and Dodge Billingsley. *Operation Anaconda: America's First Major Battle in Afghanistan*. Lawrence: University Press of Kansas, 2011.

Grau, Lester W., and Hernán Vázquez. "Ground Combat at High Altitude." *Military Review* (January–February 2002): 22–31.

Graydon, Don, ed. *Mountaineering: The Freedom of the Hills*. 5th ed. Seattle: The Mountaineers, 1992.

Graydon, Don, and Kurt Hanson, eds. *Mountaineering: The Freedom of the Hills*. 6th ed. Seattle: The Mountaineers, 1997.

Greenfield, Ken Roberts, Robert R. Palmer, and Bell I. Wiley. *The Organization of Ground Combat Troops*. Washington, DC: United States Army Center of Military History, 1987.

Greer, John D. *Mountain Infantry—Is There a Need?* Fort Leavenworth, KS: US Army Command and General Staff College, 1988.

Gregory, Barry. *Mountain and Arctic Warfare: From Alexander to Afghanistan*. Bath, UK: Bath Press, 1989.

Gross, Rachel S. "Bob Gore's Cozy Revolution: Gore-Tex Changed the Way Americans Went Outside." *Distillations Magazine* (December 1, 2020). https://sciencehistory .org/stories/magazine/bob-gores-cozy-revolution/.

———. "Layering for a Cold War: The M-1943 Combat System, Military Testing, and Clothing as Technology." *Technology and Culture* 60 (2019): 378–408.

Grotelueschen, Mark E. "Joint Planning for Global Warfare: The Development of the RAINBOW Plans in the United States, 1938–1941." *Army History* (Fall 2015): 9–26.

Hard, William H. *Operations of the Tenth Mountain Division on Monte Belvedere, 18–26 February 1945 (North Apennines Campaign) (Personal Experience of a Regimental Adjutant)*. Fort Benning, GA: Infantry School, 1947.

Harper, Frank. *Military Ski Manual: A Handbook for Ski and Mountain Troops*. Harrisburg, PA: Military Service Publishing Co., 1943.

Hastings, Andrew D. "Mountain Research." *Army Research and Development Newsmagazine* (April 1966): 34–35.

Hays, George P. "U.S. Forces in Austria." *Army, Navy, & Air Force Journal* (September 20, 1952): 65, 68.

Hays, J. J. *United States Army Ground Forces: Tables of Organization and Equipment World War II, Vol. 5: The 10th Mountain Division, 1942–1945.* 2 vols. Milton Keynes, UK: Military Press, 2008.

Henderson, Kenneth A. *The American Alpine Club's Handbook of American Mountaineering*. Boston: Houghton Mifflin, 1942.

Henry, Charles D. "Meeting Our Enemies in the Mountains." *Infantry* (October–December 2018): 36–39.

Herrington, William F. *The Operations of the 10th Mountain Division on Mount Belvedere, 18–25 February 1945 (North Apennines Campaign)*. Fort Benning, GA: Infantry School, 1950.

Hickey, Charles A., Jr., William E. Hanlon, and Thomas Oblak. *Mobility and Human Factors in Evaluation of Three Prototype Assault Snowshoes*. Aberdeen, MD: U.S. Army Research Laboratory, 1994.

Hinterstoisser, Hermann. "Soldaten im Hochgebirge." *Truppendienst* (March 2006). www.bundesheer.at/truppendienst/ausgaben/artikel.php?id=464. Accessed October 10, 2019.

Hobbs, Reginald A. *The Role of the Marine Amphibious Unit, Special Operations Capable in Low Intensity Conflict*. Fort Leavenworth, KS: US Army Command and General Staff College, 1988.

Hogan, David W., Jr., Robert K. Wright Jr., and Arnold G. Fisch Jr. *The Story of the Noncommissioned Officer Corps*. Washington, DC: United States Army Center of Military History, 2007.

Holden, John S. "Let's Get Together." *American Ski Annual* (1945): 52–59.

Holly, James F. "Military Aerial Tramways." *Military Engineer* 45 (1953): 40–46.

House, William P. "Mountain Equipment for the U.S. Army." *American Alpine Journal* (1946): 51–60.

Howe, Steve. "Stone Cold Campers." *Backpacker* (August 1, 2003). https://www.backpacker.com/gear-item/stone-cold-campers/.

Hughes, Whitney. "Legacies of Excellence." *Defense Visual Information Distribution Service* (January 24, 2020). https://www.dvidshub.net/news/414795/legacies-excellence.

Hyndman, Jerry. "U.S. Marine Corps Cold Weather Combat Operations Study." Arlington, VA: Northrop Services, November 1980.

Isserman, Maurice. *Continental Divide: A History of American Mountaineering*. New York: W. W. Norton, 2016.

———. *The Winter Army: The World War II Odyssey of the 10th Mountain Division, America's Elite Alpine Warriors*. New York: Houghton Mifflin Harcourt, 2019.

ITS Crew. "The PCU Protective Combat Uniform: A Buyer's Guide and Clothing System History." *Imminent Threat Solutions* (August 30, 2018). https://www.itstactical.com/gearcom/apparel/comprehensive-guide-protective-combat-uniform/.

Jackman, Albert H. "The Tenth Mountain Division: A Successful Experiment." *American Alpine Journal* (1946): 13–18.

Jenkins, Harry W. *Challenges: Leadership in Two Wars, Washington DC, and Industry*. Fortis, 2020.

Jenkins, Mark. "Winter to the Corps." *Outside* (January 2, 2002). https://www.outsideonline.com/1906321/winter-corps.

Jenkins, McKay. *The Last Ridge: The Epic Story of the U.S. Army's 10th Mountain Division and the Assault on Hitler's Europe*. New York: Random House, 2003.

Jones, Chris. *Climbing in North America*. Berkeley: University of California Press, 1976; Seattle: The Mountaineers, 1997.

Jones, James Earl, and Penelope Niven. *Voices and Silences*. New York: Charles Scribner's Sons, 1993.

Kesselring, Albert. *The Memoirs of Field-Marshal Kesselring*. Stroud, UK: History Press, 2015.

Kidney, Micah. "The Army Mountain Warfare School and the Past, Present, and Future of Military Mountaineering." *Infantry* (Winter 2022–23): 15–20.

Kinser, Patrick. "The Making of a Mountain Warfare Instructor" (February 26, 2010). https://www.29palms.marines.mil/Articles/Article/498757/the-making-of-a-mountain-warfare-instructor/.

Kirkpatrick, Charles E. *An Unknown Future and a Doubtful Present: Writing the Victory Plan of 1941*. Washington, DC: United States Army Center of Military History, 1992.

Kumes, Tom. "Making It Mountain: Opportunities in Army Mountain Warfare Capabilities." *Infantry* (Winter 2022–23): 7–9.

Labelle, Joseph C. *Mountaineering Equipment Evaluation*. Washington, DC: Arctic Institute of North America, 1972.

LaChapelle, Ed R. *The ABCs of Avalanche Safety*. 1961. Reprint, Seattle: The Mountaineers, 1978.

———. *The ABCs of Avalanche Safety*. 2nd ed. Seattle: The Mountaineers, 1985.

Lackenbauer, P. Whitney, and Peter Kikkert, eds. *Lessons in Arctic Operations: The Canadian Army Experience, 1945–1956*. Calgary, AB: University of Calgary, 2016.

Lang, Otto. *Downhill Skiing*. New York: Henry Holt, 1936.

Lauer, G. Stephen. *Forging the Anvil: Combat Units in the US, British, and German Infantries of World War II*. Boulder, CO: Lynne Rienner, 2022.

Leach, David M. "The Impact of the Tenth Mountain Division on the Development of a Modern Ski Industry in Colorado and Vermont: 1930–1965." Bachelor's thesis, Middlebury College, April 2005.

Lechner, Raimund, Thomas Küpper, and Markus Tannheimer. "Challenges of Military Health Service Support in Mountain Warfare." *Wilderness & Environmental Medicine* 29 (2018): 266–74.

Leonard, Richard. "War in the Snow?" *California: Magazine of the Pacific* 30 (December 1940): 24, 40.

Lied, Karstein. "The Avalanche Accident at Vassdalen, Norway, 5 March 1986." *Cold Regions Science and Technology* 15 (1988): 137–50.

Lillquist, Karl. "The Post–World War II Origin and Evolution of Mountain Snowshoes and Mountain Snowshoeing in North America." *Yearbook of the Association of Pacific Coast Geographers* 75 (2013): 140–66.

Lund, Morten. "Combat Ski Patrols." *Skiing Heritage* 7, no. 2 (1995): 20–21.

Maduschka, Leo. "Modern Rock Technique." Trans. E. A. Stewardson. *Mountaineering Journal* 1 (March–May 1933): 156–64.

Mahon, John K., and Romana Danysh. *Army Lineage Series Infantry, Part I: Regular Army.* Washington, DC: Office of the Chief of Military History, 1972.

Malik, Muhammad Asim. "Mountain Warfare: The Need for Specialist Training." Master of Military Art and Science thesis, US Army Command and General Staff College, Fort Leavenworth, KS, 2003.

———. "Mountain Warfare—The Need for Specialist Training." *Military Review* (September–October 2004): 94–102.

Mangrum, Daniel E. "The Marine Corps Needs a Better Mountain Warfare Training Center." *Proceedings* (March 2019). https://www.usni.org/magazines/proceedings/2019/march/marine-corps-needs-better-mountain-warfare-training-center.

Manning, Harvey, ed. *Mountaineering: The Freedom of the Hills.* Seattle: The Mountaineers, 1960.

———. *Mountaineering: The Freedom of the Hills.* 2nd ed. Seattle: The Mountaineers, 1967.

Mansoor, Peter R. *The GI Offensive in Europe: The Triumph of American Infantry Divisions, 1941–1945.* Lawrence: University Press of Kansas, 1999.

"Marines' Cold Weather Gear Faces Overhaul after Poor Showing in Arctic." *Military.com* (May 12, 2017). https://www.military.com/kitup/2017/05/marines-cold-weather-gear-faces-overhaul-poor-showing-arctic.html.

Marzoli, Nathan A. "'The Best Substitute': U.S. Army Low-Mountain Training in the Blue Ridge and Allegheny Mountains, 1943–1944." *Army History* (Fall 2019): 6–24.

Masia, Seth. "Release! History of Safety Bindings." *Skiing History.* https://www.skiinghistory.org/history/release-history-safety-bindings.

Matloff, Maurice, and Edwin M. Snell. *Strategic Planning for Coalition Warfare, 1941–1942.* Washington, DC: United States Army Center of Military History, 1990.

McClung, David, and Peter Schaerer. *The Avalanche Handbook.* 2nd ed. Seattle: The Mountaineers, 1993.

McGilvray, Evan. *Narvik and the Allies: The Polish Brigade at Narvik 1940.* Solihull, UK: Helion & Company, 2017.

McGrath, John J. *The Brigade: A History, Its Organization and Employment in the US Army.* Fort Leavenworth, KS: Combat Studies Institute Press, 2004.

McLane, Charles. "Of Mules and Skis." *American Ski Annual* (1943): 21–34.

McNeil, Fred H. "Skiing and National Defense." *American Ski Annual* (1942): 5–21.

Millett, John D. "The War Department in World War II." *American Political Science Review* 40 (1946): 863–89.

Mitscherling, Russell, Marcus Elledge, and David O'Rear. "The Tactical Application of Military Mountaineering." *Infantry* (July–September 2014): 36–40.

Mulherin, Michael. "Planning for Support Operations in a Mountainous Environment." *Infantry* (January–February 2008): 32–33.

Myers, W. Michael. "Rucksack History." *Rucksack.* http://www.mountaintroops.us
/history_rucksack.html.

"National Defence." *American Alpine Journal* (1941).

Neiberg, Michael S. *When France Fell: The Vichy Crisis and the Date of the Anglo-American Alliance.* Cambridge, MA: Harvard University Press, 2021.

Neidner, William S. *The Operations of Company A (Less One Platoon), 86th Mountain Infantry Regiment (10th Mountain Division) in Attack on Mancinello-Campiano Ridge, Italy, 18–22 February 1945 (North Apennines Campaign) (Personal Experience of a Company Commander).* Fort Benning, GA: Infantry School, 1950.

Nenye, Vesa, Peter Munter, and Toni Wirtanen. *Finland at War: The Winter War, 1939–1940.* New York: Osprey, 2015.

Ney, Virgil. *Evolution of the US Army Infantry Battalion: 1939–1968.* Fort Belvoir, VA: HQ US Army Combat Developments Command, 1968.

Nilsson, Erwin G. *The Operations of the First Battalion, 86th Mountain Infantry Regiment (10th Mountain Division) on Riva Ridge, 17–22 February 1945 (North Apennines Campaign, Italy) (Personal Experience of a Heavy Weapons Company Commander).* Fort Benning, GA: Infantry School, 1947.

———. "Post War Mountain Training." *American Alpine Journal* (1955).

Norton, Steve, et al. *Battle Analysis: Operation Encore—the 10th Mountain Division in Action, Limited Offensive in Mountains, 18 February to 5 March 1945.* Fort Leavenworth, KS: Combat Studies Institute, 1984.

O'Brien, Chris. "Constructing a Platoon FOB in Afghanistan." *Infantry* (January–February 2008): 34–37.

Oliver, Peter. "Bindings: Vive la Difference." *Skiing* (September 1990): 148–58.

Palmer, Robert R., Bell I. Wiley, and William R. Keast. *The Procurement and Training of Ground Combat Troops.* Washington, DC: United States Army Center of Military History, 1991.

Pasdermadjian, Henry G. "Mountain Warfare." *Military Engineer* 29 (1937): 428–33.

Pennell, John. "Northern Warfare Training Center Courses Teach the Ropes of Military Mountaineering" (September 22, 2020). https://www.pacom.mil/Media/News/News-Article-View/Article/2356869/northern-warfare-training-center-courses-teach-the-ropes-of-military-mountainee/.

Peters, Ed, ed. *Mountaineering: The Freedom of the Hills.* 4th ed. Seattle: The Mountaineers, 1982.

Pierce, Scott W. *Mountain and Cold Weather Warfighting: Critical Capability for the 21st Century.* Fort Leavenworth, KS: US Army Command and General Staff College, 2008.

Polartec. "Alpha Direct." https://www.polartec.com/fabrics/insulation/alpha-direct.

———. "Power Grid Technical Fleece." https://www.polartec.com/fabrics/base/power-grid.

Protective Combat Uniform Visual User Guide. Alexandria, VA: Kwikpoint, 2007.

Putnam, William Lowell. *Green Cognac: The Education of a Mountain Fighter.* New York: AAC Press, 1991.

Reeder, David. "Arc'teryx LEAF—What Is It and Why Should You Care?" *Recoil* (January 18, 2015). https://www.recoilweb.com/arcteryx-leaf-what-is-it-and-why-should-you-care-56711.html.

Reiss, Sami. "Do Outdoors Companies Really Need to Cater to Police?" *GQ* (July 15, 2020). https://www.gq.com/story/outdoors-companies-policing.

Richardson, Eudora Ramsay, and Sherman Allen. *Quartermaster Supply in the Fifth Army in World War II*. Fort Lee, VA: Quartermaster School, 1950.

Richmond, Melvin E. *Combat Operations in Mountainous Terrain—Are United States Army Light Infantry Divisions Preparing Properly?* Fort Leavenworth, KS: US Army Command and General Staff College, 1987.

Ringholz, Raye C. *On Belay! The Life of Legendary Mountaineer Paul Petzoldt*. Seattle: The Mountaineers, 1997.

Risch, Erna, and Thomas M. Pitkin. *Clothing the Soldier of World War II*. Washington, DC: Government Printing Office, 1946.

Roberts, Charles C., Jr., and Seth Masia. "The 10th Mountain Division Ski Technique of World War II." *Skiing History* (November–December 2017): 13–15.

Roberts, David. *The Last of His Kind: The Life and Adventures of Bradford Washburn, America's Boldest Mountaineer*. New York: Harper, 2009.

Robinson, Bestor. "Equipment and Technique for Camping on Snow." *Sierra Club Bulletin* (1937): 38–47.

———. "How the USA Is Assuring Winter Warfare Leadership." *Commonwealth* 18 (1942): 102.

Rocker, Richard. "Trooper Traverse—1944: First Person Account." *Wildsnow.* https://www.wildsnow.com/backcountry-skiing-history/trooper-traverse-history-index-aspen-leadville/richard-rocker-account-trooper-traverse/.

Roll, David L. *George Marshall: Defender of the Republic*. New York: Dutton Caliber, 2019.

Rosenburgh, Bob. "A Higher Calling: Training Curve Is Steep at the Army Mountain Warfare School." *Infantry* (January–February 2008): 38–40.

Ross, Steven T., ed. *U.S. War Plans, 1938–1945*. Boulder, CO: Lynne Rienner, 2002.

Rottman, Gordon L. *US 10th Mountain Division in World War II*. New York: Osprey, 2012.

Roulet, Louis-Édouard, Derck Engelberts, and Hervé de Weck, eds. *La guerre et la montagne/Krieg und Gerbirge/Mountains and Warfare*. 2 vols. Berne: Association suisse d'histoire et de sciences militaires, 1993.

Safer, Scott M. *The Alpini Effect: Why the US Army Should Train for Mountain Warfare*. Fort Leavenworth, KS: US Army Command and General Staff College, 2014.

Sanders, Charles J. *The Boys of Winter: Life and Death in the U.S. Ski Troops during the Second World War*. Boulder: University Press of Colorado, 2005.

Sayen, John J. *US Army Infantry Divisions, 1942–43*. New York: Osprey, 2006.

Schepe, Gerhard. *Mountain Warfare in Europe*. Kingston, ON: Centre for International Relations, 1983.

Schifferle, Peter J. *America's School for War: Fort Leavenworth, Officer Education, and Victory in World War II*. Lawrence: University Press of Kansas, 2017.

Scott, John M. "Power of Place and Landscape: The US 10th Mountain Division, from Colorado to the Apennines." In *Conflict Landscapes: Materiality and Meaning in Contested Places*, ed. Nicholas J. Saunders and Paul Cornish. New York: Routledge, 2021, 221–40.

Seligman, Gerald. *Snow Structures and Ski Fields*. 1936. Reprint, Brussels: Jos. Adams, 1963.

Selters, Andy. *Ways to the Sky: A Historical Guide to North American Mountaineering*. Golden, CO: American Alpine Club Press, 2004.

Serket. "Bindings." https://serketusa.com/bindings/.

———. "Skis." https://serketusa.com/skis/.

Shelton, Peter. *Climb to Conquer: The Untold Story of World War II's 10th Mountain Division Ski Troops.* New York: Scribner, 2003.

Siler, Wes. "What the Special Forces Can Teach Us about Layering: Beyond Clothing Is Turning Protective Combat Uniforms into Stylish Outdoor Gear." *Outside* (May 9, 2019). https://www.outsideonline.com/2395575/beyond-clothing-special-forces.

Simonson, Curtis R. *Creating the 10th Mountain Division: The National Ski Patrol's Role.* Carlisle Barracks, PA: US Army War College, 2015.

Simpson, Edward. *The Operations of the 1st Battalion, 85th Mountain Infantry (10th Mountain Division) North of Bagni di Lucca, Italy, 20 January—12 February 1945 (North Apennines Campaign).* Fort Benning, GA: Infantry School, 1947.

"Six Ways to Invade U.S.: Axis Powers Can Try It If They Combine Fleets to Win Sea Superiority." *Life* (March 2, 1942): 16–20.

Skoog, Lowell. *Written in the Snows: Across Time on Skis in the Pacific Northwest.* Seattle: The Mountaineers, 2021.

Soldier Systems Daily. "Forgeline Solutions Announces New Ownership." *Soldier Systems* (June 8, 2022). https://soldiersystems.net/2022/06/08/forgeline-solutions-announces-new-ownership/.

———. "The Lost Arrow Project by Patagonia—Military Alpine Recce System: Program History." *Soldier Systems* (May 16, 2018). https://soldiersystems.net/2018/05/16/the-lost-arrow-project-by-patagonia-military-alpine-recce-system-program-history/.

———. "PEO Soldier Works with Industry to Rapidly Field New Cold Weather Clothing to 11th Abn Div." *Soldier Systems* (March 6, 2023). https://soldiersystems.net/2023/03/06/peo-soldier-works-with-industry-to-rapidly-field-new-cold-weather-clothing-to-11th-abn-div-2/.

———. "The United States Marine Corps Has Awarded Provengo, LLC the Military Ski System (MSS) Contract for a Total Value of Up to $9,085,675." *Soldier Systems* (September 28, 2018). https://soldiersystems.net/2018/09/28/the-united-states-marine-corps-has-awarded-provengo-llc-the-military-ski-system-mss-contract-for-a-total-value-of-up-to-9085675/.

Soles, Clyde. *Rock and Ice Gear: Equipment for the Vertical World.* Seattle: The Mountaineers, 2002.

Stanton, Shelby. *U.S. Army Uniforms of the Cold War, 1948–1973.* Mechanicsburg, PA: Stackpole Books, 1994.

———. *U.S. Army Uniforms of World War II.* Mechanicsburg, PA: Stackpole Books, 1991.

Statiev, Alexander. *At War's Summit: The Red Army and the Struggle for the Caucasus Mountains in World War II.* New York: Cambridge University Press, 2018.

Steele, Orlo K., and Michael I. Moffett. *U.S. Marine Corps Mountain Warfare Training Center, 1951–2001.* Washington, DC: United States Marine Corps History Division, 2011.

Stephan, Scott E. "Changing the Mountain and Cold Weather Training Paradigm." USMC Command and General Staff College, Quantico, VA, 2006.

Stevenson, David. "Higher Calling." *Adventure Journal* (Summer 2020): 54–59.

Sumner, Ian, and François Vauvillier. *The French Army, 1939–45 (1): The Army of 1939–40 and Vichy France.* London: Osprey, 1998.

Taylor, Joseph E., III. *Pilgrims of the Vertical: Yosemite Rock Climbers and Nature at Risk*. Cambridge, MA: Harvard University Press, 2010.

Tejada-Flores, Lito. *Backcountry Skiing: The Sierra Club Guide to Skiing Off the Beaten Track*. San Francisco: Sierra Club, 1981.

Teuscher, Carson. "Life on the Line: Reevaluating 10th Mountain Division Patrol Actions in the Northern Italian Apennines, January to February 1945." Manuscript in author's possession.

Thomas, Paul A. "Ambush in Gumbad Valley." *Infantry* (January–February 2008): 27–31.

Thompson, George Raynor, Dixie R. Harris, Pauline M. Oaks, and Dulany Terrett. *The Signal Corps: The Test (December 1941 to July 1943)*. Washington, DC: Office of the Chief of Military History, 1957.

Thompson, Mark. *The White War: Life and Death on the Italian Front*. New York: Basic Books, 2010.

Tremper, Bruce. *Avalanche Essentials: A Step-by-Step System for Safety and Survival*. Seattle: The Mountaineers, 2013.

Truscott, Lucian K., Jr. *Command Missions: A Personal Story*. New York: E. P. Dutton, 1954.

Tuunainen, Pasi. "Training the US Army to Fight the Red Army in Winter—Former Finnish Officers and Military Knowledge Transfer from Finland to the United States during the Early Cold War, 1947–1964." *Journal of Slavic Military Studies* 29 (2016): 110–38.

Twight, Mark F., and James Martin. *Extreme Alpinism: Climbing Light, Fast, and High*. Seattle: The Mountaineers, 1999.

Underhill, Robert L. M. "On the Use and Management of the Rope in Rock Work." *Sierra Club Bulletin* (1931): 67–88.

Van Dyke, Carl. *The Soviet Invasion of Finland, 1939–1940*. Portland, OR: Frank Cass, 1997.

Verde Brand Communications. "Outdoor Research Launches OR Pro™." January 18, 2022. https://outdoorindustry.org/press-release/outdoor-research-launches-or-pro/.

Vermont National Guard. "Construction of New Army Mountain Warfare School Facility Begins." *Defense Visual Information Distribution Service* (November 1, 2020). https://www.dvidshub.net/news/382161/construction-new-army-mountain-warfare-school-facility-begins.

Vives, Jean. *Backcountry Skier: Your Complete Guide to Ski Touring*. Champaign, IL: Human Kinetics, 1998.

———. *Ski Randonée: Backcountry Skiing for the Alpine Skier*. Fraser, CO: Ice Box Books, 2006.

Volken, Martin, Scott Schell, and Margaret Wheeler. *Backcountry Skiing: Skills for Ski Touring and Ski Mountaineering*. Seattle: The Mountaineers, 2007.

Vollmer, A., trans. "The Attack in Mountain Warfare." *Review of Military Literature* (March 1934): 61–65.

Wade, Andrew M. "Winter Is Coming: Ensuring U.S. Special Forces Are Prepared to Fight and Win in a Cold Weather Environment." Thesis, Naval Postgraduate School, Monterey, CA, 2018.

Ware, Wilson. "Italy: The Riva Ridge." *American Alpine Journal* (1946): 34–46.

Watson, Mark Skinner. *Chief of Staff: Prewar Plans and Preparations*. Washington, DC: US Army Center of Military History, 1951.

Wellborn, Charles. *History of the 86th Mountain Infantry in Italy, 10 December 1944–30 June 1945.* 1945. Reprint, edited by Barbara Imbrie, 2004.

Westover, John G. *Combat Support in Korea.* Washington, DC: US Army Center of Military History, 1987.

Whitlock, Flint, and Bob Bishop. *Soldiers on Skis: A Pictorial Memoir of the 10th Mountain Division.* Boulder, CO: Paladin Press, 1992.

Whittaker, Jim. *A Life on the Edge: Memoirs of Everest and Beyond.* Seattle: The Mountaineers, 1999.

Wilson, John B. *Armies, Corps, Divisions, and Separate Brigades.* Washington, DC: US Army Center of Military History, 1999.

———. *Maneuver and Firepower: The Evolution of Divisions and Separate Brigades.* Washington, DC: US Army Center of Military History, 1998.

Witte, David R. *World War II at Camp Hale: Blazing a New Trail in the Rockies.* Charleston, SC: History Press, 2015.

Wojdakowski, Walter. "Adaptability—the Key to Success in Mountain Operations." *Infantry* (January–February 2008): 1.

———. "Mountain Operations: The High Altitude Challenge." *Infantry* (September–October 2006): 1.

Woodruff, John. *History of the 85th Mountain Infantry in Italy, 4 January 1945–31 May 1945.* 1945. Reprint, edited by Barbara Imbrie, 2004.

Woodward, John B. Interview with Lowell Skoog. August 18, 2001. Alpenglow Ski History. http://www.alpenglow.org/ski-history/notes/comm/woodward-john.html.

Works, Robert C. "Postwar Mountain Training." *Military Review* (May 1946): 71–77.

Wray, Timothy A. *The Army's Light Infantry Divisions: An Analysis of Advocacy and Opposition.* Washington, DC: National War College, 2005.

Young, Geoffrey Winthrop. *Mountain Craft.* New York: Charles Scribner's Sons, 1920.

Index

Italicized references indicate illustrations.
For additional reference, see "Acronyms and Abbreviations" on pages xiii–xiv.

www.ingramcontent.com/pod-product-compliance
Lightning Source LLC
Chambersburg PA
CBHW032341210225
22387CB00010B/112/J